THE GLOBAL MINOTAUR

THE GLOBAL MINOTAUR

America, Europe and the
Future of the Global Economy

YANIS VAROUFAKIS

with a foreword by Paul Mason

Zed Books

LONDON

For Danae Stratou,
my global partner

The Global Minotaur was first published in 2011 by Zed Books Ltd,
Unit 2.8, The Foundry, 17 Oval Way, London, SE11 5RR, UK.

www.zedbooks.co.uk

This edition published in 2015
Copyright © Yanis Varoufakis 2011, 2013, 2015

The right of Yanis Varoufakis to be identified as the author of this work
has been asserted by him in accordance with the Copyright, Designs
and Patents Act, 1988

Typeset in Monotype Bulmer
Index by Sally Phillips
Cover design: Liam Chapple
Cover photo © EPA/Andy Rain

A catalogue record for this book is available from the British Library

ISBN 978-1-78360-610-8 pb
ISBN 978-1-78360-612-2 epub
ISBN 978-1-78360-611-5 mobi
ISBN 978-1-78360-664-1 pdf

Printed and bound by CPI Group (UK) Ltd, Croydon, CR0 4YY

MIX
Paper from
responsible sources
FSC
www.fsc.org
FSC® C013604

Contents

Abbreviations

AC	alternating current
ACE	aeronautic–computer–electronics complex
AIG	American Insurance Group
ATM	automated telling machine
CDO	collateralized debt obligation
CDS	credit default swap
CEO	chief executive officer
DC	direct current
ECB	European Central Bank
ECSC	European Coal and Steel Community
EFSF	European Financial Stability Facility
EIB	European Investment Bank
EMH	Efficient Market Hypothesis
ERAB	Economic Recovery Advisory Board
EU	European Union
FDIC	Federal Deposit Insurance Corporation
GDP	gross domestic product
GM	General Motors
GSRM	global surplus recycling mechanism
IBRD	International Bank for Reconstruction and Development
ICU	International Currency Union
IMF	International Monetary Fund

LTCM	Long-Term Capital Management (hedge fund)
MIE	military–industrial establishment
NAFTA	North American Free Trade Agreement
NATO	North Atlantic Treaty Organization
OECD	Organisation for Economic Co-operation and Development
OEEC	Organisation for European Economic Co-operation
OMT	outright monetary operations
OPEC	Organization of the Petroleum Exporting Countries
RBCT	Real Business Cycle Theory
RBS	Royal Bank of Scotland
REH	Rational Expectations Hypothesis
RMB	renminbi – Chinese currency
SME	small and medium-sized enterprise
SPV	Special Purpose Vehicle
TARP	Troubled Asset Relief Program

Foreword

Paul Mason

On 20 February 2015 Yanis Varoufakis entered the HQ of
the European Union alone – both literally and figuratively.
He came without advisers, press liaison or bodyguards – and
with the Brussels press corps salivating over what seemed
like a certain and abject surrender. Sixteen days before that,
the European Central Bank had punctured the euphoria of
Syriza's election victory by suddenly withdrawing its regular
loan facility to the Greek banks, putting them on life support,
and triggering a silent run on bank deposits.

By the time Varoufakis arrived in Brussels, he knew that
up €1 billion a day were draining from the Greek banking
system: he would, without a deal, be forced to impose
capital controls, limiting ATM withdrawals and preventing
the removal of cash offshore. In the end he signed a deal
somewhat short of abject surrender. Greece would get leeway
to implement measures to counteract austerity; the high levels
of government surplus (4 per cent) demanded by the 2011
bailout were waived.

In all other senses Greece was still a debt colony of the
EU. But it had been granted a modicum of home rule, and

what we used to call the 'comprador bourgeoisie' – the pliant agents of the colonists – were gone.

Most ordinary politicians would have given a terse statement, taken a couple of questions and headed for the steam room in their hotel. Instead Varoufakis conducted a 40-minute Q&A hailing the deal as a minor victory – which, once you understand the eurozone, it was. For Varoufakis had, in those sixteen days, vaulted the minotaur.

In the original version of this book he set out an analysis of the 2008 crisis and its aftermath using the Cretan legend of the minotaur as a metaphor: the 'Global Minotaur' was US capitalism centred on Wall Street, extracting tribute from the world after 1971. Lacking a Theseus to kill it, the mythical beast was killed by unsustainable economics. But the spirit of the minotaur lives on. Austerity economics, and the primacy of the banks over households, businesses and state treasuries, have been the articles of faith guiding the eurozone since the Greek crisis began. As America imposed its one-sided deal on the world after the fall of Bretton Woods, so Germany remained determined to take only the upside of the Euro arrangement.

With the arrival of Syriza in power the Euro Minotaur awakened, looked up and took aim at the most colourful presence in its labyrinth – Varoufakis.

Though I'd been engaged with his work for years, I only met Yanis Varoufakis three days before the election of 25 January 2015. He lucidly laid out his argument, and his plan: Greece was effectively insolvent; Europe's bailout a €320 billion handout to the north European banks to protect them from that fact. Unless the eurozone acquired an effective mechanism for recycling fiscal surpluses and deficits – with the mountains of idle savings energized so that they become productive investments, particularly where investment is lagging behind – it was 'finished within two years'.

But Varoufakis remained convinced, like the majority of Syriza's economic gurus, that a 'good euro' was achievable. The auguries were positive: Mario Draghi had launched quantitative easing – a €1.6 trillion monetary stimulus – plus he had called for less austerity. Jean-Claude Juncker had launched a fund aimed at bringing €300 billion of investment to the stricken eurozone. The politics were lined up in favour of Greece. Between the election and 20 February Varoufakis learned a lesson on behalf of the entire European left: politicians do not control Europe; the Minotaur does.

As this edition goes to press, we don't know whether the reprieve Varoufakis won on 20 February will last, expand or get closed down. But we do know the power that fresh ideas alone can bring. Varoufakis's straight-talking changed the modus operandi of Euro summits, probably forever. His preparedness to expose the workings of power-summitry and pressure threatened to put out of business a press corps whose working lives had been devoted to accommodating it. In every conversation there were three audiences: Greece, its debtors, and the workers and youth of Europe.

What irked the debtors most was that Varoufakis looked and sounded like one of them. A successful professional economist in the West European tradition, who had moved left at a time when others of his generation were moving right, Varoufakis knows enough of the way the neoliberal world works to make every clash with it look and feel excruciating. Most politicians cannot be theorists. First, because they are rarely thinkers; second, because the frenetic lifestyle they impose on themselves leaves no time for big ideas. But most of all because to be a theorist you have to admit the possibility of being wrong – the provisionality of knowledge – and you know you cannot spin your way out of a theoretical problem.

In this book Varoufakis laid bare the central problem of the world economy: the lack of an agent to create new rules, new paradigms of behaviour, new reservoirs of popular consent. If China is unready, the European centre too unpopular, and America too decayed to do it, he asked the question: who will? Through the sheer incompetence and venality of the political centre in Greece, and the exasperation of its people, the answer was: the radical left.

Whether they win or lose their fight with the Euro institutions, Syriza have demonstrated the power of theory. Varoufakis predicted the catastrophic end of the Greek bonanza, the unsustainability of leveraged finance and the fragmentation of the eurozone – even while the theories acceptable to the *Wall Street Journal* and *Financial Times* said the opposite. He also told his advisers, from the very beginning, that they could expect a deal with Europe only at 'one minute past midnight'. That is, he theorized the potential accidental outcomes of the crisis too.

That's what gives this book both its power and its poignancy. We don't know how the fight between Syriza and the eurozone will end – but we can be certain it will involve compromise. Politicians live in the world of compromise; theorists do not. But by the end of it, the radical left will know what it means to fight for a new, fairer kind of capitalism, in the teeth of resistance from the old kind.

Paul Mason,
28 March 2015

Preface

This book originally aimed at pressing a useful metaphor into the service of elucidating a troubled world; a world that could no longer be understood properly by means of the paradigms that dominated our thinking before the Crash of 2008. Its purpose was to appeal to the non-specialist reader on whose behalf my metaphor was to unveil a simple, yet never simplistic, account of a very complex global tragedy. The idea was not to discount all other explanations but, rather, to provide a platform for combining many different explanations, each valid in its own way, into an overarching analysis of the global 'arrangement' that crashed and burned in 2008, leaving our world in a state of stunned disenchantment.

The Global Minotaur metaphor crept up on me in 2002, after endless conversations with friend, colleague and co-author Joseph Halevi. Our discussions on what made the world tick after the 1970s' economic crises produced a coherent, albeit complex, view of the global economic system in which America's deficits, Wall Street and the ever-declining real value of American wages played a defining and, paradoxically, a hegemonic role.

The gist of our argument was that the defining character-istic of the post-1971 era was a reversal of the flow of trade and capital surpluses between the United States and the rest of the world. The hegemon, for the first time in world history, strengthened its hegemony by wilfully enlarging its deficits. The trick was to understand *how* America ac-complished this and the tragic manner in which its success gave rise to the financialization which both reinforced US dominance and, simultaneously, implanted the seeds of its potential downfall. Part of the trick was the deployment of the Global Minotaur narrative, which was born as an attempt to simplify the argument's complexity. (See our joint article 'The Global Minotaur', *Monthly Review* 55, July–August 2003.)

When five years later, in 2008, the financial system im-ploded, Danae Stratou, my partner in everything, incited me to write this book on the strength of the main metaphor's capacity to relate my complex story to a lay readership. It was her belief in my ability to do this that gave me the idea and impetus to try it. I began writing the book in our Athens home, at a time when the dark clouds around our country were still thin and most of our friends and family would not believe that Greece was about to fall into a never-ending tailspin. Against that background of resistance to bad omens, and while writing the book's early draft, I was beginning to gain a degree of notoriety in the Greek and international media as a doomsayer who believed that not only was Greece's bankruptcy inevitable but that it was a precursor of the euro-zone's unravelling as well. Only then did I notice the irony of using a Greek metaphor (that of the Minoan Minotaur) by which to account for an international catastrophe of which Greece would be the worst-hit victim.

Nonetheless, immersed in my writing, I refused to give Greece too prominent a role therein. A dichotomy soon emerged in my daily routine: while spending hour upon hour in radio and television studios debating Greece's steady deterioration, I would return to my Minotaur script determined more than ever to keep Greece off its pages. For if my diagnosis about Greece's misfortune was right (i.e. that there is no such thing as a Greek crisis, but rather that Greece is a symptom of a broader shift in global economic history) it was imperative that my book should reflect this. Thus, the United States was, and remains in this updated edition, the focal point of the analysis.

At the level of intellectual and analytical development, it was my engagement with the larger canvas of the euro crisis that gave me an opportunity to test the Global Minotaur's capacity to throw helpful light on our post-2008 circumstances, and to elicit policy suggestions. Indeed, while working on this book's first edition, I also expended a great deal of energy writing and rewriting, together with Stuart Holland, our 'A Modest Proposal for Resolving the Euro Crisis'. The campaign that Stuart and I ran across the breadth of Europe to promote our 'Modest Proposal' (taking it even to North America and Australia) was an eye-opener, a source of insight, a testbed for the book's sub-hypotheses.

As is always the case with powerful metaphors, the danger lurked that my analysis and predictions might have been covertly influenced by the allegorical power of the Global Minotaur. Especially while completing the book (some time in January 2011), at the point when I felt compelled to state my prognosis for the future of the world economy, the anxiety that my conclusions might have been hijacked by an irresistible urge to stay loyal to the chosen metaphor intensified. Had

I allowed myself to be lulled into a false sense of analytical security in the comforting bosom of an allegory of my own creation? The fact that the Crisis was mutating and changing its colours at a frightening pace reinforced the angst and made me feel exceptionally exposed to the vagaries of our generation's turbocharged history.

In the months that intervened between completing the final draft and holding the published copy in my hands, my nerves had steadied considerably: the world seemed to have done nothing that the book's metaphor was uncomfortable with. Indeed, the book's warm reception in different parts of the world suggested that I had tapped a rich vein. Still, when a year later my publishers proposed that I revisit the text with a view to producing an updated edition, I jumped at the opportunity to carry out new research for the purposes of finding out, mainly for myself, whether my 'Global Minotaur Hypothesis' had withstood the test of time at a global scale. The result is a whole new chapter (Chapter 9), which begins by stating which facts would have falsified my narrative, before investigating the actual facts hidden within officially published statistics. Thankfully, it is now safe to report that the 'Global Minotaur Hypothesis' passes the test of empiricism with flying colours.

Lastly, on a personal note, the new edition was completed in the United States, where Danae and I now live. It is from here that, somewhat guilt-ridden, I peruse the wastelands of my country, every now and then giving the odd interview to various networks that pose the same question over and over again: what should Greece do to extricate itself from its Great Depression? How should Spain or Italy respond to demands that logic tells us will make things worse? The answer I deliver with increasing monotonousness is that there is nothing that our proud countries can do other than to say 'No!' to inane policies whose real objective is to deepen the depression for apocryphal reasons that only a close study of the Global Minotaur's legacy can reveal.

Yanis Varoufakis
February 2013

Acknowledgements

Joseph Halevi having been mentioned already, I must now turn to Nicholas Theocarakis, my great friend and colleague at the University of Athens. The three of us took the initial Global Minotaur narrative, which Joseph and I first discussed in our *Monthly Review* article in 2003, and developed it much further in a hefty academic volume under the title *Modern Political Economics: Making Sense of the Post-modern World* (published by Routledge in 2011). This was the foundation on which the book you are now holding was built. Besides thanking Joseph and Nicholas, for the shared thoughts which have trickled into the following pages, I must also thank Ken Barlow and the rest of the Zed Books crew for embracing my idea warmly and efficiently, as well as the many people around the world who have invited me to speak to the book's themes, thus enabling me to put its narrative to the test of sophisticated and highly opinionated people from all walks of life and backgrounds. Lastly, thanks are due to Michael Abrash and Gabe Newell for getting me started on the new Chapter 9 with an interesting question. (The question being that, since the US trade and budget deficits bounced back after 2009, why am I arguing that the Global Minotaur has lost its capacity, based on the twin US deficit, to recycle the rest of the world's surpluses?) Indeed, the world would be a better place if more fascinating questions were posed for every definitive answer provided...

CHAPTER 1

Introduction

The 2008 moment

Nothing humanizes us like *aporia* – that state of intense puzzlement in which we find ourselves when our certainties fall to pieces; when suddenly we get caught in an impasse, at a loss to explain what our eyes can see, our fingers can touch, our ears can hear. At those rare moments, as our reason valiantly struggles to fathom what the senses are reporting, our *aporia* humbles us and readies the prepared mind for previously unbearable truths. And when the *aporia* casts its net far and wide to ensnare the whole of humanity, we know we are at a very special moment in history. September 2008 was just such a moment.

The world had just astonished itself in a manner not seen since 1929. The certainties that decades of conditioning had led us to acknowledge were, all of a sudden, gone, along with around $40 trillion of equity globally, $14 trillion of household wealth in the US alone, 700,000 US jobs every month, countless repossessed homes everywhere... The list is almost as long as the numbers on it are unfathomable.

The collective *aporia* was intensified by the response of governments that had hitherto clung tenaciously to fiscal conservatism as perhaps the twentieth century's last surviving mass ideology: they began to pour trillions of dollars, euros, yen, etc. into a financial system that had, until a few months before, been on a huge roll, accumulating fabulous profits and provocatively professing to have found the pot of gold at the end of some globalized rainbow. And when that response proved too feeble, our presidents and prime ministers, men and women with impeccable anti-statist, neoliberal credentials, embarked upon a spree of nationalizing banks, insurance companies and car manufacturers that put even Lenin's post-1917 exploits to shame.

Unlike previous crises, such as the dotcom crash of 2001, the 1991 recession, Black Monday,[1] the 1980s Latin American debacle, the slide of the Third World into a vicious debt trap, or even the devastating early 1980s depression in Britain and parts of the US, this crisis was not limited to a specific geography, a certain social class or particular sectors. All the pre-2008 crises were, in a sense, localized. Their long-term victims were hardly ever of importance to the powers-that-be, and when (as in the case of Black Monday, the Long-Term Capital Management (LTCM) hedge fund fiasco of 1998 or the dotcom bubble of two years later) it was the powerful who felt the shock, the authorities had managed to come to the rescue quickly and efficiently.

In contrast, the Crash of 2008 had devastating effects both globally and across the neoliberal heartland. Moreover, its effects will be with us for a long, long time. In Britain, it was probably the first crisis in living memory really to have hit the richer regions of the south. In the United States, although the sub-prime crisis began in less-than-prosperous corners of that great land, it spread to every nook and cranny of the privileged middle classes, its gated communities, its leafy suburbs, the Ivy League universities where the well-off congregate, queuing up for the better socio-economic roles. In Europe, the whole continent reverberates with a crisis that refuses to go away and which threatens European illusions that had managed to remain unscathed for six decades. Migration flows were reversed, as Polish and Irish workers abandoned Dublin and London alike for Warsaw and Melbourne. Even China, which famously escaped the recession with a healthy growth rate at a time of global shrinkage, is in a bind over its falling consumption share of total income and its heavy reliance on state investment projects that are feeding into a worrying bubble – two portents that do not bode well at a time when the rest of the world's long-term capacity to absorb the country's trade surpluses is questionable.

Adding to the general *aporia*, the high and mighty let it be known that they, too, were at a loss to grasp reality's new twists. In October 2008, Alan Greenspan, the former chairman of the Federal Reserve (the Fed) and a man viewed as a latter-day Merlin, confessed to 'a flaw in the model that I perceived is the critical functioning structure that defines how the world works'.[2] Two months later, Larry Summers, formerly President Clinton's treasury secretary and at the time President-Elect Obama's chief economic adviser (head of the National Economic Council), said that '[i]n this crisis, doing too little poses a greater threat than doing too much...' When the Grand Wizard confesses to having based all his magic on a flawed model of the world's ways, and the doyen of presidential economic advisers proposes that caution be thrown to the wind, the public 'gets' it: our ship is sailing in treacherous, uncharted waters, its crew clueless, its skipper terrified.

Thus we entered a state of tangible, shared *aporia*. Anxious disbelief replaced intellectual indolence. The figures in authority seemed bereft of authority. Policy was, evidently, being made on the hoof. Almost immediately, a puzzled public trained its antennae in every possible direction, desperately seeking explanations for the causes and nature of what had just hit it. As if to prove that supply needs no prompting when demand is plentiful, the presses started rolling. One after another, the books, the articles, the long essays – even the movies – churned through the pipeline, creating a flood of possible explanations for what had gone wrong. But while a world in shock is always pregnant with theories about its predicament, the overproduction of explanations does not guarantee the *aporia*'s dissolution.

Six explanations for why it happened

1. *'Principally a failure of the collective imagination of many bright people...to understand the risks to the system as a whole'*

That was the gist of a letter sent to the Queen by the British Academy on 22 July 2009, in response to a question she had put to a gathering of red-faced professors at the London School of Economics: 'Why had you not seen it coming?' In their letter, thirty-five of Britain's top economists answered in effect: 'Whoops! We mistook a Great Big Bubble for a Brave New World.' The gist of their response was that, while they had their finger on the pulse and their eye on the data, they had made two related diagnostic mistakes: the error of extrapolation and the (rather more sinister) error of falling prey to their own rhetoric.

Everyone could see that the numbers were running riot. In the United States, the financial sector's debt had shot up from an already sizeable 22 per cent of national income (Gross Domestic Product or GDP) in 1981 to 117 per cent in the summer of 2008. In the meantime, American households saw their debt share of national income rise from 66 per cent in 1997 to 100 per cent ten years later. Put together, aggregate US debt in 2008 exceeded 350 per cent of GDP, when in 1980 it had stood at an already inflated 160 per cent. As for Britain, the City of London (the financial sector in which British society had put most of its eggs, following the rapid deindustrialization of the early 1980s) sported a collective debt almost two and a half times Britain's GDP, while, in addition, British families owed a sum greater than one annual GDP.

So, if an accumulation of inordinate debt infused more risk than the world could bear, how come no one saw the crash coming? That was, after all, the Queen's reasonable question. The British Academy's answer grudgingly confessed to the combined sins of smug rhetoric and linear extrapolation. Together, these sins fed into the self-congratulatory conviction that a paradigm shift had occurred, enabling the world of finance to create unlimited, benign, riskless debt.

The first sin, which took the form of a mathematized rhetoric, lulled authorities and academics into a false belief that financial innovation had engineered risk out of the system; that the new instruments allowed a new form of debt with the properties of quicksilver. Once loans were originated, they were then sliced up into tiny pieces, blended together in packages that contained different degrees of risk,[3] and sold all over the globe. By thus spreading financial risk, so the rhetoric went, no single agent faced any significant danger that they would be hurt if some debtors went bust. It was a New Age faith in the financial sector's powers to create 'riskless risk', which culminated in the belief that the planet could now sustain debts (and bets made on the back of these debts) that were many multiples of actual, global income.

Vulgar empiricism shored up such mystical beliefs: back in 2001, when the so-called 'new economy' collapsed, destroying much of the paper wealth made from the dotcom bubble and the Enron-like scams, the system held together. The 2001 new economy bubble was, in fact, worse than the sub-prime mortgage equivalent that burst six years later. And yet the ill effects were

contained efficiently by the authorities (even though employment did not recover until 2004–05). If such a large shock could
be absorbed so readily, surely the system could sustain smaller
shocks, like the $500 billion sub-prime losses of 2007–08.

According to the British Academy's explanation (which, it
must be said, is widely shared), the Crash of 2008 happened
because by then – and unbeknownst to the armies of hyper-
smart men and women whose job was to have known better – the
risks that had been assumed to be riskless had become anything
but. Banks like the Royal Bank of Scotland, which employed
4,000 'risk managers', ended up consumed by a black hole
of 'risk gone sour'. The world, in this reading, paid the price
for believing its own rhetoric and for assuming that the future
would be no different from the very recent past. Thinking that
it had successfully diffused risk, our financialized world created
so much that it was consumed by it.

2. *Regulatory capture*

Markets determine the price of lemons. And they do so with
minimal institutional input, since buyers know a good lemon
when they are sold one. The same cannot be said of bonds or,
even worse, of synthetic financial instruments. Buyers cannot
taste the 'produce', squeeze it to test for ripeness, or smell its
aroma. They rely on external, institutional information and
on well-defined rules that are designed and policed by dispas-
sionate, incorruptible authorities. This was the role, supposedly, of the credit rating agencies and of the state's regulatory
bodies. Undoubtedly, both types of institution were found not
just wanting but culpable.

When, for instance, a *collateralized debt obligation* (CDO) – a
paper asset combining a multitude of slices of many different
types of debt[4] – carried a triple-A rating and offered a return

1 per cent above that of US Treasury Bills,[5] the significance was twofold: the buyer could feel confident that the purchase was not a dud and, if the buyer was a bank, it could treat that piece of paper as indistinguishable from (and not an iota riskier than) the real money with which it had been bought. This pretence helped banks to attain breathtaking profits for two reasons.

1   If they held on to their newly acquired CDO – and remember, the authorities accepted that a triple-A rated CDO was as good as dollar bills of the same face value – the banks did not even have to include it in their capitalization computations.[6] This meant that they could use with impunity their own clients' deposits to buy the triple-A rated CDOs without compromising their ability to make new loans to other clients and other banks. So long as they could charge higher interest rates than they paid, buying triple-A rated CDOs enhanced the banks' profitability without limiting their loan-making capacity. The CDOs were, in effect, instruments for bending the very rules designed to save the banking system from itself.

2   An alternative to keeping the CDOs in the bank vaults was to pawn them off to a central bank (e.g. the Fed) as collateral for loans, which the banks could then use as they wished: to lend to clients, to other banks, or to buy even more CDOs for themselves. The crucial detail here is that the loans secured from the central bank by pawning the triple-A rated CDO bore the pitiful interest rates charged by the central bank. Then, when the CDO matured, at an interest rate of 1 per cent above what the central bank was charging, the banks kept the difference.

The combination of these two factors meant that the issuers of CDOs had good cause:

(a) to issue as many of them as they physically could;
(b) to borrow as much money as possible to buy other issuers'
     CDOs; and
(c) to keep vast quantities of such paper assets on their books.[7]

Alas, this was an open invitation to print one's own money! No
wonder Warren Buffet took one look at the fabled CDOs and
described them as WMDs (weapons of mass destruction). The
incentives were incendiary: the more the financial institutions
borrowed in order to buy the triple-A rated CDOs, the more
money they made. The dream of an ATM in one's living room
had come true, at least for the private financial institutions and
the people running them.

With these facts before us, it is not hard to come to the conclusion that the Crash of 2008 was the inevitable result of granting
to poachers the role of gamekeeper. Their power was blatant
and their image as the postmodern wizards conjuring up new
wealth and new paradigms was unchallenged. The bankers paid
the credit rating agencies to extend triple-A status to the CDOs
that they issued; the regulating authorities (including the central
bank) accepted these ratings as kosher; and the up-and-coming
young men and women who had secured a badly paid job with
one of the regulating authorities soon began to plan a career
move to Lehman Brothers or Moody's. Overseeing all of them
was a host of treasury secretaries and finance ministers who had
either already served for years at Goldman Sachs, Bear Stearns,
etc. or were hoping to join that magic circle after leaving politics.

In an environment that reverberated with the popping of
champagne corks and the revving of gleaming Porsches and
Ferraris; in a landscape where torrents of bank bonuses flooded
into already wealthy areas (further boosting the real estate boom
and creating new bubbles from Long Island and London's
East End to the suburbs of Sydney and the high-rise blocks of

Shanghai); in that ecology of seemingly self-propagating paper wealth, it would take a heroic – a reckless – disposition to sound the alarm bells, to ask the awkward questions, to cast doubt on the pretence that triple-A rated CDOs carried zero risk. Even if some incurably romantic regulator, trader or senior banker were to raise the alarm, she would be well and truly trumped, ending up a tragic, crushed figure in history's gutter.

The Brothers Grimm had a story involving a magic pot that embodied industrialization's early dreams – of automated cornucopias fulfilling all our desires, unstoppably. It was also a bleak and cautionary tale that demonstrated how those industrial dreams might turn into a nightmare. For, towards the end of the story, the wondrous pot runs amok and ends up flooding the village with porridge. Technology turned nasty, in much the same way as Mary Shelley's ingenious Dr Frankenstein had his own creation turn viciously against him. In similar fashion, the virtual automated telling machines (ATMs) conjured up by Wall Street, the credit rating agencies and the regulators who connived with them flooded the financial system with a modern-day porridge, which ended up choking the whole planet. And when, in autumn of 2008, the ATMs stopped working, a world addicted to synthesized porridge juddered to a grinding halt.

3. Irrepressible greed

'It's the nature of the beast', goes the third explanation. Humans are greedy creatures who only feign civility. Given the slightest chance, they will steal, plunder and bully. This dim view of our human lot leaves no room even for a modicum of hope that intelligent bullies will consent to rules banning bullying. For even if they do, who will enforce them? To keep the bullies in awe, some Leviathan with extraordinary power will be necessary. But then again, who will keep tabs on the Leviathan?

Such are the workings of the neoliberal mind, yielding the conclusion that crises may be necessary evils; that no human design can avert economic meltdowns. For a few decades, beginning with President Roosevelt's post-1932 attempts to regulate the banks, the Leviathan solution became widely accepted: the state could and should play its Hobbesian role in regulating greed and bringing it into some balance with propriety. The Glass–Steagall Act of 1933 is possibly the most often quoted example of that regulatory effort.[8]

However, the 1970s saw a steady retreat away from this regulatory framework and toward the re-establishment of the fatalistic view that human nature will always find ways of defeating its own best intentions. This 'retreat to fatalism' coincided with the period when neoliberalism and financialization were rearing their unsightly heads. This meant a new take on the old fatalism: the Leviathan's overwhelming power, while necessary to keep the bullies in their place, was choking growth, constraining innovation, putting the brakes on imaginative finance, and thus keeping the world stuck in a low gear just when technological innovations offered the potential to whisk us onto higher planes of development and prosperity.

In 1987, President Reagan decided to replace Paul Volcker (a Carter administration appointment) as chairman of the Fed. His choice was Alan Greenspan. Some months later, the money markets experienced their worst single day ever, the infamous 'Black Monday' episode. Greenspan's deft handling of the consequences earned him a reputation for cleaning up efficiently after a money market collapse.[9] He was to perform the same 'miracle' again and again until his retirement in 2006.[10]

Greenspan had been chosen by Reagan's staunch neoliberals not *in spite of* but *because of* his deeply held belief that the merits and capacities of regulation were overrated. Greenspan truly doubted that any state institution, including the Fed, could rein in human nature and effectively restrain greed without, at the same time, killing off creativity, innovation and, ultimately, growth. His belief led him to adopt a simple recipe, which shaped the world for a good nineteen years: since nothing disciplines human greed like the unyielding masters of supply and demand, let the markets function as they will, but with the state remaining ready and willing to step in to clean up the mess when the inevitable disaster strikes. Like a liberal parent who lets his children get into all sorts of mischief, he expected trouble but thought it better to remain on the sidelines, always ready to step in, clean up after a boisterous party, or tend to the wounds and the broken limbs.

Greenspan stuck to his recipe, and this underlying model of the world, in each and every downturn that occurred on his watch. During the upturns, he would sit by, doing almost nothing, save for giving the occasional sibyllic pep talk. Then, when some bubble burst, he would rush in aggressively, lower interest rates precipitously, flood the markets with cash and generally do anything it took to refloat the sinking ship. The recipe seemed to work nicely – at least until 2008, a year and a half into his golden retirement. Then it stopped working.

To his credit, Greenspan confessed to having misunderstood capitalism. If only for this *mea culpa*, history ought to treat him kindly, for there are precious few examples of powerful men willing and able to come clean – especially when the people who used to be their minions remain in denial. Indeed, Greenspan's model of the world, which he himself renounced, is still alive, well and making a comeback. Aided and abetted by a resurgent Wall Street bent on derailing any serious post-2008 attempt to regulate its behaviour, the view that human nature cannot be restrained without simultaneously jeopardizing our liberty and our long-term prosperity is back. Like a criminally negligent doctor whose patient survived by luck, the pre-2008 establishment is insisting on being absolved on the grounds that capitalism, after all, survived. And if some of us continue to insist on apportioning blame for the Crash of 2008, why not censure human nature? Surely honest introspection would reveal to each and every one of us a culpable dark side. The only sin to which Wall Street confessed is that it projected that dark side onto a larger canvas.

4. Cultural origins

In September 2008, Europeans looked smugly over the pond, shaking their heads with a self-serving conviction that the Anglo-Celts, at long last, were getting their comeuppance. After years and years of being lectured on the superiority of the Anglo-Celtic model, on the advantages of flexible labour markets, on how inane it was to think that Europe could retain a generous social welfare net in the era of globalization, on the wonders of an aggressively atomistic entrepreneurial culture, on the wizardry of Wall Street and on the brilliance of the post-Big Bang City of London, the news of the Crash, its sights and sounds as they were beamed all over the world, filled the European heart with an ambiguous mix of *Schadenfreude* and fear.

Of course, it was not too long before the crisis migrated to Europe, metamorphosing in the process into something far worse and more threatening than Europeans had ever anticipated. Nevertheless, most Europeans remain convinced of the Crash's Anglo-Celtic cultural roots. They blame the fascination that English-speaking people have with the notion of home ownership at all costs. They find it hard to wrap their minds around an economic model which generates silly house prices by stigmatizing rent-paying non-homeowners (for being in thrall to landlords) while celebrating pretend homeowners (who are even more deeply indebted to bankers).

Europeans and Asians alike saw the obscene relative size of the Anglo-Celtic financial sector, which had been growing for decades at the expense of industry, and became convinced that global capitalism had been taken over by lunatics. So when the meltdown began in precisely those locations (the US, Britain, Ireland, the housing market and Wall Street), they could not help but feel vindicated. While the Europeans' sense of vindication was dealt a savage blow by the ensuing euro crisis, Asians can afford a large dose of smugness. Indeed, in much of Asia the Crash of 2008 and its aftermath are referred to as the 'North Atlantic Crisis'.

5. Toxic theory

In 1997, the Nobel Prize for Economics went to Robert Merton and Myron Scholes for developing 'a pioneering formula for the valuation of stock options'. 'Their methodology', trumpeted the awarding committee's press release, 'has paved the way for economic valuations in many areas. It has also generated new types of financial instruments and facilitated more efficient risk management in society.' If only the hapless Nobel committee had known that, in a few short months, the much-lauded 'pioneering formula' would cause a spectacular multi-billion-dollar debacle, the collapse of a major hedge fund (the infamous LTCM, in which Merton and Scholes had invested all their kudos) and, naturally, a bail-out by the reliably obliging US taxpayers.

The true cause of the LTCM failure, which was a mere test run for the larger Crash of 2008, was simple enough: huge investments that relied on the untestable assumption that one can estimate the probability of events that one's *own* model assumes away not just as improbable but, in fact, as untheorizable. To adopt a logically incoherent assumption in one's theories is bad enough. But to gamble the fortunes of world capitalism on such an assumption is bordering on the criminal. So how did the economists get away with it? How did they convince the world, and the Nobel committee, that they could estimate the probability of events (such as a string of defaults by debtors) which their own models assumed to be inestimable?

The answer lies more in the realm of mass psychology than in economics itself: economists relabelled *ignorance* and marketed it successfully as *a form of provisional knowledge*. The financiers then built new forms of debt on that relabelled ignorance and erected pyramids on the assumption that risk had been removed. The more investors were convinced, the more money everyone involved made and the better placed the economists became to silence anyone who dared to doubt their underlying assumptions. In this manner, *toxic finance* and *toxic economic theorizing* became mutually reinforcing processes.

As the Mertons of the financial world were sweeping up Nobel Prizes and accumulating fabulous profits in the same breath, their counterparts who remained in the great economics departments were changing the economic theory 'paradigm'. Whereas, once upon a time, leading economists were in the business of explanation, the new trend was toward relabelling. Copying the financiers' strategy of disguising ignorance as provisional knowledge and uncertainty as riskless risk, the economists relabelled unexplained joblessness (e.g. an observed rate of 5 per cent that refused to budge) as the *natural rate of unemployment*. The beauty of the new label was that, suddenly, unemployment seemed natural, and therefore no longer in need of explanation.

It is worth, at this point, delving a little deeper into the economists' elaborate scam: whenever they were unable to explain the observed deviations of human behaviour from their predictions, they (a) labelled such behaviour 'out of equilibrium', and then (b) assumed that it was random and best modelled as such. So long as the 'deviations' were subdued, the models worked and the financiers profited. But when panic set in, and the run on the financial system began, the 'deviations' proved anything but random. Naturally, the models collapsed, along with the markets that they had helped create.

Any fair-minded investigator of these episodes must, many believe, conclude that the economic theories that dominated the thinking of influential people (in the banking sector, the hedge funds, the Fed, the European Central Bank (ECB) – everywhere) were no more than thinly veiled forms of intellectual fraud, which provided the 'scientific' fig leaves behind which Wall Street tried to conceal the truth about its 'financial innovations'. They came with impressive names, like the Efficient Market Hypothesis (EMH), the Rational Expectations Hypothesis (REH) and Real Business Cycle Theory (RBCT). In truth, these were no more than impressively marketed theories whose mathematical complexity succeeded for too long in hiding their feebleness.

Three toxic theories underpinning pre-2008 establishment thinking

EMH: No one can systematically make money by second-guessing the market. Why? Because financial markets contrive to ensure that current prices reveal all the privately known information that there is. Some market players overreact to new information, others underreact. Thus, even when everyone errs, the market gets it 'right'. A pure Panglossian theory!

REH: No one should expect any theory of human action to make accurate predictions in the long run if the theory presupposes that humans systematically misunderstand or totally ignore it. For example, suppose a brilliant mathematician were to develop a theory of bluffing at poker and schooled you in its use. The only way it would work for you is if your opponents either had no access to the theory or misunderstood it. For if your opponents also knew the theory, each could use it to work out when you were bluffing, thus defeating the bluff's purpose. In the end, you would abandon it and so would they. REH assumes that such theories cannot predict behaviour well because people will see through them and will eventually violate their edicts and predictions. No doubt this sounds radically anti-patronizing. It assumes that not much light can be shed on society by theorists who believe they understand its ways better than Joe Bloggs. But note the sting in the tail: for REH to hold, it must be true that people's errors (when they predict some economic variable, such as inflation, wheat prices, the price of some derivative or share) must *always* be random – i.e. unpatterned, uncorrelated, untheorizable. It only takes a moment's reflection to see that the espousal of REH, especially when taken together with EMH, is tantamount to never expecting recessions, let alone crises. Why? Because recessions are, by definition, systematic, patterned events. However surprising when they hit, they unfold in a patterned manner, each phase highly correlated with what preceded it. So how does a believer in EMH–REH respond when her eyes and ears scream to her brain: 'recession, crash, meltdown!'? The answer is by turning to RBCT for a comforting explanation.

RBCT: Taking EMH and REH as its starting point, this theory portrays capitalism as a well-functioning *Gaia*. Left alone, it will remain harmonious and never go into a spasm (like that of 2008). However, it may well be 'attacked' by some 'exogenous' shock (coming from a meddling government, a wayward Fed, heinous trades unions, Arab oil producers, aliens, etc.), to which it must respond and adapt. Like a benevolent *Gaia* reacting to a large meteor crashing into it, capitalism responds efficiently to exogenous shocks. It may take a while for the shockwaves to be absorbed, and there may be many victims in the process, but, nonetheless, the best way of handling the crisis is to let capitalism get on with it, without being subjected to new shocks administered by self-interested government officials and their fellow travellers (who pretend to be standing up for the common good in order to further their own agendas).

To sum up, *toxic derivatives* were underpinned by *toxic economics*, which, in turn, were no more than motivated delusions in search of theoretical justification; fundamentalist tracts that acknowledged facts only when they could be accommodated to the demands of the lucrative faith. Despite their highly impressive labels and technical appearance, economic models were merely mathematized versions of the touching superstition that markets know best, both at times of tranquillity and in periods of tumult.

6. Systemic failure

What if neither human nature nor economic theory was to blame for the Crash? What if it did not come about because bankers were greedy (even if most are), or because they made use of toxic theories (even though they undoubtedly did), but because capitalism was caught in a trap of its own making? What if capitalism is not a 'natural' system but, rather, a particular system with a propensity to systemic failure?

The Left, with Marx its original prophet, has always warned that, as a system, capitalism strives to turn us into automata and our market society into a *Matrix*-like dystopia. But the closer it comes to achieving its aim, the nearer it gets to its moment of ruin, very much like the mythical Icarus. Then, after the Crash (and unlike Icarus) it picks itself up, dusts itself down, and embarks upon the same path all over again.

In this final explanation on my list, it is as if our capitalist societies were designed to generate periodic crises, which get worse and worse the more they displace human labour from the production process and critical thinking from public debate. To those who blame human avarice, greed and selfishness, Marx replied that they are following a good instinct but are looking in the wrong place; that capitalism's secret is its penchant for contradiction – its capacity to produce at once massive wealth and unbearable poverty, magnificent new freedoms and the worst forms of slavery, gleaming mechanical slaves and depraved human labour.

Human will, in this reading, may be dark and mysterious; but, in the Age of Capital, it has become more of a derivative than a prime mover. For it is *capital* that usurped the role of the primary force shaping our world, including our will. Capital's self-referential momentum makes a mockery of the human will, of entrepreneur and labourer alike. Though inanimate and mindless, *capital* – shorthand for machines, money, securitized derivatives and all forms of crystallized wealth – quickly evolves as if it were in business for itself, using human actors (bankers, bosses and workers in equal measure) as pawns in its own game. Not unlike our subconscious, capital also instils illusions in our minds – above all, the illusion that, in serving it, we become worthy, exceptional, potent. We take pride in our relationship with it (either as financiers who 'create' millions in a single day, or as employers on whom a multitude of working families depend, or as labourers who enjoy privileged access to gleaming machinery or to puny services denied to illegal migrants), turning a blind eye to the tragic fact that it is *capital* which, in effect, owns us all, and that it is *we* who serve *it*.

The German philosopher Schopenhauer castigated us modern humans for deceiving ourselves into thinking that our beliefs and actions are subject to our consciousness. Nietzsche concurred, suggesting that all the things we believe in, at any given time, reflect not truth but someone else's power over us. Marx dragged economics into this picture, reprimanding us all for ignoring the reality that our thoughts have become hijacked by capital and its drive to accumulate. Naturally, although it follows its own steely logic, capital evolves mindlessly. No one designed capitalism and no one can civilize it now that it is going at full tilt.

Having simply evolved, without anyone's consent, it quickly liberated us from more primitive forms of social and economic organization. It bred machines and instruments (material and financial) that allowed us to take over the planet. It empowered us to imagine a future without poverty, where our lives are no longer at the mercy of a hostile *nature*. Yet, at the same time, just as nature spawned Mozart and HIV using the same indiscriminate mechanism, so too did capital produce catastrophic forces with a tendency to bring about discord, inequality, industrial-scale warfare, environmental degradation and, of course, financial freefalls. In one fell swoop, it generated – with neither rhyme nor reason – wealth and crises, development and deprivation, progress and backwardness.

Could the Crash of 2008, then, be nothing more than our periodic chance to realize how far we have allowed our *will* to be subjugated to *capital*? Was it a jolt that ought to awaken us to the reality that capital has become a 'force we must submit to', a power that developed 'a cosmopolitan, universal energy which breaks through every limit and every bond and posits itself as the only policy, the only universality, the only limit and the only bond'?[11]

The parallax challenge

A stick half submerged in a river looks bent. As one moves around it, the angle changes and every different location yields a different perspective. If, in addition, the river's flow gently moves the stick around, both the 'reality' of the 'bent' stick and our understanding of it are in constant flux. Physicists refer to the phenomenon as the *parallax*. I enlist it here to make the simple point that many different observations about the Crash of 2008 may be both accurate *and* misleading.

This is not to deny the objective reality either of the stick (i.e. that it is not bent at all) or of the Crash and its aftermath, the *Crisis*. It is simply to note that different viewpoints can all generate 'true' observations, yet fail to unveil the basic *truth* about the phenomenon under study. What we need is something beyond a variety of potential explanations and perspectives from which to grasp the stick's reality. We need a theoretical leap, like the one the physicist makes, which will allow us to rise above the incommensurable observations before landing in a conceptual place from which the whole thing makes perfect sense. I call this 'leap' the *parallax challenge*.

Coming to terms with the Crash of 2008 is like coming face to face with the parallax challenge at its most demanding. Who could credibly deny that economists and risk managers miscalculated systemic risk big time? Is there any doubt that Wall Street, and the financial sector at large, *did* grow fat on insidious voracity, on quasi-criminal practices, and on financial products that any decent society ought to have banned? Were the credit rating agencies not textbook cases of conflict of interest in action? Was greed not hailed as the new good? Did the regulators not fail spectacularly to resist the temptation to stay on the 'right' side of the bankers? Were Anglo-Celtic societies not more prone than others to neoliberalism's cultural trickery, acting as a beachhead from which to spread the word to the rest of the globe that 'scruples' meant nothing and self-interest was the only way, the only motive? Is it not true that the Crash of 2008 affected the developed world more acutely than it did the so-called emerging economies? Can anyone refute the simple proposition that capitalism, as a system, has an uncanny capacity to trip itself up?

Just as in a simple optical parallax, where all perspectives are equally plausible depending on one's standpoint, here, too, each of the explanations listed above illuminates important aspects of what happened in 2008. And yet they leave us dissatisfied, with a nagging feeling that we are missing something important; that, while we have glimpsed many crucial manifestations of the Crash, its quintessence still escapes us. Why did it happen, *really*? And how could legions of keenly motivated, technically hyper-skilled market observers miss it? If it was not greed and profligacy, loose morals and even looser regulation that caused the Crash and the ensuing Crisis, what was it? If the Marxists' expectation that capitalism's internal contradictions will always strike back is too simple an explanation for the events leading to 2008, what is the missing link there?

My figurative answer is: the Crash of 2008 was what happened when a beast I call the *Global Minotaur* was critically wounded. While it ruled the planet, its iron fist was pitiless, its reign callous. Nevertheless, so long as it remained in rude health, it kept the global economy in a state of *balanced disequilibrium*. It offered a degree of stability. But when it fell prey to the inevitable, collapsing into a comatose state in 2008, it plunged the world into a simmering crisis. Until we find ways to live without the beast, radical uncertainty, protracted stagnation and a revival of heightened insecurity will be the order of the day.

The Global Minotaur: a first glimpse

The collapse of communism in 1991 saw the conclusion of a tragedy with classical overtones, a fatal inversion (a *peripeteia*, as Aristotle would have called it) which began when the noble intentions of revolutionary socialists were first usurped by power-hungry zealots, before giving way to an unsustainable industrial feudalism containing only victims and villains. By contrast, the Crash of 2008 exuded the air of a pre-classical, more mythological and thus cruder sequence of events. It is for this reason that this book adopts a title alluding to a period before tragedy was invented.

I might have called this book *The Global Vacuum Cleaner*, a term that captures quite well the main feature of the second post-war phase that began in 1971 with an audacious strategic decision by the US authorities: instead of reducing the twin deficits that had been building up in the late 1960s (the budget deficit of the US government and the trade deficit of the American economy), America's top policy makers decided to increase both deficits liberally and intentionally. And who would pay for the red ink? Simple: the rest of the world! How? By means of a permanent tsunami of capital that rushed ceaselessly across the two great oceans to finance America's twin deficits.

The twin deficits of the US economy thus operated for decades like a giant vacuum cleaner, absorbing other people's surplus goods and capital. While that 'arrangement' was the embodiment of the grossest imbalance imaginable on a planetary scale, and required what Paul Volcker described vividly as 'controlled disintegration in the world economy', nonetheless it did give rise to something resembling *global balance*: an international system of rapidly accelerating asymmetrical financial and trade flows capable of creating a semblance of stability and steady growth.

Powered by America's twin deficits, the world's leading surplus economies (e.g. Germany, Japan and, later, China) kept churning out goods that Americans gobbled up. Almost 70 per cent of the profits made globally by these countries were then transferred back to the United States, in the form of capital flows to Wall Street. And what did Wall Street do with them? It instantly turned these capital inflows into direct investments, shares, new financial instruments, new and old forms of loans and, last but not least, a 'nice little earner' for the bankers themselves. Through this prism, everything seems to make more sense: the rise of financialization, the triumph of greed, the retreat of regulators, the domination of the Anglo-Celtic growth model. All these phenomena that typified the era suddenly appear as mere by-products of the massive capital flows necessary to feed the twin deficits of the United States.

Clearly, 'the global vacuum cleaner' would have been an accurate description of this book's theme. Its humble origins in the world of domestic appliances might prove a marketing demerit but should not disqualify it *per se*. However, at a more symbolic level, it would have failed to connect with the dramatic, almost mythological, aspects of the international design under which we all laboured prior to the ill-fated 2008 – a design too unstable to survive in perpetuity but, at the same time, one that helped maintain global tranquillity for decades, based upon a constant flow of tribute from the periphery to the imperial centre – tribute that sustained the mutual reinforcement between the US twin deficits and overall demand for the surplus nations' goods and services.

Such were the features of a global beast that roared from the 1970s until so very recently. They lend themselves, I believe, more readily to the Minotaur metaphor than to one involving domestic chores.

Box 1.1
The Cretan Minotaur

The Minotaur is a tragic mythological figure. Its story is packed with greed, divine retribution, revenge and much suffering. It is also a symbol of a particular form of political and economic equilibrium straddling vastly different, faraway lands; a precarious geopolitical balance that collapsed with the beast's slaughter, thus giving rise to a new era.

According to the myth's main variant, King Minos of Crete, the most powerful ruler of his time, asked Poseidon for a fine bull as a sign of divine endorsement, pledging to sacrifice it in the god's honour. After Poseidon obliged him, Minos recklessly decided to spare the animal, captivated as he was by its beauty and poise. The gods, never allowing a good excuse for horrible retribution to go begging, chose an interesting punishment for Minos: using Aphrodite's special skills, they had Minos's wife, Queen Pasiphaë, fall in lust with the bull. Using various props constructed by Daedalus, the legendary engineer, she managed to impregnate herself, the result of that brief encounter being the Minotaur: a creature half-human, half-bull (Minotaur translates as 'Minos's Bull', from the Greek *taurus*, 'bull').

When the Minotaur grew larger and increasingly unruly, King Minos instructed Daedalus to build a labyrinth, an immense underground maze where the Minotaur was kept. Unable to nourish itself with normal human food, the beast had to feast on human flesh. This proved an excellent opportunity for Minos to take revenge on the Athenians, whose King Aegeus, a lousy loser, had had Minos's son killed after the young man had won all races and contests in the Pan-Athenian Games. After a brief war with Athens, Aegeus was forced to send seven young boys and seven unwed girls to be devoured by the Minotaur every year (or every nine years, according to another version). Thus, so the myth has it, a *Pax Cretana* was established across the known lands and seas on the basis of regular foreign tribute that kept the Minotaur well nourished.

Beyond myth, historians suggest that Minoan Crete was the economic and political hegemon of the Aegean region. Weaker city-states, like Athens, had to pay tribute to Crete regularly as a sign of subjugation. This may well have included the shipment of teenagers to be sacrificed by priests wearing bull masks.

Returning to the realm of myth, the eventual slaughter of the Minotaur by Theseus, son of King Aegeus of Athens, marked the emancipation of Athens from Cretan hegemony and the dawn of a new era.

Aegeus only grudgingly allowed his son to set off for Crete on that dangerous mission. He asked Theseus to make sure that, before sailing back to Piraeus, he replaced the original mournful black sails of his vessel with white ones, as a signal to his waiting father that the mission had been successful and that Theseus was returning from Crete victorious. Alas, consumed by joy at having slaughtered the Minotaur, Theseus forgot to raise the white sails. On spotting the ship's black sails from afar, and thinking that his son had died in the clutches of the Minotaur, Aegeus plunged to his death in the sea below, thus giving his name to the Aegean Sea.

A quick perusal of the ancient myth (see Box 1.1) confirms its suitability as a tale of unbalanced might stabilized and sustained by one-sided tribute; of a hegemonic power projecting its authority across the seas, and acting as custodian of far-reaching peace and international trade, in return for regular tribute that keep nourishing the beast within.

In the misty world of Cretan myth, the beast was a sad, unloved, vicious creature, and the tribute was young people, whose sacrifice preserved a hard-won peace. To end its reign, a brave prince, Theseus, had to perform the ugly deed – to slay the Minotaur and usher in a new post-Cretan era. No such heroics were necessary in our more complicated world. The role of the beast was played by America's twin deficits, and the tribute took the form of incoming goods and capital. As for our Global Minotaur's end, it came suddenly, with no physical agent intentionally striking out. The potentially fatal wound was inflicted by the cowardly, spontaneous collapse of the banking system. While the hit was just as dramatic, ending global capitalism's second post-war phase in no uncertain terms, the new era is stubbornly refusing to show its face. Until it does, we shall all remain in the state of *aporia* brought on by 2008.

CHAPTER 2

Laboratories of the future

Our two great leaps forward

Humanity owes its first great leap forward to a crisis. Indeed, we have it on good authority that the farming revolution was brought on by severe food shortages, triggered when population size rose beyond a level that nature could sustain.[1] While we tend to identify progress with gadgets and assorted machinery, none of our proud industrial achievements can compare with the audacity of those prehistoric hunter-gatherers to grow their own food in the face of nature's declining capacity to satisfy their hunger. No innovation behind our gleaming gizmos is equal to the impudent genius of some long-dead early human who aspired to enslave a mammal (often mightier and larger than herself) so as to drink its milk every morning.

Thus food crises of often famine proportions begat brilliant interventions in nature's ways which, about 12,000 years ago, set us on the path to *socialized agricultural production*. And it was this socialized work with soil, seeds and water that gave rise to *surpluses* – i.e. to the production of quantities of food, clothes and other materials that, over a season, exceeded the quantities necessary to replace the food, the clothes and the other materials consumed or used up during that same season. In turn, the ensuing surpluses provided the foundation of 'civilization' as we now know it and the backbone of recorded history.

Indeed, surpluses gave rise to bureaucracies and organized religion (by affording a large minority the privilege of systematically shunning food production), to the written word (whose original purpose was to assist in the book-keeping necessary for keeping tabs on who produced what within clans and families), to sophisticated metal tools (for ploughing the land, harnessing the cows and, ultimately, arming the guardians of the surplus), to biological weapons of mass destruction (as new strands of lethal bacteria evolved in the presence of so much biomass), as well as to differential immunity levels that made farming societies invincible colonizers of non-farming valleys, islands and even continents (recall the hideous encounter of native Americans and Australian aborigines with the bacteria-infested European settlers).

The second great leap forward of our species brought us industrialization. It, too, was a chaotic, unsavoury affair occasioned by another crisis – this time a crisis in which nature had no part. Its roots are deep and extend well into the fifteenth century, if not earlier. Back then, improvements in navigation and ship-building had made possible the establishment of the first truly global trading networks. Spanish, Dutch, British and Portuguese traders began to exchange British wool for Chinese silk, silk for Japanese swords, swords for Indian spices, and spices for much more wool than they had started with. Thus, these goods established themselves as *commodities* and, eventually, as *global currencies*.

Unlike the aristocrats, whose wealth was appropriated from the peasantry or looted from their defeated neighbours, the emerging merchant class benefited from long-distance arbitrage: they transported commodities that were undervalued in one market and sold them at a high price in some remote market. Tragically, the trade in commodities was soon to be augmented by another kind of trade – the trade in slaves, whose heart-wrenching unpaid labour was to generate more of these global commodities (e.g. cotton in the Americas). At some stage landowners in Britain joined this lucrative global trading network in the only way they could: they produced wool, the global commodity that the British Isles could deliver at the time. To do so, however, they expelled most of the peasants from their ancestral lands (to make room for sheep) and built great fences to stop them from returning – the enclosures.

At a single stroke, land and labour had become commodities: each acre of land acquired a rental price that depended on the global price of the wool that one acre could generate in a season. And as for labour, its price was the puny sum the dispossessed ex-peasants could get for doing odd jobs. The coalescence of the merchants' wealth (which was stock-piling in the City of London, seeking ways of breeding more money), a potential working class (the expelled ex-peasants pleading to work for a loaf of bread), unique quantities of coal close to the surface (in England), and some clever tech-nological advances spurred on by the trading opportuni-ties made possible by the ongoing globalization (the steam engine, the mechanical loom, etc.) eventually led to the inven-tion of a new locus of production – the factory. A frenzy of industrialization followed.

Had history been democratic in its ways, there would have been no farming and no industrial revolution. Both leaps into the future were occasioned by unbearably painful crises that made most people wish they could recoil into the past. At *our* moment of Crisis, it is perhaps soothing to recall how crises act upon history as the laboratories of the future.

Condorcet's secret in the Age of Capital

If crisis is history's laboratory, consent is its main driving force. Although violence was never far below the surface, it is remarkable how consensual the resolution of great tensions has been, at least following the second great leap forward that culminated in today's market societies. Despite the organized killing sprees (known also as wars), the famous revolutions and the violent enslavement of whole peoples, explicit force has generally been used only occasionally (even if to devastating effect), and by rulers whose power was on the wane.

Indeed, the power to compel, the power to privatize a large part of the collectively produced surplus and the authority to set the agenda are not forms of might that can be maintained for long on the basis of brute force. The French thinker Marquis de Condorcet put this point deftly at the time of another great convulsion of history, back in 1794, as the French Revolution was preparing to yield its place to a new despotism. Condorcet suggested that 'force cannot, like opinion, endure for long unless the tyrant extends his empire far enough afield to hide from the people, whom he divides and rules, the secret that real power lies not with the oppressors but with the oppressed'. The 'mind forg'd manacles', as William Blake called them, are as real as the hand-forged ones.

Condorcet's secret, as I like to call this noteworthy insight, illuminates much of what makes societies tick. From the fertile agricultural lands which underwrote the pharaohs' reign to the astonishing cities financed by surplus production in the Andes; from the magnificent Babylonian gardens to the golden age of Athens; from the splendour of Rome to the feudal economies that erected the great cathedrals – in all that is nowadays described as 'civilization', the rulers' command over the surplus and its uses was based on a combination of their capacity to make compliance seem individually inescapable (indeed, attractive), ingenious divide-and-rule tactics, moral enthusiasm for the maintenance of the status quo (especially among the underprivileged) and the promise of a pre-eminent role in some afterlife. Only very infrequently was it based on brute force.

All dynamic societies founded their success on two production processes that unfolded in parallel: *the manufacturing of a surplus* and *the manufacturing of consent* (regarding its distribution). However, the feedback between the two processes grew to new heights in the Age of Capital. The rise of *commodification*, which also led to the flourishing of *finance*, coincided with a subtler, more powerful, form of consent. And here lies a delicious paradox: consent grew more powerful the more economic life was financialized. And as finance grew in importance, the more prone our societies became to economic crises. Hence the interesting observation that modern societies tend to produce both more consent and more violent crises.

Why is this? Under feudalism, surplus production and its distribution was a fairly transparent affair. After having piled up the very corn that *they* had produced, the peasants would watch the sheriff depart with the master's share of a resource he had had no hand in producing. Put simply, distribution happened *after* the harvest was in. Who got what chunk of it depended on visible power and customs that everyone understood quite well. But when the market extended its reign into the fields and the workshops, things changed drastically. A veil of obfuscation descended upon the emerging commercial societies, resulting in both new forms of consent and crises (i.e. misfortunes of a purely economic variety).

What was it exactly that made the difference? Why were market societies more prone to economic meltdowns? The main difference occurred when, some centuries before, both land and labour stopped being mere productive inputs. They were, instead, transformed into commodities (traded in specialist markets at free-floating prices). At that point a great inversion occurred: distribution no longer came *after* production. Increasingly, it preceded it. Put simply, the labourers were paid wages in advance of the harvest. By whom? By their 'employers', of course. By people who no longer commanded labour, but instead hired it. By people who, come the nineteenth century, came to be known as *capitalists*.

What is fascinating is that many of the early capitalists had not chosen to be capitalists. Just as, during humanity's first great leap forward, hunter-gatherers did not *choose* to become farmers but were led to agriculture by hunger, so too a large number of former peasants or artisans had no alternative (especially after the enclosures) but to rent land from landlords – and make it pay. To that effect, they borrowed from moneylenders to pay for rent, seeds and, of course, wages. Moneylenders turned into bankers, and a whole panoply of financial instruments became an important part of the business of surplus production and its distribution. Thus *finance* acquired a mythical new role as a 'pillar of industry', a lubricant of economic activity, and a contributor to society's surplus production.

Unlike the landed gentry, the new capitalist employers, not all of them rich, went to bed every night and woke up every morning with an all-pervasive anxiety: would the crop allow them to pay their debts to the landlord and the banker? Would something be left over for their own families after the produce was sold? Would the weather be kind? Would customers buy their wares? In short, they took risks. And these risks blurred everyone's vision regarding the role of social power in determining the distribution of the surplus between the employer, the landowner, the banker and the worker.

Whereas the feudal lord understood that he was *extracting* part of a surplus produced by others, thanks to his political and military might, the anxious capitalist naturally felt that his sleepless nights were a genuine input into the surplus, and that any profit was his just reward for all that angst and for the manner in which he orchestrated production. The moneylender, too, bragged about his contribution to the miracle economy that was taking shape on the back of the credit line he was making available to the capitalist. At least at the outset, as Shakespeare's *Merchant of Venice* illustrates, lending money was not without its perils. Shylock's tragedy was emblematic of the risks that one had to take in order to be the financier of other people's endeavours. But as the Age of Capital progressed, finance became entrenched both in practice and in established ideology.

Meanwhile, the labourers were experiencing formal freedom for the first time ever, even if they struggled to make sense of their new-found liberty's coexistence with another new freedom – the freedom to a very private death through starvation. Those who did find paid work (and they were by no means in the majority) saw their labour diverted from the farms to the workshops and the factories. There, separated from the countryside of their ancestors by the tall walls of the noisy, smoke-filled, grey industrial buildings, their human effort was blended with the mechanical labour of technological wonders such as the steam engine and the mechanical loom. They became participants in production processes over which they had no control and which treated them as small cogs in a vast machine that produced an assortment of products, many of which they would never own.

In this brilliantly challenging world, which encompasses both nineteenth-century Manchester and twenty-first-century Shenzhen, Condorcet's secret appears as an impossible riddle. The exercise of social power retreats behind multiple veils that no amount of rational thinking may penetrate easily. Employer and worker, moneylender and artisan, destitute peasant and dumbfounded local dignitary – they are all stunned by the pace of change. Each feels like a powerless plaything of forces beyond their control or understanding.

The Crash of 2008 also left our world floating in a pool of bewilderment. Its roots are to be found at the dawn of industrial, market societies. Our current *aporia* is a variant of the puzzlement engendered by the simultaneous progression of commodification, financialization, and the crises these processes inevitably occasion.

The paradox of success and redemptive crises

The dynamic of crises was understood well before markets began to dominate and to yield purely economic crises. Nature's keen observers noticed that, when prey is plentiful, the number of predators rises, thus putting the prey population under pressure. Once prey numbers begin to fall, the predators' population shrinks, too. But not for long. For when the decline turns into a crisis, then the prey numbers rebound and the whole cyclical process starts again.

Back in the fourteenth century, Ibn Khaldun (1332–1406) was probably the first scholar carefully to project the prey–predator dynamic onto political society. Based on his close study of the history of the Arab states of Spain and North Africa, he told a story of the rise and fall of regimes, in which rulers play the role of the predator and there is something called *asabiyyah* in the role of prey.[2] *Asabiyyah* is defined as a form of solidarity, group feeling, or cohesion that emerges within small groups as a result of the urge to cooperate in the struggle against need and danger. *Asabiyyah* thus confers power and success on the groups within which it takes root. These groups then rise to power in the urban centres and found great city-states. But, as in the case of predators, success is pregnant with the seeds of its destruction.

Before too long, claimed Ibn Khaldun, the rulers lose touch with their subjects and *asabiyyah* begins to recede. The rituals of power, the hubris that comes with absolute authority and the gratification afforded by amassed riches all conspire to sap the rulers' vigour. Thus *asabiyyah* fades and, at some point, the rulers discover that their authority and power have weakened. Strife and anarchy follow, hope diminishes and optimism fades. Then some other group that has developed *asabiyyah* elsewhere takes over and the cycle continues.

Commercial society is anything but immune to the prey–predator dynamic. Joseph Schumpeter (1883–1950), the doyen of liberal economists (though, paradoxically, he was much influenced by Marx's economics), warned that it is in capitalism's nature periodically to generate violent crises. The reason? Capital's tendency to coalesce into large corporations with significant monopoly power. Successful corporations grow big; then they grow complacent (in ways Ibn Khaldun would have recognized), are usurped by hungry, innovative upstarts, and subsequently fail. While their death causes much pain, the dinosaurs' extinction gives rise to new, more vibrant 'species' of enterprise. In this sense, crises play a crucial, redemptive role in the story of capitalist development.

Interestingly, this dynamic storyline has its roots in Marx's critique of capitalism as a crisis-generating system. Richard Goodwin (1913–96) was a Cambridge economist who summed up Marx's view as follows:

- Capitalism is ruled by two parallel dynamics.
- The *first* dynamic determines the wage share (total wages as a share of national income): as employment increases above a certain threshold, say E, labour becomes scarce, workers' bargaining power rises, and therefore so does the wage share.
- The *second* dynamic determines employment growth: as the wage share surpasses another threshold (W), so employment suffers.

To see how the combination of these two dynamics produces a regular cycle (boom to bust to boom), suppose the economy is growing and employment is on the rise. According to the first dynamic, once employment exceeds threshold level E, wages rise too. But when wages rise above level W, the second dynamic kicks in, reducing employment. At some point, employment falls below E and, as a result, the first dynamic operates in reverse, causing wages to fall. The cycle has, at this point, reached its most depressed state – wages have fallen and unemployment is at its highest. However, with wages below W, it is the second dynamic's turn to go into reverse, boosting employment once again. Once it reaches E again wages are lifted. The economy is in recovery mode, albeit a recovery pregnant with the next crisis.

Note that this cycle was 'produced' without saying anything about money and finance. When finance is added to the mix, the cycle becomes more volatile and a new, unprecedented, systemic risk appears on the horizon: the risk of a catastrophic fall (as opposed to a gradual recessionary decline), followed by a stubborn, long-lasting, depression.

Raising the stakes: crashes, crises and the role of finance

The paradox of success is based on the tendency of some valuable common good, trait or bond to fade. The inevitable crisis thus plays a *redemptive* role, which brings about the revival of the very thing whose demise it was that put the 'system' into a downturn and delivered the crisis itself. From the fluctuations in the relative size of prey and predator populations in the wild, through political power in the Arab city-states, to the wage and employment dynamics in our market societies, crises deliver both retribution and redemption. Famine among predators helps restore the prey population, political downfalls reignite lost solidarity, unemployment leads to new employment via a squeeze on wages, and so on and so forth. Nemesis thus becomes the new source of hubris, and crisis is a prerequisite for the next upturn, for a revitalization of the whole 'ecology' of power, wealth and domination. In this sense, periodic crises, rather than avoidable accidents, constitute 'natural' plunges into some abyss and help history along its path.

Undoubtedly, both nature and history are replete with such cycles. But not all crises can be understood as the passing phase of a regular cycle. Once in a while, a Crisis with a capital C strikes. And then the cycle ends, at least in its existing form. Take, for instance, the Easter Island civilization. Archaeologists tell us that it experienced many cyclical crises in its history. But alas, one big, whopping Crisis wiped it out: once Easter Islanders had chopped down their last tree, the ecological *cum* economic cycle that their activities had been subject to reached a tragic end. All that was left were the magnificent statues as constant reminders of the destructive and disruptive power of Crises.

So what makes a Crisis different from run-of-the-mill crises? A radical inability to act as its own medicine is the answer. Or, put slightly differently, the lack of anything redemptive about it. In short, while crises are phases of some cycle, co-conspirators in its perpetuation, a Crisis spells the end of the current cycle. The year 1929 was just such a discontinuity. This book has been written in the conviction that 2008 is another such discontinuity. If so, the post-2008 world will not be another recapitulation of the Global Minotaur's reign, but the harbinger of a new era, which we can only vaguely make out through the mists of the present. But before anything can be properly discerned, we need to bring finance into the narrative.

The preceding discussion of the Age of Capital has already touched on the way in which commodification of land and labour begat financialization. Let us now see how the newly pivotal role of finance brought about capital-C economic Crises. The key to this is finance's immense capacity to inflate risk. It is one thing to bet one's daily wage on a horse, but quite another to have access to financial instruments that allow one to bet a lifetime's wages on that same horse. *Leveraging* of that sort makes possible fabulous winnings and calamitous losses. John Maynard Keynes (1883-1946) put the same thought more elegantly in his 1936 (Great Depression-inspired) book, known as the *General Theory*:

> Speculators may do no harm as bubbles on a steady stream of enterprise. But the position is serious when enterprise becomes a bubble on a whirlpool of speculation. When the capital development of a country becomes a by-product of the activities of a casino, the job is likely to be ill-done.

Prophetic words indeed.

In the 1970s, Hyman Minsky (1919-96) took Keynes' point a little further, blending it with the cyclical narrative coming out of our paradox of success. Minsky's suggestion was that periods of financial stability and growth cause the rate of defaults on loans to drop and, for this reason, inspire confidence in banks that loans will be repaid. Interest rates thus fall. This encourages investors to take increasing risks, in order to improve their returns. More risks generate a bubble. When the bubble bursts, there are disagreeable effects on the rest of the economy. Interest rates rise fast, financial markets become insanely risk averse, asset prices plunge and a state of depressed stability, or *stagnation*, ensues. However, in this tale, the crisis plays its usual redemptive role: once risk aversion has set in, only 'good' investment projects seek finance. This steadies the financiers' nerves, confidence is restored and the cycle is given another whirl.

However, once in a while the financial bubble inflates so much that its bursting leads to the cycle's collapse – pretty much as the Easter Islanders' volatile economic activity came to a crashing halt when the last tree was felled. When the dust settles, the whole economy lies in ruin, often unable to pick itself up, dust itself down and begin rebuilding.[3] A well-used metaphor is apt: think of what happens as cars get safer: we tend to speed more. While minor accidents make us more careful for a while, every improvement in the car's active (handling, brakes) and passive (airbags) safety features increases our average speed. Though accidents become rarer, when the big one happens our chances of walking away are slim. This is precisely what caused, at least in part, the Crashes of 1929 and 2008: new financial instruments had fuelled speedy growth and had made wild investments seem safer than ever before. Until the accident that we had to have happened.

The Crash of 1929

On a cold January day, back in 1903, a crowd of New Yorkers assembled at Coney Island's Luna Park. They had come not to enjoy the rides or munch the popcorn, but to witness a grotesque scene: Topsy, an elephant who had not taken to captivity gracefully, was to be electrocuted by Thomas Edison, the great inventor. What business did such a brilliant man have killing an elephant in public?

Edison epitomized the new entrepreneur at the heart of a brand-new phase in the development of market societies: an inventor who innovated in order to create monopoly power for himself – not so much for the riches that it provided, but for its own sake; for the sheer glory and the sheer power of it all. He was an entrepreneur who inspired, in equal measure, incredible loyalty from his overworked staff and loathing from his adversaries. He was a friend of Henry Ford, who also famously played a key role in bringing machinery into the lives of ordinary people while, at the same time, turning workers into the nearest a person can come to a machine.

Topsy's execution was a move on an oversized chessboard between two industrial behemoths. Edison's invention of the light bulb had been only the first step in creating electricity generating stations and the network of wires which took that electricity into every American home to light up the bulbs produced en masse by his own factories. Without control of the generation and distribution of electricity, his bulbs would not have made him King of the Electron. Thus occurred the so-called War of the Currents against his great adversary, George Westinghouse.

In a tussle over whose standard would prevail, Edison and Westinghouse bet on different types of electrical current: Edison on DC (direct current) and Westinghouse on AC (alternating current). Both knew that this was a winner-takes-all game. So they fought tooth and nail. Poor Topsy was mere collateral damage, as were a number of other animals that Edison and his employees electrocuted in a bid to besmirch AC by demonstrating its lethal nature, and thus drum up public support for the safer, albeit dearer, DC.

Men like Edison, Westinghouse and Ford were part of the avant-garde of a new era, in which innovations produced new sectors and companies that resembled corporate mini-states. The game they played continues unabated to this day. Think, for instance, of Steve Jobs and his great success with iTunes – an internet-based platform that started life as an online music store but went on to furnish Apple with immense monopoly power over MP3 players and smartphones.[4]

Now, the problem with such vast networked corporations is that they are big enough to subvert the market's normal rules in at least two important ways. First and foremost, the role of price diminishes substantially. In your local farmers' market, for instance, if demand for lemons falls, their price will follow suit, until no lemons remain unsold. Flexible prices help clear the

---

Box 2.1

Pre-1929 crises

Growth spurts generated bubbles from the very beginning. The whole period of the rise of corporate, financialized capitalism was punctuated by one financial crisis after another. In 1847, the end of the first boom in railway building in Britain caused a major banking implosion. In 1873, a six-year-long depression began in the United States as a result of the bursting of a speculative bubble over the building of railways at the end of the American Civil War. A mere three years after the US economy had recovered, another recession struck in 1882 which was to last for three years. In its midst, a major investment firm and the Penn Bank (of Pittsburgh) went under, together with around ten thousand businesses. In 1890, back in the 'old country', Barings Bank's investments in Argentina went bad and nearly brought the London bank down. Though the Bank of England intervened to save Barings, the loss in business confidence reverberated around the world. Three years later, another financial bubble had grown on the back of railway overbuilding in the US. A run on gold reserves followed, and unemployment rose fast (from 4 per cent to 18 per cent), causing a series of industrial strikes that changed the US industrial relations scene. The depression lasted until 1896, when a new gold rush raised the economic tempo, thus ushering in a period of rapid growth which lasted until 1907, at which point a fresh financial crisis, involving a 50 per cent drop in the New York stock exchange, whipped up mass panic, widespread unemployment, business closures, etc. Indeed, it was the Crash of 1907 that led to the creation of America's central bank in 1913, the Federal Reserve System (or Fed) with an explicit remit to prevent similar crises.

shelves of unsold goods and act, in essence, as capitalism's shock absorbers: when demand drops, flexible prices ensure that output does not go to waste. In contrast, corporate giants have another option in the face of lower demand: rather than reduce prices, they can choose to cut production massively, so much so that prices hardly move. So from Edison's time onwards, as prices became 'stickier', capitalism's shock absorbers faded.

Second, colossal projects (like the construction of power stations and telephone networks) require similarly colossal financing. So again, from that time on, banks had to cooperate, syndicate, merge, take each other over, do whatever it took to come up with the rivers of cash that the corporations were willing to borrow, at very attractive rates, given their exuberant profit expectations. It is, therefore, no great surprise that the world of finance began to grow even faster than the corporations.

By the early 1920s, a new boom phase was in evidence. For the first time American workers were told that the cure to poverty had been found: if only they hitched themselves to the bandwagon of corporate, financialized capitalism, life would be good. All it would take was hard work, confidence in Wall Street, and trust in the corporations nestling in its listings.

For a while, it seemed a plausible dream. A worker who, in 1921, started to invest $15 a week from his wages in blue-chip shares, could look forward to having, by 1941 (on the basis of performance between 1921 and 1929), a nice portfolio of shares worth $80,000 and a healthy monthly dividend of $400. These were not empty promises: by 1926, our thrifty worker's stream of monthly savings (which took $3,900 out of his income) had grown to almost $7,000. Three years later, just before the bubble burst, his shares were worth a heart-warming $21,000 (for a cumulative investment of $6,240).

But then the dream turned sour. In short order, $40 billion disappeared from Wall Street. Our parsimonious friend's shares fell, and fell, and fell. By 1932, they were down in value to $4,000. Had he instead stuffed his weekly $15 inside the mattress, he would have amassed more than double the sum in that same eleven-year period.

After the initial shock, expectations of a quick recovery grew. Everyone wanted to believe that 1929 was a mere downturn in the usual cycle. Alas, the stricken economy never managed to react redemptively in response to the shock. National income in the United States continued its free fall. In 1930 it fell by almost 14 per cent in dollar terms; in 1931 it plummeted 25.3 per cent. And when everyone thought the bottom had been reached, it shed yet another 25 per cent. By 1933, all the gains corporate capitalism had made during its most vibrant years had fizzled out. Banks went to the wall in droves for four years running. In 1929 659 banks went out of business; in 1930 another 1,350 followed. In 1931 everyone hoped that things would improve – but to no avail: 2,293 more banks closed their doors permanently. Even in 1932, some 1,453 banks went under. With very few banks surviving, 1933 saw only another thirty-nine bank closures. By then, the United States economy resembled a desert – stable but barren:

> Men who have created new fruits in the world cannot create a system whereby their fruits may be eaten. And the failure hangs over the State like a great sorrow. [A]nd in the eyes of the people there is the failure; and in the eyes of the hungry there is a growing wrath. In the souls of the people the grapes of wrath are filling and growing heavy, growing heavy for the vintage.[5]

Thus poverty was back with a vengeance, only this time the shattered promise of the 1920s made it more unbearable. Meanwhile, Washington was clueless. President Herbert Hoover, his ears ringing with the economists' hollow reassurances (that the self-correcting stabilizers of the market economy were about to kick in), responded like a distressed shopkeeper.

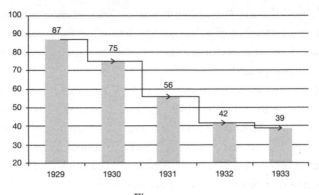

Figure 2.1
US national income (GDP in $ billions)

Indeed, his administration tried to do what every shopkeeper does in lean times: tighten the belt. The only problem was that 1929 was not just another crisis. It was a capital-C variant, during which market faith, belt tightening and money fetishism are ruinous.

Midas loses his touch: the collapse of the Gold Standard

The idea of doing something to arrest the Crisis by exploiting the state's monopoly on money was alien to the elites. At the time of the Crash of 1929, capitalist economies were running what was, in essence, a common currency, much like today's euro in the seventeen countries of the eurozone. It was called the *Gold Exchange Standard*, and it prevented governments from doing what the G20 governments did following the Crash of 2008: pumping money into the economy in a bid to arrest the descent into deflationary chaos.

The rationale behind the Gold Standard was simple: if governments were allowed to print money at will, they would not be able to resist the temptation to do so. The quantity of money would then rise, and more dollars, pounds, francs, etc. would be chasing after the same quantity of goods. Therefore, prices would rise in a relentless tide, boosting inflation, reducing the competitiveness of the country's exports and generally messing with the value of people's hard-earned money. To prevent themselves from diminishing the standing of the currency, politicians tried to find some way of lashing themselves to some imaginary mast – just as Odysseus had done so that he could listen to the Sirens' bewitching song without falling prey to the temptation to disembark onto their island. That mast was the Gold Standard.

It worked as follows: governments agreed to fix the dollar-sterling, the dollar–franc, etc., exchange rates, and also to fix the rate at which all these currencies could be traded for ounces of gold. Moreover, each government agreed to tie the quantity of money it printed to an agreed quantity of gold. Since no one can produce gold at will (with only small amounts being mined every year), this Gold Standard system seemed to guarantee a stable, almost constant, supply of money in each participating country.

Despite many hiccups, especially during the First World War, during which it was suspended, the Gold Standard seemed to deliver the intended price stability. Indeed, inflation was kept at bay, even if we now know that this price stability was bought at the cost of lower growth and employment. Then the Crash of 1929 struck at a time when, because of the Gold Standard, governments' hands were tied. Banks were failing, businesses were collapsing, workers were being laid off in droves, tax takes were falling fast, but the government could not create more money to help either labour or capital weather the storm.

In 1931, Britain and the Scandinavian countries bailed out of the Gold Standard and, as a result, lessened the impact of the Depression on their people. President Hoover steadfastly refused to follow them, convinced that inflation was around the corner. Instead, in order to do something, he acted as many a beleaguered leader acts: he turned against the foreigners. In June 1930, a bill was rushed through Congress raising tariffs on imports in an ill-fated attempt to increase demand for domestically produced goods. When other countries retaliated, world trade suffered, things got worse and the malaise spread further afield.

In the 1932 presidential election, Franklin Delano Roosevelt swept to power with his promised *New Deal*. One of his first measures was to take the United States out of the Gold Standard. Soon, the common currency of the era had collapsed and the New Deal began to take shape. Sadly, despite the many excellent ideas – and the even better intentions – the New Deal did not end the Great Depression. It took industrial-scale carnage (aka the Second World War), and similarly sized public 'investment' in mega-death, to lift the world economy out of the slump.

The two gremlins: the labour and money markets

The Crash of 1929 taught us an important lesson that we seem to have forgotten: the capitalist machine is infested with two gremlins. They render it unstable and prone to crises – and every now and then a capital-C Crisis. What are the two gremlins? Money and labour. Both are, seemingly, commodities not dissimilar to cheese and hammers. When one borrows money to buy a house, one suffers a cost (known as interest) and pays a price (the interest rate). Similarly, hiring labour requires the payment of a fee, not unlike the hiring of an electricity generator. But then come the differences.

A friend of mine once complained that he could not sell his stunning holiday home. I offered him $10 for it to make the pedantic (but not inconsequential) point that it was not that he could not sell it, but rather that he could not sell it at a price of his choosing. A similar point could be made about an idle generator: if the hiring fee is lowered substantially, someone will hire it. These 'points' – however obvious in the case of my friend's house or of the generator – fail to carry through to money loans or to the employment of humans. Let's see why.

In an economy whose rhythm is set by large corporations, the captains of industry make decisions that largely determine the overall economic climate. When the corporations invest freely, the smaller players – resembling the pilot fish that follow the great sharks and feed off their leftovers – follow suit. Demand for both money and labour rides the crest of the corporate investment wave. But what determines the corporate moguls' decision to invest? The answer is optimism!

When chief executive officers (CEOs) ponder a large-scale investment in some new plant or product line, they spend sleepless nights trying desperately to peer into the future. To see what? To see whether there will be sufficient demand for their final product. And what does that ultimately depend on? It depends – and the CEOs know this – on whether other CEOs like them invest now en masse. For if many of them invest, then order books will be full, employment will rise, people will have money to spend, and the economy will be buoyant when they bring their gleaming new product to market. But if not enough of them invest, then orders will be few, employment sluggish and final demand low.

Thus CEOs are caught in the *prophecy paradox*: if each foretells good times, then good times will come and their optimistic forecasts will be confirmed. But if they prophesy bad times, then bad times will ensue, thus validating the original pessimism. Prophecy, therefore, becomes self-fulfilling, and this means that corporate magnates cannot base their decisions either on some scientific analysis of the markets or on rational trains of thought. Box 2.2 outlines a simple game that captures their impossible dilemma.

Box 2.2

When reason defers to expectation

Tom, Dick and Harriet are invited to play a simple game. They are seated in different rooms, isolated from one another. Each is given $100 and the option either of keeping it or of putting it in a joint 'kitty'. The rules are simple: they must contribute either the whole $100 to the kitty or nothing. In the end, if there is $300 in the kitty, that sum is multiplied by ten and the resulting amount is divided equally. Conversely, if the kitty contains less than $300, the whole amount is lost and each player leaves with whatever money they have left (i.e. nothing if they contributed their $100 to the kitty or $100 if they did not contribute).

The best scenario is that each puts $100 into the kitty, the total is multiplied by ten to yield $3,000, and Tom, Dick and Harriet walk away with $1,000 each. But will they contribute $100 each? Let us tap into Harriet's thoughts just before she reaches her decision: 'If I think that *both* Tom and Dick will contribute their $100 each to the kitty, then of course it makes perfect sense for me to contribute my $100 as well. But if one of them fails to do so, then I shouldn't hand over my $100, because $100 is better than nothing!'

So, for Harriet to decide to contribute her $100, she must think: (a) that Tom will predict that both she and Dick will contribute; *and* (b) that Dick will predict that both she and Tom will contribute. Optimism prevails when each expects everyone else to contribute their $100, while pessimism means the opposite. It turns out that the best strategy depends on one's estimation of the degree of optimism among one's co-players.

This game offers an example of what philosophers refer to as an *infinite regress* – a situation where it is impossible to work out what to do rationally. Even if Tom, Dick and Harriet were hyperrational, and respected each other's intelligence to the full, they would still not know what to do. It is the stuff of true human drama played out on a stage where the prophecy paradox makes safe prediction impossible.

The game in Box 2.2 captures neatly the prophecy paradox and resonates powerfully with the experience of a complex, dynamic, corporate capitalism, where, at the first sniff of an impending recession, capitalists go on an investment strike and the recession occurs, confirming their gloomy forecasts. It also echoes John Maynard Keynes' famous description of investment decisions as a realm 'where we devote our intelligences to anticipating what average opinion expects average opinion to be'.[6]

The alert reader will have noticed that something important is missing from this story of growth and crisis: wages and the interest rate! They do not feature at all. While CEOs, employers, industrialists, etc. would *love* to pay lower wages and less interest on their loans, neither gets much of a look in when it comes to the large investment decisions, which depend on the overall business climate. If the business climate is positive, and expectations are buoyant, CEOs will give the green light to large investment projects. If not, no drop in the wage rate and no fall in the rate of interest can persuade them to invest. Period.

As if this were not enough, once a recession has begun, following a Crisis, falling wage and interest rates may cause corporations to panic, to fire workers and to cancel whatever investment projects are already in train. Why? Is this not counter-intuitive? Surely they will hire *more* people if the going wage falls, and will borrow *more* at the new, lower interest rate, won't they? Not at all! Recalling that CEOs have their antennae trained on future demand, worrying almost exclusively about whether future product lines will attract enough paying customers, a fall in wages *today* may be interpreted as a bad omen for future demand. The very fact that trades unions and independent workers have acquiesced in lower wages signals to business leaders that things are bad. And this then translates into a lower expectation of demand. It is a similar story with an interest rate reduction: any such announcement by the central bank, rather than filling a CEO with enthusiasm (because the company's interest payments will fall), may horrify her and lead her to think: 'For the central bank to take this action, things must be truly bad!'

To recap, 1929 ought to have taught us that money and labour are special commodities: those who are in a position to hire their value-creating powers may well actually want less of them if their price drops. The paradox dissolves when one grasps the fact that these two commodities are troublesome gremlins in the capitalist machine because they are truly, radically, different from all other commodities: *nobody wants them for themselves.* They are, in fact, deeply *unwanted.* As Marx put it in the second volume of *Das Kapital*,

> [t]he process of production appears merely as an unavoidable intermediate link, as a necessary evil for the sake of money-making. All nations with a capitalist mode of production are therefore seized periodically by a feverish attempt to make money without the intervention of the process of production.

Come to think of it, no one likes being in debt either. And no employer likes the chore of managing more employees. Loans and workers are necessary evils whose 'services' businesspeople hire only for what they can get out of them: profit. But then profit can only be envisaged if the level of overall (or aggregate) future demand is strong. Unfortunately, the future is unknowable. The only thing business folk know for sure is that demand is never strong for long at a time of falling wages and interest rates. The result is an interesting, albeit tragic, conundrum: at a time of recession, when there is a mounting glut of labour and uninvested savings, a reduction in wages and interest rates does not help. In fact, it deepens the recession.

The ghost in the machine

Judging by our popular culture, we seem obsessed with the fear of losing out to our creations. From the 'Sweet Porridge' story of the Brothers Grimm to Goethe's 'Sorcerer's Apprentice', from the Jewish 'Golem' tales and Mary Shelley's *Frankenstein* to films like *Blade Runner* and the *Terminator* series, the evidence is huge that we fear our own artefacts. However, one tale stands out for its capacity to illustrate the greatest paradox of our post-modern condition: *The Matrix*, a 1999 film by Larry and Andy Wachowski.

In *The Matrix*, our artefacts' rebellion is not just a simple case of 'creator-cide'. Unlike Frankenstein's 'Thing', which attacks humans irrationally out of its sheer existentialist angst, or the machines in the *Terminator* series, which just want to exterminate all humans in order to consolidate their future dominance of the planet, in *The Matrix* the emergent empire of machines is keen to *preserve* human life for its own ends – to keep us alive as a *primary resource*, a source of thermal energy that will allow the machines to power themselves up and continue growing their machine society.

Setting aside the engaging storyline (which revolves around the inevitable human rebellion), this foray into science fiction has, I feel, a serious purpose: to reveal a ghost inside our *current* economic system that undermines the stability of *our* economies. What ghost? *Human labour.*

Question: Do the machines depicted in the economy of *The Matrix* produce value? The answer, of course, depends on what value means and how it differs from price. One definition of value is the price towards which the actual price tends under normal market conditions. Another derives from the idea that the value of things reflects the true costs of producing them. One thing is certain: just like love, poetry, porn and beauty, one knows value when one sees it, even if one finds it impossible to define it analytically.

If you have seen *The Matrix*, you will recall that machines are divided into groups, each playing a different role in sustaining a growing, multifarious machine economy. There is division of labour among them, and the output of each different machine is an indispensable component of the world of machinery it belongs to. But are they producing *value*? I think not.

Why not? Consider the following related questions. Do the tiny springs and cogs inside an old mechanical watch produce *value*? Does the sophisticated software inside some computer create *value* by itself (without a human doing something with it)? More generally, in a world without humans (or in a world where humans have lost control of their minds completely and utterly, as in *The Matrix*), could we speak meaningfully of *value creation*? To me, in each case the answer seems unequivocally negative.

Indeed, what would be the sense in invoking the 'difficult' notion of *value* in the context of systems that feature no humans, especially when the word *function* will do nicely? When watchmakers discuss the wheels, pinions and springs of their object of study, they speak of their *function*. When computer engineers discuss some fully automated system, they have no use for a term like *value* to describe the role or output of the system's components. They, too, speak of functions, outputs, inputs, etc. Value, in that context, would be a superfluous and unnecessarily confusing term. Indeed, it would be quite absurd to speak of the relative value of each unit of machinery produced by the different species of machines (save perhaps as an allegorical word play).

The significance of these thoughts is that if value requires human agency, then we have just spotted a major source of instability buried deep in the foundations of our market societies:

the more successful corporations are at replacing human labour with magnificent machines, and at disciplining human labour to perform with machine-like efficiency, the lower the value that our societies will be producing. They may churn out huge *quantities* of goods and shiny artefacts that we all crave. But the *value* of this avalanche of goodies will be tending to zero, just as the machine economy in *The Matrix* is a value-free zone, despite the vast output of its mechanized workforce.

We are now ready to take a long, hard look at the ghost inside *our* 'machine' (i.e. our corporatized, financialized market societies). Corporations are forced, by competition and by the fear of predators, to try to turn workers into machine-like production units; to make the hiring of a worker no different from the hiring of an electricity generator. And yet, however hard they try to turn humans into machines and to extract output from their 'work' (in the same way as they extract effort from a horse or electricity from a generator), it is an impossible task. The worker *cannot* discard her innate human quirks, rebelliousness, indeterminateness – not even if she honestly wants to. All the things that make her contribution to production inherently unpredictable are part of who she is. Independently of her *will*, one moment she is capable of sloth and the next of brilliant creativity (which no machine can ever understand).

Unable to be liberated from her humanity, incapable of swallowing a blue pill that lifts the weight of consciousness from her weary shoulders (such as the one that the protagonist in *The Matrix* is offered at the start of the film), the human worker remains the last bastion, refusing to be penetrated fully by the market. Her 'humanness' is just not for sale. The result of this stubborn perseverance is the continued prevalence of the *labour contract* – a hopelessly incomplete agreement between labour and capital that acts at once as the *source of instability* and as the *fountain of value*.

Have you ever wondered why markets doggedly refuse to work like clockwork? The answer may lie here, in this simple truth about human nature: even if we wanted to, we are unable to transform ourselves into a fully fledged commodity. This inability may even explain why our economic systems, unlike those we observe in nature, are prone to (capital-C) Crises. The more successful corporations are at turning labour into machine-like intensive activity, the lower the overall value that they generate in the long run and the closer our market society edges to a Crisis.

The process resembles a subterranean, almost ironic, conspiracy between the paradox of success and the prophecy paradox: growth and wealth creation require the utilization of machinery, the development of new technologies and the intensification of labour productivity. Market societies flourish when commodification, financialization and technological innovation are on the rise. The more streamlined and mechanized production gets, the lower the human contribution to its existence becomes and the cheaper it gets. But then the more output that is squeezed from a given amount of human creative input, the less the per-unit value of the output. If mobile phones and all sorts of other gadgets are getting cheaper, it is because their production is increasingly being automated, involving next to no human labour. Thus profit margins decline. When they fall below a certain threshold, the first bankruptcies occur. Like gentle snowflakes at first, their steady fall finally triggers an avalanche. The Crisis then starts. Once it has society in its iron grip, the gremlins in the system (the labour and money markets) refuse to let it escape before humanity has paid a huge price in the form of a wasted generation.

In short, so long as human work resists full commodification, society can produce value; but only under circumstances that also produce crises – and sometimes Crises, too, like that of 1929, or indeed of 2008.

Epilogue: incubation of the Global Plan

Regular crises perpetuate the past by reinvigorating cycles which started long ago. In contrast, (capital-C) Crises are the past's death knell. They function like laboratories in which the future is incubated. They have given us agriculture and the industrial revolution, technology and the labour contract, killer germs and antibiotics. Once they strike, the past ceases to be a reliable predictor of the future and a brave new world is born.

During the past three hundred years or so, the world changed fast and furiously. Commodification began when the peasants were fenced off their ancestral lands. Later, it accelerated when the expelled peasants' labour was immured behind factory walls. Once human labour was blended with the labour of steam engines and mechanical looms, an unstoppable stream of commodities oozed out, spreading to the four corners of the planet. Since then commodification has taken the world by storm. Today, its tentacles have reached into the microcosm, patenting genomes and claiming hybrid organisms as someone's 'property'. Given time, it will privatize the moon and the planets, even the sun and the stars. Yet, its most significant intervention in society's functioning came early on.

From the very beginning, commodification gave rise to an inversion in the production–distribution cycle. Whereas in the past production always preceded the harvest's division between those who laboured to produce it and the powerful elites who claimed part of it on the basis of some socially established convention, the commodification of land and labour meant that the labourers' share was paid in advance (in the form of wages). Distribution, therefore, began even before the harvest was in.

The effect of this inversion cannot be exaggerated. It simultaneously stabilized and destabilized the newly created market societies. Whereas it ushered in a new version of Condorcet's secret, which stabilized the new order no end, it also infused into the fledgling capitalism the potential dynamite that is known as finance. And, as if this were not enough, it added two troublesome gremlins and a frightful ghost for good measure.

The availability of finance, as Dr Faustus was to discover to his detriment, makes the highs soar and the lows unbearable.[7] In addition, the ghost of human free labour haunts market societies by generating a wicked dynamic, which tries, for the sake of profitability, to mechanize human activity, only to find that the more it succeeds the less valuable are the products produced.

The result of these peculiar features of market societies, of capitalism, has been remarkable progress, punctuated with hundreds of crises – some tiny, others painful. The first real Crisis took its time to strike. It awaited the rise of the great corporations and the concomitant dawn of large-scale financialization. When these substantial institutions – Edison, the Wall Street banks, etc. – became prominent players, spreading the good news of the 'end of poverty', 1929 descended on humanity, crushing its great expectations. It felt as if the sky had fallen in.

After Roosevelt's 1932 victory, and despite his New Deal's valiant efforts, the Great Depression clung on tenaciously. The social projects, the new banking regulations, the large public employment programmes, the attempts to help stressed homeowners save their houses, the healthcare provision, the social benefits – all these made a difference, but not as big a difference as had been hoped. Indeed, as late as 1938, a second crisis lashed out – one that was almost as significant as that of 1929. Had it not been for the carnage of the Second World War, the Crash of 1929 would have maintained its grip well into the 1940s.

The war liberated state finances from all political constraints. The government spent money as though there was no tomorrow, the federal debt doubled, but the cycle of self-confirming pessimism was broken. Indeed, the prophecy paradox was defeated in the boardrooms well before the Germans and the Japanese were cornered on the battlefield. Old factories were powered up again, new factories sprang up on green fields, innovation reached its apotheosis, output went through the roof, business boomed. What a pity millions had to die before politics could allow government to act properly and fully.

Once the war began to lose its momentum and peace seemed within reach, US officials began to panic. In a majestic reaction to the fear that the Crisis (during which they had cut their teeth) might rear its ugly head again once the war ended, they got down to business. They planned for the most far-reaching socio-economic engineering human history has ever seen. I call it the *Global Plan*.

CHAPTER 3

The Global Plan

The remarkable opportunity

The United States of America came out of the Second World War as the major (indeed, if one excludes Switzerland, the *only*) creditor nation. For the first time since the rise of capitalism, all of the world's trade relied on a single currency (the dollar) and was financed from a single epicentre (Wall Street). While half of Europe was under the control of the Red Army and Europeans generally were openly questioning the merits of the capitalist system, the New Dealers who had been running Washington since 1932 realized that history had presented them with a remarkable opportunity: to erect a post-war global order that would cast American hegemony in stainless steel. It was an opportunity that they seized upon with glee.

Their audacious scheme sprang from the two sources that lie behind every great achievement – fear and power. The war endowed the United States with unprecedented military and economic might. But, at the same time, it acted as a constant reminder of America's failure properly to come to terms with the legacy of 1929 before the Japanese navy unleashed its bombs

and torpedoes on Pearl Harbor. The New Dealers never forgot
the unexpectedness of the Great Depression and its resistance
to 'treatment'. The more power they felt they had in their hands,
the greater was their fear that a new 1929 could turn it into ash
that trickled through their fingers.

Even before the guns had fallen silent in Europe, and even
before the Soviet Union emerged as a dragon to be slain, the
United States understood that it had inherited the historic role
of reconstructing, in its own image, the world of global capitalism. For if 1929 nearly ended the dominion of capital at a time
of multiple capitalist centres, what would a new 1929 do when
the larger game, global capitalism, revolved around a single axis,
the dollar?

In 1944, the New Dealers' anxieties led to the famous Bretton
Woods conference. The idea of designing a new global order
was not so much grandiose as essential. At Bretton Woods a new
monetary framework was designed, acknowledging the dollar's
centrality but also taking steps to create international shock
absorbers in case the US economy wavered. It took fifteen years
before the agreement could be fully implemented. During that
preparatory phase, the United States had to put together the
essential pieces of the jigsaw puzzle of the Global Plan, of which
Bretton Woods was an important piece.

Bretton Woods

While the war was still raging in Europe and the Pacific, in July
1944, 730 delegates converged on the plush Mount Washington
Hotel located in the New Hampshire town of Bretton Woods.
Over three weeks of intensive negotiations, they hammered out
the nature and institutions of the post-war global monetary order.

They did not come to Bretton Woods spontaneously, but at the
behest of President Roosevelt, whose New Deal administration

was determined to win the peace, after having almost lost the war against the Great Depression. The one lesson the New Dealers had learned was that capitalism cannot be managed effectively at the national level. In his opening speech, Roosevelt made that point with commendable clarity: 'The economic health of every country is a proper matter of concern to all its neighbors, near and far.'

The two issues that were ostensibly central to the conference were the design of the post-war monetary system and the reconstruction of the war-torn economies of Europe and Japan. However, under the surface, the real questions concerned (a) the institutional framework that would keep a new Great Depression at bay, and (b) who would be in control of that framework. Both questions created significant tensions, especially between the two great allies represented, in the US corner, by Harry Dexter White[1] and, in the British corner, by none other than John Maynard Keynes. In the aftermath of the conference, Keynes remarked:

> We have had to perform at one and the same time the tasks appropriate to the economist, to the financier, to the politician, to the journalist, to the propagandist, to the lawyer, to the statesman – even, I think, to the prophet and to the soothsayer.

Two of the institutions that were designed at Bretton Woods are still with us and still in the news. One is the International Monetary Fund (IMF), the other the International Bank for Reconstruction and Development (IBRD), today known simply as the World Bank.[2] The IMF was to be the global capitalist system's 'fire brigade' – an institution that would rush to the assistance of any country whose house caught (fiscal) fire, handing out loans on strict conditions that would ensure that any balance of payments deficits would be fixed and the loans repaid. As for the World Bank, its role would be that of an international investment bank, with a remit to channel productive investments to regions of the world devastated by the war.

However, the one institution that left the greatest mark on post-war history is no longer with us, its demise in 1971 marking the end of the Global Plan and the beginning of the Global Minotaur's reign. This was the new exchange rate regime that came to be known as the 'Bretton Woods system' – a system of fixed exchange rates, with the dollar at its heart. The main idea was that each currency would be locked to the dollar at a given exchange rate. Fluctuations would be allowed only within a narrow band of plus or minus 1 per cent, and governments would strive to stay within this band by buying or selling their own dollar reserves. A renegotiation of the exchange rate of a particular country was only allowed if it could be demonstrated that its balance of trade and its balance of capital flows could not be maintained, given its dollar reserves. As for the United States, to create the requisite confidence in the international system, it committed itself to pegging the dollar to gold at the fixed exchange rate of $35 per ounce of gold and to guarantee full gold convertibility for anyone, American or non-American, who wanted to swap their dollars for gold.

During the debate on what that new system should look like, John Maynard Keynes made the most audacious proposal that has ever reached the bargaining table of a major international conference: to create an International Currency Union (ICU), a single currency (which he even named – the *bancor*) for the whole capitalist world, with its own international central bank and matching institutions. Keynes' proposal was not as impudent as it seemed. In fact, it has withstood the test of time quite well. In a recent BBC interview, Dominique Strauss-Kahn, the IMF's then managing director, called for a return to Keynes' original idea as the only solution to the troubles of the post-2008 world economy.[3] But what was the nub of the proposal? It was to bring on the benefits of a common currency (trade facilitation and convenience, price stability, predictability in international trading) without suffering the main demerits that come when disparate economies are monetarily bound together.

The lost opportunity

The problem with currency unions, as Argentina was to discover in the late 1990s and Europe in the aftermath of the Crash of 2008, is the simple fact of life that trade and capital flows can remain systematically unbalanced for decades, if not centuries. Come what may, some regions within a country (e.g. the Stuttgart area in Germany, the Greater London area in Britain, or the Shanghai region in China) will *always* post a surplus in their trading with other regions (e.g. with eastern *Länder*, with Yorkshire, or with the western provinces of China). So it is with states within federations: California will never balance its trade with Arizona, and Tasmania will always be in deficit vis-à-vis Victoria and New South Wales. Given that these trade imbalances are chronic, something has to take the slack; something must give.

When each of these entities has its own currency, it is the exchange rate that gradually shifts in order to absorb the strain caused by the trade imbalances. Before the euro was established, Germany's persistent surplus vis-à-vis countries like Greece and Italy resulted in a gradual devaluation of the drachma and the lira relative to the Deutschmark. Thus balance was maintained, as the growing trade asymmetries were cancelled out by analogously deepening imbalances in the exchange rates.

However, once these economic regions are bound together by the same currency (as in the United States or the eurozone), something else is required to release the tension caused by unbalanced trade and capital flows – some mechanism for recycling surpluses from the surplus regions (e.g. London or California) to the deficit regions (e.g. Wales and Delaware). Such recycling might be in the shape of simple transfers (e.g. paying unemployment benefits in

Yorkshire through taxes raised in Sussex). Or – and this is much more desirable for both the surplus and the deficit regions – it might be in the form of productive and profitable investments in the deficit regions (e.g. directing business to build factories in the north of England or Ohio).

In a sense, the reason why the dollar-zone (i.e. the United States) is a successful currency union whereas the eurozone is plagued with crises is that America features at least two surplus recycling mechanisms, whereas Europe boasts none (see Box 3.1). Indeed, without an effective surplus recycling mechanism in place, a currency union is bound to succumb to tectonic shifts, which eventually cause great cracks to form before finally the union shatters.

At Bretton Woods, where the whole post-war order was being blueprinted, Keynes was a concerned man. He knew that, just like the pre-war Gold Standard, an international system of fixed exchange rates would not be able to sustain serious shocks. He predicted that even minor crises could bring on a major Crisis. To avert that, the new international system ought to feature a global surplus recycling mechanism (GSRM). Its purpose? To prevent the build-up of systematic surpluses in some countries and of persistent deficits in others.

Why were trade imbalances such a source of worry? Keynes believed that, if global trade was badly imbalanced, with some countries (e.g. the United States) enjoying large surpluses and others in deep deficit, a small crisis anywhere could easily turn into another global catastrophe. To begin with, we should note that trade deficits usually go hand in hand with governments that are also in deficit. Suppose a crisis occurred anywhere in the Bretton Woods system. The fall in demand would trickle down to the deficit countries. And then all hell would break loose.

Once the crisis began, whether in a surplus country or not, it would inevitably soon reach a deficit nation. Even if it arrived in the form of a small downturn, some debtors would be made to feel that they were carrying too much debt. Keen to reduce their exposure, they would cut spending. But since, at the level of the national economy, society's overall demand is the sum of private and public expenditure, when a large segment of the business community tries to reduce debt (by cutting expenditure), overall demand declines, sales drop, businesses close their doors, unemployment rises and prices fall. As prices fall, consumers decide to wait for them to fall further before buying costly items. A vicious debt–deflation cycle thus takes hold.

Now, since this is a deficit country, the government is more likely than not to be labouring under an already considerable budget deficit (with tax revenue less than expenditure) and a large accumulated public debt. The recession squeezes taxes, boosts the state's deficit and forces the government to pay higher interest rates to service its increasing debts. Politicians react instinctively by cutting public spending in the midst of the recession. Thus, with both private and public expenditure falling fast, domestic demand collapses.

In a knee-jerk reaction, the stricken government, unable to increase public expenditure itself, will seek ways to 'import' demand from abroad. Keynes surmised that it would purposely violate the rules of the Bretton Woods system. Why? The 'system' requires that, in order to counter the tendency of the currency to fall during the debt–deflationary crisis, the government should use its dollar reserves to stabilize it within the original ±1 per cent band. But the government, desperate to increase exports as the only way to counter the recession, would have every incentive to do precisely the opposite – to hoard its dollar reserves and instead to approach the Bretton Woods system's administrators, begging them to allow the currency to be devalued.

Box 3.1
Surplus recycling mechanisms: capitalism's *sine qua non*

Surplus recycling is an integral component of any society that organizes production through the market. In feudal times, it was unnecessary: the peasants tilled the land, and once the harvest was collected the sheriff would extract a portion of it on the lord's behalf. Thus, distribution came after production. Later, the lord's share would be sold in markets and the proceeds would enrich the aristocrat. Part of that profit was occasionally loaned, contributing to the nascent capital markets of the day.

However, especially after the enclosures, and once the peasants lost their access to land, production was organized by small-scale tenant entrepreneurs (often ex-peasants). They would bring in hired labour and pay rent to the landlord. But to do so they had to borrow money (to advance wages and buy raw materials), in the hope that their future revenue would show a small surplus (i.e. would exceed the sum of the loans, the interest and the rent payments). Thus, suddenly, and courtesy of an enhanced credit system, income distribution was largely determined *before* the harvest was in.

This meant that the value of 'things' not yet produced, and the anticipated surplus from their production, was recycled from the future to the present. It is in this sense that *surplus recycling* was always an integral component of capitalism. Indeed, it took at least two different forms: recycling from the future to the present (as described above) and recycling from one region to another. Surpluses produced in Manchester were recycled in faraway places, e.g. India, where they were invested for the purposes of creating markets for linen and other Mancunian industrial products.

In general, any economic system contains units that are prone to showing surpluses and others that are more likely to report deficits. To maintain balance, the system must feature surplus recycling mechanisms that maintain the flow of surpluses from the future to the present, from the urban centres to the rural areas, from the developed regions to the less developed ones, etc.

Surplus recycling becomes, however, ever more pressing when the various regions are tied together by a common currency or some form of fixed exchange rate. The persistent deficits and surpluses within such a currency union are like tectonic plates pushing against one another. Once currency devaluations are no longer possible, to take some of the strain, the forces generated by ever-expanding trade imbalances threaten the union with earthquakes of increasing strength. Since a currency cannot be devalued to lessen the accumulating trade deficits of the union's 'poor relations', the strains on the fixed exchange rate or on the common currency will grow and grow until the system cracks. This is what happened in Argentina in the late 1990s, when, in the absence of a surplus recycling mechanism, the country's deteriorating trade deficit eventually took its toll on the fixed exchange rate with the US dollar. The same negative dynamic is currently at play within the eurozone – see chapter 8.

The two surplus recycling mechanisms characteristic of the United States since the Second World War have been the simple transfer union instituted by the New Deal in the late 1930s and the complicated military-industrial complex, which developed in the 1940s. The former works straightforwardly, by ensuring that the unemployment and health benefits of deficit states are paid for by Washington, dipping into taxes raised in surplus states, e.g. California and New York. The second mechanism, too, turns on a political arrangement: whenever a conglomerate like Boeing receives a large Pentagon contract to build a new fighter jet or missile system, it is stipulated that some of the production facilities must be located in depressed, deficit states. This recycling takes the form not of loans and transfers but of productive investments in deficit regions that utilize surpluses produced in the surplus regions.

All sorts of excuses could be made in support of this demand (e.g. that the country has run out of dollars). Keynes knew that, at a time of crisis, it would be politically impossible to force the deficit countries to apply the agreed rules. Other deficit countries would follow suit and the system of fixed exchange rates would collapse. Just as it did on 15 August 1971.

With these troubled thoughts in mind, Keynes designed and proposed the ICU so as to deal with two potential problems at once: to avert systematic trade imbalances and to endow the commonwealth of capitalist nations with the flexibility necessary to deal with future catastrophic crashes (like that of 1929). The proposal was both simple and audacious: the ICU would grant each member country an overdraft facility, i.e. the right to borrow at zero interest from the international central bank. Loans in excess of 50 per cent of a deficit country's average trade volume (measured in *bancors*) would also be made, but at the cost of a fixed interest rate. In this manner, deficit countries would be given the flexibility to boost demand in order to arrest any debt–deflation cycle without having to devalue the currency.

At the same time, there would be a penalty for excess trade surpluses: recognizing that a systematic surplus is the obverse of a systematic deficit, Keynes' proposal stipulated that any country with a trade surplus that exceeded a certain percentage of its trade volume should be charged interest, which would force its currency to appreciate. These penalties would, in turn, finance the loans to the deficit countries, acting as an automatic GSRM.

Lionel Robbins, an influential British economist and the pioneer behind the rise of the London School of Economics and Political Science, wrote that, upon hearing Keynes' proposals, the conference participants were stunned: '[I]t would be difficult to exaggerate the electrifying effect on thought throughout the whole relevant apparatus of government...nothing so imaginative and so ambitious had ever been discussed.' Nevertheless, the intellectual value and technical competence of this well-laid plan was not in tune with America's priorities.[4]

The United States, which emerged from the war as the world's powerhouse, had no interest in restraining its own capacity to run large, systematic trade surpluses with the rest of the world. The New Dealers, however respectful they might have been of John Maynard Keynes, had another plan: a Global Plan, according to which the dollar would effectively become the world currency and the United States would export goods *and* capital to Europe and Japan in return for direct investment and political patronage – a hegemony based on the direct financing of foreign capitalist centres in return for an American trade surplus with them.[5]

The rise of the fallen

The Global Plan started life as an attempt to kick-start international trade, create markets for US exports, and address the dearth of international investment by private US companies. But before long it had developed into something bigger and supposedly better.

To give Bretton Woods a strong backbone, the New Dealers were determined to support the dollar by creating, within the Bretton Woods fixed exchange system, at least two additional strong currencies that would act as shock absorbers in case the American economy took one of its many periodic downturns. The idea was to find ways to absorb such shocks until Washington managed to reverse the downturn in its own backyard. Without these supporting pillars, the Bretton Woods system, they feared, would be too precariously balanced.

However, strong currencies cannot be willed into existence. They must be underpinned by heavy industry, as well as by adjacent trade zones, a form of *Lebensraum* (or vital space) that provides the requisite demand for manufacturing products. The New Dealers, thus, understood that their work was cut out for them. Had they not been energized by the experience of running the war economy for four long years, it is doubtful whether they would have taken on a task of such scope and ambition.

It is history's wont to turn unforeseeable developments into apparent inevitabilities. At war's end, Germany was left smouldering, divided into different occupation zones, devastated and despised by the whole world; Japan was still numb with the humiliation of surrender, wounded by the nuclear attacks on Hiroshima and Nagasaki, struggling to come to terms with the immense death

---

Box 3.2
The Global Plan's architects

Four New Dealers played crucial roles in fashioning the Global Plan. They were, not by chance, also the architects of the Cold War. They shared a pragmatic view that was conceived in the shadow of the Great Depression and forged during the war. Convinced that 'free market capitalism' had to be planned meticulously by Washington, and in a manner not too dissimilar to the successful running of the war economy, they sought to project onto a global canvas the successful recipe that had brought America out of the doldrums. Intent on winning the peace, they sought to empower US business through a combination of New Deal-inspired interventions and the technological advances achieved by the military-industrial complex. The four men were:

- **James Forrestal**, secretary of defence (and previously secretary of the navy)
- **James Byrnes**, secretary of state
- **George Kennan**, director of policy planning staff at the State Department and renowned 'prophet' of Soviet containment
- **Dean Acheson**, leading light in all major post-war designs (the Bretton Woods agreement, the Marshall Plan, the prosecution of the Cold War, etc.) and secretary of state from 1949 onwards.

toll on the east Asian and Polynesian battlefields, and labouring under an American occupation. At this time the writing of the eventual post-war script was definitely *not* on the wall!

No one had any inkling of the role that these once proud but now ruined countries would be playing within a few years. The notion that Germany and Japan would become pillars of the new Global Plan was as outlandish as it was outrageous. And yet, it was the notion on which the New Dealers converged around 1947. How did that choice come about? The answer is gradually.

At first it seemed inconceivable, at least to the British, that Britain would not be a central pillar of the Global Plan. However, the chances of London being kept at the centre of the post-war international design by Washington were always slim. Even before the war, President Roosevelt was aghast at Britain's imperial demeanour. It can be argued that the United States, having extracted large payments from Britain during the war, manoeuvred immediately after the end of the war to ensure that London was deprived of a dominant position in relation to Middle East oil. At the same time, Washington effectively underfinanced Britain during the early post-war period, while insisting on sterling convertibility. So, when the fiscal weakness of the British state came to the fore, its fast-declining industry proved unable to provide London with the necessary revenues, the Labour Party swept to power in 1945, and Britain's political elite displayed a certain reluctance to come to terms with the impending end of empire, the scene was set for Britain's marginalization. The final straw was the slide of the pound to eventual non-convertibility. It gave the New Dealers an excuse to leave Britain on the margins of the Global Plan. It took the 1956 Suez Canal trauma and the CIA's constant undermining of its colonial rule in Cyprus throughout the 1950s for Britain to realize this turn in US thinking.[6]

Once Britain was deemed 'inappropriate', the choice of Germany and Japan appeared increasingly logical. Both countries had been rendered dependable (thanks to the over-whelming presence of the US military); both featured solid industrial bases; and both offered a highly skilled workforce and a people that would jump at the opportunity of rising, phoenix-like, from the ashes. Moreover, they both offered considerable geostrategic benefits vis-à-vis the Soviet Union.

Nonetheless, there was a good deal of resistance to this idea to be overcome – resistance grounded in the urge to punish Germany and Japan by forcing them to deindustrialize and return to an almost pastoral state from which they would never again be able to launch an industrial-scale war. Indeed, Harry White, the US representative at Bretton Woods, had advocated the effective removal of Germany's industry, forcing German living standards down to those of the country's less-developed neighbours. In 1946, the Allies, under the auspices of the Allied Control Council, ordered the dismantling of steel plants with a view to reducing German steel production to less than 6 million tons annually, i.e. around 75 per cent of Germany's pre-war steel output. As for car production, it was decided that output should dwindle to around 10 per cent of what it had been before Germany invaded Poland.

Things were a little different in Japan. Since Japan was administered as an occupied country by one man, General Douglas MacArthur, supreme commander of the allied powers, US policy could be dictated directly, unencumbered by the need to negotiate with other allies (as was the case in Germany). MacArthur decided that Japan should not go through an equiv-alent process of de-Nazification and went to great lengths to exonerate the emperor and the Japanese political, military and economic elites. Nevertheless, during the first two years of occu-pation, he, too, had to argue vigorously with Washington policy makers against punishing Japan by destroying, or severely circumscribing, its industrial base.

The sea change against the idea of flattening the industrial sectors of Germany and Japan came with the increasing tension between the United States and the Soviet Union. It was George Kennan's 'Long Telegram' from Moscow in February 1946, heralding the Cold War spirit, that created the circumstances for a change of heart about Germany. The pivotal moment came in 1947, when President Harry Truman (who had taken over in 1945 after President Roosevelt's death) announced his notorious 'Doctrine': the United States would, from that moment onwards, make the containment of Soviet influence its top priority.

The first on-the-ground manifestation of the Truman Doctrine was the American involvement in the brutal Greek Civil War (which the British had started but could not afford to finish). After a few months of proxy war in the mountains of Greece, there was nearly a direct confrontation elsewhere, when the Western occupiers of West Berlin tussled with the Soviet occupiers of East Berlin – a mêlée which led to a prolonged airlift of supplies from West Germany to West Berlin, over the lines of the Red Army.

The Cold War had begun. From the perspective of the Global Plan, the Truman Doctrine, the Greek Civil War and the Berlin crisis signalled the end of any plan to level West Germany or to maintain a grudge against the Japanese. The road was thus clear to turn the two conquered industrial nations, Germany and Japan, into the Global Plan's pillars.

The Marshall Plan to dollarize Europe and rehabilitate Germany

The speech in which President Truman announced his Doctrine on 12 March 1947 contained some firm financial data:

the United States was committing $400 million to a civil war that haunts Greeks to this very day. A few months later, on 5 June, George Marshall, Truman's secretary of state, addressed a Harvard audience with a speech that marked the beginning of the Marshall Plan, a massive aid package that was to change Europe forever.

Its formal name was the European Recovery Program and it was the brainchild of the Global Plan's four architects mentioned above (see Box 3.2). The fact that it was meant as a game-changing intervention, the purpose of which was clearly to establish a new Global Plan, can be gleaned from some key words employed by Marshall in that important speech: 'The modern system of the division of labor upon which the exchange of products is based is in danger of breaking down.' The point of the Marshall Plan was, put simply, to save global capitalism from some future 1929-like Crisis.

During the first year of the Marshall Plan, the total sum involved was in the order of $5.3 billion, a little more than 2 per cent of US GDP. By 31 December 1951, when the Marshall Plan came to an end, $12.5 billion had been expended. The end result was a sharp rise in European industrial output (about 35 per cent) and, more importantly, political stabilization and the creation of sustainable demand for manufacturing products, both European and American.

Not all of the New Dealers, it must be said, bought into the Truman Doctrine and the Marshall Plan. For instance, Henry Wallace, the former vice president and secretary of agriculture, who was fired by Truman for disagreeing with the Cold War's imperatives, referred to the Marshall Plan as the 'Martial Plan'. He warned against creating a rift with America's wartime ally, the Soviet Union, and remarked that the conditions attached to the Soviet Union's invitation to be part of the Marshall Plan were intentionally so designed that Stalin would be obliged to reject them (which, of course, he did). A number of academics of the New Deal generation, among them Paul Sweezy and John Kenneth Galbraith, also rejected Truman's cold-warrior tactics. However, they were soon to be silenced by the witch-hunt orchestrated by Senator Joseph McCarthy and his House Committee on Un-American Activities.

The Marshall Plan involved not only a great deal of money but also vital institutions. On 3 April 1948, Truman established the Economic Cooperation Administration, and thirteen days later the United States and its European allies created the Organisation for European Economic Co-operation (OEEC), with a remit to work out where to channel the funding, under what conditions, and to what purpose. The first chair of the OEEC (which later, in 1961, evolved into what we know today as the Organisation for Economic Co-operation and Development, the OECD) was Robert Marjolin.[7] One of the most unsung yet lasting legacies of the Marshall Plan was the integration of defeated and despised Germany into the institutions of European integration.

Indeed, the Americans' condition for parting with about 2 per cent of their GDP annually was the erasure of intra-European trade barriers and the commencement of a process of economic integration that would increasingly be centred around Germany's reviving industry. In this sense, the Marshall Plan may be regarded as the progenitor of today's European Union (EU). Indeed, from 1947 onwards, the US military (and in particular the Joint Chiefs of Staff at the Pentagon) called for the 'complete revival of Germany industry, particularly coal mining' and pronounced that the latter was acquiring 'primary importance' for the security of the United States.

However, it would be a while longer before the rejuvenation of Germany's industrial might became an openly declared aim. For even as the Marshall Plan unfolded, the dissolution of

German factories was continuing. It is indicative of the period that in 1949 German Chancellor Konrad Adenauer pleaded with the Allies to put an end to factory liquidations.

The most resistant of the Allies to the notion of an industrialized post-war Germany was, as one might have expected, France. The French demanded the implementation of the agreement of 29 March 1946, by which the Allies had ruled that half of Germany's industrial capacity should be destroyed (involving the demolition of 1,500 plants). And it was implemented, or at least in part. By 1949, more than 700 plants had been dismantled and West Germany's annual steel output was reduced by a massive 6.7 million tons.

So what was it that convinced the French to accept the reindustrialization of Germany? The simple answer is – the United States of America. When the New Dealers formed the view, around 1947, that a new currency must rise in Europe to support the dollar, and that this currency would be the Deutschmark, it was only a matter of time before the plan to destroy German industry would be scrapped. The price France had to pay for the great benefits of the Marshall Plan, and for its central administrative role in the management of the whole affair (through the OEEC), was the gradual acceptance that Germany would be restored to grace, courtesy of the new US Global Plan.

In this context, it is useful to think of the Marshall Plan as the Global Plan's foundation stone. And when the Marshall Plan began to run out of steam in 1951, Phase 2 of the American design for Europe was commencing: integration of its markets and its heavy industry. That second phase came to be known as the European Coal and Steel Community (ECSC), the precursor to today's European Union. As was intended by the New Dealers, the new institution was soon to provide the vital space that the resurgent German industry required in its immediate economic environment.

The European Union and the Japanese miracle

Students of European integration are taught that the European Union started life in the form of the ECSC. What they are less likely to come across is the well-kept secret that it was the United States that cajoled, pushed, threatened and sweet-talked the Europeans into putting it together.

Technically speaking, the ECSC was a common market for coal and steel, linking West Germany, France, Italy, Belgium, Luxembourg and Holland. Not only did it involve the dismantling of all trade barriers between these countries for coal and steel products, but, moreover, it featured supra-national institutional links, whose purpose was to regulate production and price levels. In effect, and despite the propaganda to the contrary, the six nations formed a coal and steel cartel.

European leaders like Robert Schuman (a leading light in the ECSC's creation) stressed the importance of this coming-together from the (pertinent) perspective of averting another European war and forging a modicum of political union. Creating a shared heavy industry across, primarily, France and West Germany would, Schuman rightly believed, both remove the causes of conflict and deprive the two countries of the means by which to prosecute it.

Thus, West Germany was brought in from the cold and France gradually accepted its reindustrialization – a development essential to the New Dealers' Global Plan. Indeed, it is indisputable that, without the United States' guiding hand, the ECSC would not have materialized. Contrary to the Europeans' self-adulatory narrative (according to which European unification was a European dream made real thanks to European diplomacy and an iron will to put the continent's violent past behind it), the reality is that European integration was a grand American idea implemented by American diplomacy of the highest order. That the Americans who effected it enlisted in their cause enlightened politicians like Schuman does not change this reality.

There was one politician who saw this clearly: General Charles de Gaulle, the future president of France, who was to come to blows with the United States in the 1960s – so much so that he removed France from the military wing of the North Atlantic Treaty Organization (NATO). When the ECSC was formed, de Gaulle denounced it on the basis that it was creating a united Europe in the form of a restrictive cartel and, more importantly, that it was an American creation, under Washington's influence, and better suited to serving *its* Global Plan than to providing a sound foundation for a New Europe. For these reasons, de Gaulle and his followers voted against the formation of the ECSC in the French parliament.

Let us turn now to the second pillar that was intended to support the dollar, this time on the other side of the northern hemisphere. The restoration of Japan as an industrial power proved less problematic for the New Dealers than Germany had. The eastern version of the Global Plan was helped significantly by the onslaught of Chairman Mao's Chinese Communist Party against Chiang Kai-shek's nationalist government army.

The more Mao seemed to evade attacks on his guerrillas, invoking the fabled pre-war Long March, and the closer his final showdown with Chiang Kai-shek came, the more General MacArthur edged toward a resolution to bolster Japanese industry, rather than succumbing to pressures to weaken it. However, there was a snag: while Japan's industry (and infrastructure) emerged from the war almost intact (in sharp contrast to Europe's), it was plagued by a dearth of demand. The New Dealers' original idea was that the Chinese mainland would provide the yen-zone with its much-needed vital space, just as the rest of Europe was to provide Germany's factories with the requisite markets. Alas, Mao's eventual victory threw a spanner in those works.

General MacArthur understood the problem and tried to convince Washington to embark upon a second Marshall Plan, within Japan itself. However, the New Dealers could not see how enough demand might ever be created within Japan alone, without significant trade links with its neighbours. In any case, at that time they had enough on their plate, preoccupied as they were with the struggle to convince Congress to keep pumping dollars into Europe. However, MacArthur's luck changed when, on 25 June 1950, North Korean and Chinese communists attacked South Korea, with a view to unifying the peninsula under their command.

Suddenly, the Truman Doctrine shifted focus from Europe to Asia, and the great beneficiary was Japanese industry. Mindful of the difficulty Japan was having in developing its industry due to the lack of consumer purchasing power, the New Dealers had been seeking ways to boost demand within Japan well before Kim Il Sung's escapade in Korea.

The Marshall Plan was, initially, to last until 1953. But the war in Korea encouraged the New Dealers to alter course: they would wind the Marshall Plan down in Europe and shift funds to Japan, whose new role would be to produce the goods and services required by US forces in Korea. A fascinating case of indirect war-financing of an old foe!

As for looking after Europe, the idea was that the first three years of the Marshall Plan had dollarized Europe sufficiently, and that from 1951 onwards, the cartelization centred on Germany's resurgent industry (in the context of the newly instituted ECSC) would generate enough surplus for Europe to move ahead under its own steam.[8]

The US transfers to Japan were quite handsome: from day one, they amounted to almost 30 per cent of Japan's total trade. And, just as in Europe, the United States did not just pour money in. It also created institutions and used its global power to bend existing institutions to the Global Plan's will. Within Japan, the United States wrote the country's new constitution and empowered the famed Ministry for International Trade and Industry to create a powerful, centrally planned (but privately owned), multi-sectoral industrial base. Overseas, the New Dealers clashed with, among others, Britain to have Japan admitted to the General Agreement on Tariffs and Trade (the ancestor of today's World Trade Organization). The importance of this manoeuvre cannot be underestimated, as it allowed Japanese manufactures to be exported, with minimal restrictions, wherever the United States considered would be a good destination for its new protégé's goods.

In conclusion, the New Dealers' central organizing principle was that American global hegemony meant 'looking after', nursing and nurturing two ex-enemy countries. This they did by ensuring that there was strong demand for German and Japanese industrial output among other capitalist countries. It also meant that Europe and US-controlled Asia were well stocked with US dollars, so that they could buy selected high-value-added American goods (e.g. aeroplanes, armaments, construction equipment). Stabilizing global capitalism was essential to maintain the Bretton Woods system and to enhance US prosperity and power.

With this in mind, US administrators took audacious steps to create zones for the Deutschmark and the yen, to provide their ex-enemies with the initial liquidity necessary to restart their industrial engines, and to found the political institutions that would allow the green shoots to flourish and grow into the mighty pillars that the dollar-zone required for long-term support. Never before in history has a victor supported the societies that it had so recently defeated in order to enhance its own long-term power, turning them, in the process, into economic giants.

The Global Plan's geopolitical ideology

The United States emerged from the Second World War with a healthy respect for the colonized and considerable hostility toward their European colonizers. Britain's stance in India and Cyprus, and even its incitement of the Greek Civil War (as early as 1944), was thoroughly criticized by the New Dealers. France, Holland and Belgium, too, were chastised for their ludicrous ambitions to remain the colonial masters in Africa, Indochina and Indonesia, despite the sorry state in which the war had left them.

Yet, the Global Plan put the United States' liberal attitude toward liberation movements under strain. Indeed, the interests of many national liberation movements were deemed antagonistic to the interests of America's European and East Asian creations. Washington decided, early on, that Europe and Japan could only be 'stabilized' politically if some rather unsavoury characters were co-opted.[9] Moreover, securing unhindered energy supplies to Europe and Japan, as well as sources of plentiful demand for their industrial output, put the United States on a collision course with various liberation movements that would otherwise appear quite benign to Washington (e.g. Vietnamese anti-colonialists).

The loss of China, the escalation of liberation movements in South East Asia that Mao's victory was inspiring, the stirrings in Africa which gave the Soviet Union an opening into that continent – all these developments enticed the United States into developing an aggressive stance toward liberation movements in the Third World, which Washington soon came to identify with the threat of rising input prices not so much for itself but rather for its two important protégés, Japan and Germany.

In short, the US took it upon itself to relegate the periphery, and the Third World *in toto*, to the role of supplier of raw materials to Japan and Western Europe. The result was a series of coups and wars, which the New Dealers and their successors in government pursued as part of consolidating the Global Plan. In due course, distrusted elected governments were overthrown, military interventions were authorized, nasty dictatorships were either installed or supported, large-scale wars were fought in Korea and Vietnam. Partly in the context of pursuing the Cold War, and partly in order to maintain the Global Plan, the geopolitical plot was thickening by the day. With every new twist the stakes got higher, but the rewards seemed to be proliferating, too.

In the process, American multinationals in energy and other mining activities came to count themselves among the beneficiaries, as did many sectors of the US domestic economy. However, the Global Plan's architects saw much further than the narrow interests of any American company. Their audacious policies to promote capital accumulation in distant lands, over which they had no personal or political interest (in the narrow sense), can only be explained if we take onboard the weight of history under which they laboured.

Indeed, to understand the scale of the New Dealers' ethical ambition, we must again take pause and look briefly for clues as to what motivated them in their own (not too distant) past – in the Great Depression that formed their mindset. The Global Plan, we must not forget for a moment, was the work of individuals who belonged to a damaged generation – a generation that had experienced poverty, a deep sense of loss, the anxieties engendered by the near collapse of capitalism, and a consequent war of inhuman proportions.

In addition, they were educated men who understood in their bones how prone labour and money markets are to instant meltdown. Their experiences steeled their determination not to allow capitalism to slip and fall again on their watch. They would do anything it took to avert another Crisis, especially now that the Soviet bear was straining at the leash, ready to pounce the moment the Global Plan faltered.

Although most of the New Dealers had been influenced by the writings of John Maynard Keynes, and had taken note of his crucial advice not to trust markets to organize themselves in a manner that can bring about prosperity and stability, the Cold War, which they had to pursue at the same time as managing the Global Plan, and their closeness to the military-industrial complex prevented them from seeing as clearly as Keynes had the imperative of creating a formal, cooperative system for recycling surpluses.

Many observers note the deep chasm separating the New Deal mindset from European, or British, Keynesianism. To begin with, whereas Keynes had become convinced that global capitalism required a cooperative, non-imperial global surplus recycling mechanism (GSRM), the New Dealers both wanted and were obliged to tailor their Global Plan in the context of Cold War imperatives and in clear pursuit of American hegemony.

It is also helpful to recall that the New Dealers had very early shed their willingness seriously to confront corporate power. Once the carnage had started, the war effort had brought officials closer together with both the financiers and the captains of industry. In order to emerge from the war as victors, and in order to prevent another Great Depression while they constructed a new post-war global order, the New Dealers felt it was important to keep the US government at the helm, both domestically and internationally, with American multinationals as effective agents of the state both at home and abroad. But this meant a hegemony that could not allow some *international* agency (like Keynes' proposed ICU) the right to curtail either America's surpluses or its government's capacity to mediate between conflicting interests.

What makes their story so fascinating is the combination of their sophisticated, discursive Keynesianism, their audacious initiatives and the interaction of their economic planning with the demands of the Cold War. In this sense, the Global Plan comprised not only the creation of the Deutschmark- and yen-zones by means of economic injections and political interference for the benefit of Germany and Japan, but also the careful management of overall demand within the United States, always with a clear view to its effects on these two zones in Europe and the Far East.

American domestic policies during the Global Plan

The fear that the end of the Second World War would spell the beginning of a new slump energized the New Dealers to pursue two solutions. The first we have already looked at in some detail: dollarizing the world in order to create foreign demand for America's exports. The second set of policies concerned the domestic economy and comprised three major, government-led sources of stimulus:

- the intercontinental ballistic missile programme
- the Korean and Vietnam Wars
- President John F. Kennedy's *New Frontier* and, more importantly, President Lyndon Johnson's *Great Society*.

The first two spending programmes substantially strengthened US corporations and kept them onside at a time when their own government was going out of its way to look after foreign capitalists. The greatest benefits, of course, accrued to companies somehow connected to what President Dwight Eisenhower (though a celebrated former army commander himself) disparagingly labelled the *military-industrial establishment* (MIE).

The MIE, and its special treatment by government, contributed heftily to the development of the aeronautic–computer–electronics (ACE) complex – an economic powerhouse largely divorced from the rest of the US economy, but central to its growing power.

Despite the positive impact of the Global Plan on the domestic American economy, it was an uneven impact. That it was uneven is evidenced by the fact that segments of the economy not linked to the MIE or the ACE never recovered in step either with Germany and Japan or with the rest of the US economy. That it was not Washington's *main* aim to bolster American companies across the board (though it was certainly *one* of its aims) can be gleaned from the ruthlessness with which the United States government introduced, whenever it saw fit, harsh regulations which ultimately discriminated against American multinationals, in pursuit of its *top* priority: the augmentation of the Deutschmark- and the yen-zones through the reinforcement of German and Japanese industry.

The unevenness with which prosperity was distributed within the United States, at a time of rising aspirations (not all of them income related), caused significant social tensions. These tensions, and their gradual dissolution, were the target of the Great Society spending programmes of the 1960s. First President Kennedy and then his successor, Lyndon Johnson, pushed hard for a series of domestic spending programmes that would address the fact that the Global Plan's domestic benefits were so unfairly spread as to undermine social cohesion in important urban centres and regions. To prevent these centrifugal forces from damaging the Global Plan, social welfare programmes acquired a momentum of their own.

To put the importance of the Kennedy–Johnson social programmes in perspective, it helps to note that, from 1955 until Kennedy's election in 1960, economic growth tailed off in the

United States – a petering out that affected mostly the poor and the marginal. After eight years of Republican rule (1952–60), Kennedy was elected on a New Deal-alluding platform. His New Frontier manifesto promised to revive the spirit of the New Deal by spending on education, health, urban renewal, transportation, the arts, environmental protection, public broadcasting, research in the humanities, etc.

After Kennedy's assassination, President Johnson, especially after his 1964 landslide victory, incorporated many of the (largely un-enacted) New Frontier policies into his much more ambitious Great Society proclamation. While Johnson pursued the Vietnam War abroad with increasingly reckless vigour, domestically he attempted to stamp his authority by means of the Great Society, a programme that greatly inspired progressives when it set centre stage the goal of eliminating not only poverty for the white working class, but also racism.

The Great Society will be remembered for its effective dismantling of American apartheid, especially in the southern states. Between 1964 and 1966, four pieces of legislation saw to this major transformation of American society. Moreover, the Great Society had a strong Keynesian element that came to the fore as Johnson's unconditional war on poverty. In its first three years, 1964–66, $1 billion were spent annually on various programmes to boost educational opportunities and to introduce health cover for the elderly and various vulnerable groups.

The social impact of the Great Society's public expenditure was mostly felt in the form of poverty reduction. When it began, more than 22 per cent of Americans lived below the official poverty line. By the end of the programme, that percentage had fallen to just below 13 per cent. Even more significantly, the respective figures for black Americans were 55 per cent (in 1960) and 27 per cent (in 1968). While such improvements cannot be explained solely as the effect of Great Society funding, this did play a major role in relieving some of the social tensions during an era of generalized growth.

Conclusion: capitalism's Golden Age

Gore Vidal once said that the trouble with golden ages is that, if you live in one, everything looks a little yellow. The countless Americans who took to the streets to protest against their government in the 1960s undoubtedly did not see their era as golden. Yet, in retrospect, at least through our current lens, it looks like a remarkable period: an era in which administrators truly believed they could create a rational world order that would promote intercontinental stability, growth and relative equality. When we look at our current crop of poll-driven politicians, whose *raison d'être* is to stay on the right side of Wall Street, lobbyists and assorted business interests, it is easy to romanticize the first post-war phase – the Global Plan era.

The Global Plan lasted from around 1950 to 1971. It boiled down to a simple idea: a system of fixed exchange rates binding together the capitalist economies, complete with a particular type of GSRM that guarantees the system's immunity from centrifugal forces that would otherwise tear it apart. How did that particular GSRM emerge? The idea was that the United States would retain its large post-war trade surplus but, in return, would export its surplus capital (or profits) to its protégés in the form of direct investment, aid or assistance, thus enabling them to continue to buy American products. At the same time, the United States would ensure that Japan and Germany could maintain a similar surplus position at a regional level, even at the expense of America's own bottom line.

The Global Plan's most impressive feature was its incredible adaptability – successive US administrations amended it every time bits of it came unstuck. Their policies toward Japan are an excellent example: after Mao's unexpected victory, and the demise of the original plan to turn the Chinese mainland into a huge market for Japanese industrial output, US policy makers responded with a variety of inspired responses.

First, they utilized the Korean War, turning it into an excellent opportunity to inject demand into the Japanese industrial sector. Secondly, they used their influence over America's allies to allow Japanese imports freely into their markets. Thirdly, and most surprisingly, Washington decided to turn America's own market into Japan's vital space. Indeed, the penetration of Japanese imports (cars, electronic goods, even services) into the US market would have been impossible without a nod and a wink from Washington's policy makers. Fourthly, the successor to the Korean War, the war in Vietnam, was also enlisted to boost Japanese industry further. A useful by-product of that murderous escapade was the industrialization of South East Asia, which further strengthened Japan by providing it, at long last, with the missing link – a commercial vital zone in close proximity.

My argument here is not that the cold warriors in the Pentagon and elsewhere were pursuing the New Dealers' Global Plan. While not innocent of the idea (as the heavy involvement of military leaders in the Marshall Plan shows), they naturally had their own geopolitical agenda. The point is that, while the generals, the Pentagon and the State Department were putting together their Cold War strategic plans, Washington's economic planners approached the wars in Korea and Vietnam from a quite distinct perspective.

At one level, they saw these wars as crucial to maintaining a continuous supply of cheap raw materials to Europe and Japan. At another level, however, they recognized a great chance to bring into being, through war financing, the vital economic space that Mao had robbed 'their' Japan of. It is indeed impossible to overstate the point made earlier that the South East Asian 'tiger economies' (South Korea, Thailand, Malaysia and Singapore, which were soon to become for Japan what France and Spain were to Germany) would never have emerged without these two US-financed wars, which left the US as the only sizeable market for Japanese industrial output.

In retrospect, by the standards of large-scale human design, the Global Plan was a grand success. Not only did the end of the Second World War not plunge the United States and the rest of the West into a fresh recession (as it was feared that the winding down of war spending would do), but instead the world experienced a period of legendary growth. Figure 3.1 offers a glimpse of these golden years. The developed nations, victors and losers in the recent war alike, grew and grew and grew.

The Europeans and Japan, starting from a much lower level than the United States, grew faster and made up for lost ground. At the same time, the United States continued along a path of healthy growth. However, this was not a simple case of

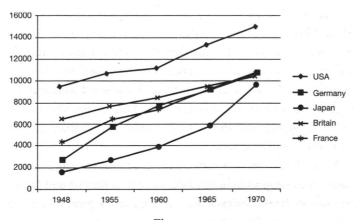

Figure 3.1
Real GDP per capita during the period of the Global Plan ($US)

a spontaneously growing world economy. There was a Global Plan behind it – one that involved a large-scale and impressively ambitious effort to overcome and supplant the multiple, conflicting imperialisms that had characterized the world political economy until the Second World War.

While the Global Plan was put together to establish and bolster American hegemony, the United States was happy to pay the price of intentionally bolstering foreign demand levels and capital accumulation, in Japan and Germany particularly. To maintain American prosperity and growth, Washington purposely served up part of the global 'pie' to its protégés: while the United States lost almost 20 per cent of its share of world income during the era of the Global Plan, Germany saw its share rise by 18 per cent and Japan watched its grow by a stupendous 156.7 per cent.

Table 3.1: Percentage change in a country's share of world GDP

	USA	Germany	Japan	Britain	France
1950–1972	–19.3%	+18%	+156.7%	–35.4%	+4.9%

Was this a form of internationalist altruism at work? Of course not. From 1945 onwards, at the heart of the New Dealers' thinking lay an intense anxiety regarding the inherent instability of a single-currency, single-zone global system. Indeed, nothing concentrated their minds like the memory of 1929 and the ensuing Depression. If a crisis of similar severity were to strike while global capitalism had but a single leg to stand on (the dollar), the future looked bleak – particularly in view of the significant growth rates of the Soviet Union (whose economy was not susceptible to contagion from capitalist crises). Thus, these same minds sought a safer future for capitalism in the formation of an interdependent network comprising three industrial-monetary zones, in which the dollar-zone would be predominant (reflecting the centrality of American finance and its military role in defending a broader realm within which inputs from the Third World would flow unhindered). To them, this Global Plan was the optimal mechanism design for the rest of the twentieth century and beyond.

In this context, the notion that European integration sprang out of a European urge to create some bulwark *against* American dominance appears to be nothing more than the European Union's 'creation myth'. Equally, the idea that the Japanese economy grew inexorably *against* the interests of the United States does not survive serious scrutiny. However strange this may seem now, behind the process of European integration and Japanese export-oriented industrialization lies a prolonged and sustained effort by Washington policy makers to plan and nurture it, despite the detrimental effects on America's balance of trade that the rise of Europe and Japan eventually entailed.

The simple lesson that the Global Plan can teach us today is that world capitalism's finest hour came when the policy makers of the strongest political union on the planet decided to play a hegemonic role – a role that involved not only the exercise of military and political might, but also the kind of massive redistribution of surpluses across the globe that the market mechanism is utterly incapable of effecting.

CHAPTER 4

The Global Minotaur

The Global Plan's Achilles heel

The Global Plan unravelled because of a major design flaw in its original architecture. John Maynard Keynes had spotted the flaw during the 1944 Bretton Woods conference but was overruled by the Americans. What was it? It was the lack of any automated global surplus recycling mechanism (GSRM) that would keep systematic trade imbalances constantly in check.

The American side vetoed Keynes' proposed mechanism, the International Currency Union, thinking that the US could, and should, manage the global flow of trade and capital itself, without committing to some formal, automated GSRM. The new hegemon, blinded by its newfangled superpower status, failed to recognize the wisdom of Odysseus's strategy of binding itself voluntarily to some Homeric mast.

Less cryptically, Washington thought that global trade imbalances would favour America in perpetuity, casting in stone its status as the world's surplus nation. Then the power bestowed upon the United States by the surpluses it extracted from all over the world would be utilized benevolently and efficiently in order to manage the world economy along the lines of an enlightened hegemony. Indeed, this is exactly what the United States did: it graciously recycled the American surpluses in the form of capital injections into Japan, Germany and other deserving regions.

Alas, US policy makers failed to foresee that global imbalances could undergo a drastic inversion, leaving the United States in the unfamiliar position of a deficit country. During the heady days of the late 1940s, the Global Plan's architects apparently neglected to take seriously the possibility that the lack of self-restraint would lead Washington to codes of behaviour that would undermine their brilliant grand design.

The Global Plan unravels

The Global Plan's path was not strewn with roses. A series of mishaps marked its evolution, with Chairman Mao's triumph delivering the first blow. Quite impressively, it reacted creatively to adversity, turning undesirable developments into a stream of welcome unintended consequences. We have already seen how the Korean War was exploited to shore up the Global Plan's Far Eastern flank. So, when the United States dragged itself into the Vietnam War, a similar wave of 'creative destruction' was on the cards.

Though it is a gross understatement to suggest that its prosecution did not go according to the original plan, the Vietnam War's silver lining is visible to anyone who has ever visited South East Asia. Korea, Thailand, Malaysia and Singapore grew fast and in a manner that confounded the pessimism of those who predicted that underdeveloped nations would find it hard to embark upon the road of capital accumulation necessary to drag them out of abject poverty. In the process, they provided Japan with valuable trade and investment opportunities that lessened the load on the US authorities, which, before the mid-1960s, had shouldered alone the burden of generating enough demand for Japanese factories' output in Europe and the US itself. Years later, the same model was copied by Deng Xiao Ping and delivered the China we know today.

The problem with unintended consequences is that they are not reliably advantageous. Ho Chi Minh's stubborn refusal to lose the Vietnam War, and Lyndon Johnson's almost manic commitment to do anything to win it, were crucial not only in creating a new capitalist region in the Far East, but also in derailing the Global Plan. The escalation of the financial costs of that war was to be a key factor in the Plan's demise.

Setting aside the appalling human suffering,[1] the war cost the US government around $113 billion and the US economy another $220 billion. Real US corporate profits declined by 17 per cent, while, in the period 1965–70, the war-induced increases in average prices forced the real average income of American blue-collar workers to fall by about 2 per cent.[2] The war took its toll not only ethically and politically, as a whole generation of American youngsters were marked by fear and loathing of Vietnam, but also in terms of tangible loss of working-class income, which fuelled social tensions. Arguably, President Johnson's Great Society social programmes were largely aimed at relieving these strains.

As the combined costs of the Vietnam War and the Great Society began to mount, the government was forced to generate mountains of US government debt. By the end of the 1960s, many governments began to worry that their own positions (which were interlocked with the dollar in the context of the Bretton Woods system) were being undermined. By early 1971, liabilities exceeded $70 billion, while the US government possessed only $12 billion of gold with which to back them up.

The increasing quantity of dollars was flooding world markets, giving rise to inflationary pressures in places like France and Britain. European governments were forced to increase the volume of their own currencies in order to keep their exchange rate constant against the dollar, as was stipulated by the Bretton Woods system. This is the basis for the European charge against the United States that, by pursuing the Vietnam War, it was exporting inflation to the rest of the world.

Beyond mere inflationary concerns, the Europeans and the Japanese feared that the build-up of dollars, against the backdrop of a constant US gold stock, might spark a run on the dollar, which might then force the United States to drop its standing commitment to swapping an ounce of gold for $35, in which case their stored dollars would lose their value, eating into their national 'savings'.

The flaw in the Global Plan was intimately connected to what Valéry Giscard d'Estaing, President de Gaulle's finance minister at the time, called the dollar's 'exorbitant privilege': the United States' unique privilege to print money at will without any global institutionalized constraints. De Gaulle and other European allies (plus various governments of oil-producing countries whose oil exports were denominated in dollars) accused the United States of building its imperial reach on borrowed money that undermined their countries' prospects. What they failed to add was that the whole point of the Global Plan was that it should revolve around a surplus-generating United States. When America turned into a deficit nation, the Global Plan could not avoid going into a vicious tailspin.

On 29 November 1967, the British government devalued the pound sterling by 14 per cent, well outside the Bretton Woods 1 per cent limit, triggering a crisis and forcing the United States government to use up to 20 per cent of its entire gold reserves to defend the $35 per ounce of gold peg. On 16 March 1968, representatives of the central banks of the seven nations that were later to form the G7 met to hammer out a compromise. They came to a curious agreement which, on the one hand, retained the official peg of $35 an ounce while, on the other hand, leaving room for speculators to trade gold at market prices.

In 1970 President Richard Nixon appointed Paul Volcker as under-secretary of the treasury for international monetary affairs. His brief was to report to the National Security Council, headed by Henry Kissinger, who was to become a most influential secretary of state in 1973. In May 1971, the taskforce headed by Volcker at the US Treasury presented Kissinger with a contingency plan, which toyed with the idea of 'suspension of gold convertibility'. It is now clear that, on both sides of the Atlantic, policy makers were jostling for position, anticipating a major change in the Global Plan.

In August 1971, the French government decided to make a very public statement of its annoyance over US policy: President Georges Pompidou ordered a destroyer to sail to New Jersey to redeem US dollars for gold held at Fort Knox, as was his right under Bretton Woods! A few days later, the British government of Edward Heath issued a similar request (though without employing the Royal Navy), demanding gold equivalent to $3 billion held by the Bank of England. Poor, luckless Pompidou and Heath: they had rushed in where angels fear to tread!

President Nixon was absolutely livid. Four days later, on 15 August 1971, he announced the effective end of Bretton Woods: the dollar would no longer be convertible to gold. Thus, the Global Plan unravelled.

Interregnum: the 1970s oil crises, stagflation and the rise of interest rates

Soon after, Nixon dispatched his secretary of the treasury (a no-nonsense Texan called John Connally) to Europe with a sharp message. According to what Connally told reporters, what he said to the Europeans was mild and affable:

We told them that we were here as a nation that had given much of our resources and our material resources and otherwise to the World to the point where frankly we were now running a deficit and have been for twenty years and it had drained our reserves and drained our resources to the point where we could no longer do it and frankly we were in trouble and we were coming to our friends to ask for help as they have so many times in the past come to us to ask for help when they were in trouble. That is in essence what we told them.

His *real* message is still ringing in European ears: *It's our currency but it's your problem!* What Connally meant was that, as the dollar was the *reserve currency* (i.e. the only truly global means of exchange), the end of Bretton Woods was not America's problem. The Global Plan was, of course, designed and implemented to be in the interests of the United States. But once the pressures on it (caused by Vietnam and internal US tensions that required an increase in domestic government spending) became such that the system reached breaking point, the greatest loser would not be the United States, but Europe and Japan – the two economic zones that had benefited most from the Global Plan.

It was not a message either the Europeans or Japan wanted to hear. Lacking an alternative to the dollar, they knew that their economies would hit a major bump as soon as the dollar started devaluing. Not only would their dollar assets lose value, but their exports would also become dearer. The only alternative was for them to devalue their currencies, too, but that would then cause their energy costs to skyrocket (given that oil was denominated in dollars). In short, Japan and the Europeans found themselves between a rock and a hard place.

Toward the end of 1971, in December, Presidents Nixon and Pompidou met in the Azores. Pompidou, eating humble pie over his destroyer antics, pleaded with Nixon to reconstitute the Bretton Woods system, on the basis of fresh fixed exchange rates that would reflect the new 'realities'. Nixon was unmoved. The Global Plan was dead and buried, and a new unruly beast, the *Global Minotaur*, was to fill its place.

Once the fixed exchange rates of the Bretton Woods system collapsed, all prices and rates broke loose. Gold was the first: it jumped from $35 to $38 per ounce, then to $42, and then off it floated into the ether. By May 1973 it was trading at more than $90, and before the decade was out, in 1979, it had reached a fabulous $455 per ounce – a twelvefold increase in less than a decade.

Meanwhile, within two years of Nixon's bold August 1971 move, the dollar had lost 30 per cent of its value against the Deutschmark and 20 per cent against the yen and the franc. Oil producers suddenly found that their black gold, when denominated in yellow gold, was worth a fraction of what it used to be. Members of the Organization of the Petroleum Exporting Countries (OPEC), which regulated the price of oil through agreed cutbacks on aggregate oil output, were soon clamouring for coordinated action (i.e. reductions in production) to boost the black liquid's gold value.

At the time of Nixon's announcement, the price of oil was less than $3 per barrel. In 1973, with the Yom Kippur War between Israel and its Arab neighbours apace, the price jumped to between $8 and $9, thereafter hovering in the $12 to $15 range until 1979. In 1979 a new upward surge began that saw oil trade above $30 well into the 1980s. And it was not just the price of oil that scaled unprecedented heights. All primary commodities shot up in price simultaneously: bauxite (165 per cent), lead (170 per cent), tin (220 per cent) and silver (1065 per cent) are just a few examples. In short, the termination of the Global Plan signalled a mighty rise in the costs of production across the world. Inflation soared, as did unemployment – a rare combination of stagnation with inflation that came to be known as *stagflation*.

The conventional wisdom about what caused the 1970s stagflation is that the OPEC countries pushed the dollar price of oil sky high against the will of the United States. It is an explanation that runs counter to logic and evidence. For if the Nixon administration had truly opposed the oil price hikes, how are we to explain the fact that its closest allies, the Shah of Iran, President Suharto of Indonesia and the Venezuelan government, not only backed the increases but led the campaign to bring them about? How are we to account for the administration's scuttling of the Tehran negotiations between the oil companies (the so-called 'Seven Sisters') and OPEC just before an agreement was reached that would have depressed prices?

Quoting an influential American observer of these crucial discussions,

> a split was announced in the talks in Tehran by a special US envoy, then-Under Secretary of State John Irwin, accompanied there by James Akins, a key State Department man on oil... [T]he real lesson of the split in negotiations with OPEC was that higher prices were not terribly worrisome to representatives of the State Department...the whole subject of what the negotiations were about began to focus not on holding the price line but on ensuring security of supply.[3]

This begs the question: why did the United States not oppose with any degree of real commitment the large increases in oil prices? The simple reason is that, just as the Nixon administration did not mourn the end of Bretton Woods, neither did it care to prevent OPEC from pushing the price of oil higher. For these hikes were not inconsistent with the administration's very own plans for a substantial increase in the global prices of energy and primary commodities! Indeed, the Saudis have consistently claimed that Henry Kissinger, keener to manage the flow of petro-dollars to America than to prevent the rise in energy prices, was encouraging them all the way to push the price of oil up by a factor of between two and four.[4] So long as oil sales were denominated in dollars, the US administration had no quarrel with the oil price increases.

Recalling that the new aim was to find ways of financing the US twin deficits without cutting US government spending, or increasing taxes, or reducing US world dominance, American policy makers understood that they had a simple task: to entice the rest of the world to finance the USA's deficits. But this meant a redistribution of global surpluses in favour of the United States and at the expense of the two economic zones it had built around Germany and Japan. There were two prerequisites for the planned reversal of global capital flows, which would see the world's capital stream into Wall Street for the purpose of financing the expanding US twin deficits: (a) improved competitiveness of US firms in relation to their German and Japanese competitors, and (b) interest rates that attracted large capital flows into the United States.

The first prerequisite could be achieved in one of two ways: either by boosting productivity in the United States or by boosting the relative unit costs of the competition. For good measure, the US administration decided to aim for *both*. Labour costs were squeezed with enthusiasm and, at the same time, oil prices were 'encouraged' to rise. The drop in US labour costs not only boosted the competitiveness of American companies, but also acted as a magnet for foreign capital that was searching for profitable ventures. Meanwhile, as oil prices rose, every part of the capitalist world was adversely affected. However, Japan and Western Europe (largely lacking their own oil) were burdened much more than the United States.

Meanwhile, the rise in oil prices led to mountainous rents piling up in bank accounts from Saudi Arabia to Indonesia, as well as huge receipts for US oil companies. All these petro-dollars soon found their way to Wall Street's hospitable bosom. The Fed's interest rate policy was to prove particularly helpful in this respect.

Turning to the second prerequisite, money (or nominal) interest rates jumped from 6 per cent, where the Global Plan's final years had left them in 1971, to 6.44 per cent in 1973 and to 7.83 per cent the following year. By 1979, President Carter's administration had begun to attack US inflation with panache. It appointed Paul Volcker as Fed chairman, with instructions to deal decisively with inflation. His first move was to push average interest rates to 11 per cent.

In June 1981, Volcker raised interest rates to a lofty 20 per cent, and then again to 21.5 per cent. While his brutal monetary policy did tame inflation (pushing it down from 13.5 per cent in 1981 to 3.2 per cent two years later), its harmful effects on employment and capital accumulation were profound, both domestically and internationally. Nevertheless, the two prereq-uisites had been met even before Ronald Reagan settled in properly at the White House.

A new phase thus began. The United States could now run an increasing trade deficit with impunity, while the new Reagan administration could also finance its hugely expanded defence budget and its gigantic tax cuts for the richest Americans. The 1980s ideology of supply-side economics, the fabled trickle-down effect, the reckless tax cuts, the dominance of greed as a form of virtue, etc. – all these were just manifestations of America's new 'exorbitant privilege': the opportunity to expand its twin deficits almost without limit, courtesy of the capital inflows from the rest of the world. American hegemony had taken a new turn. The reign of the Global Minotaur had dawned.

The Global Minotaur

The United States had neither wanted nor resigned itself readily to the collapse of the Global Plan. However, once America lost its surplus position, US policy makers were quick to read the writing on the wall: the Global Plan's Achilles heel had been pierced and its downfall was just a matter of time. They then moved on very rapidly, unwilling to countenance the prospect of jeopardizing global hegemony in a futile attempt to mend a broken design.

Perhaps the best narrative on the violent abandonment of the Global Plan comes from the horse's mouth. In 1978, Paul Volcker, the man who was among the first to recommend that Bretton Woods should be discarded, addressed an audience of students and staff at Warwick University. Not long after that speech, President Carter appointed him chairman of the Fed. One wonders if his audience grasped the significance of his words:

> It is tempting to look at the market as an impartial arbiter... But balancing the requirements of a stable international system against the desirability of retaining freedom of action for national policy, a number of countries, including the US, opted for the latter...

And as if this were not sufficiently loud and clear, Volcker added: '[A] *controlled disintegration in the world economy* is a legitimate objective for the 1980s' (my emphasis).

It was the Global Plan's best epitaph and the clearest exposition of the second post-war phase that was dawning. Volcker's speech was a blunt proclamation of the future that US authorities envisaged: unable any longer to maintain reasonably well-balanced international financial and trade flows, America was planning for a world of rapidly accelerating asymmetrical financial and trade flows. The aim? To afford it the 'exorbitant privilege' of running up boundless deficits, and thus to entrench further US hegemony – not *in spite of* but *courtesy of* its deficit position. And how would such a feat be accomplished? The answer Volcker gave, with his usual bluntness, was: by *choosing* to fling the world economy into a chaotic, yet strangely controlled, flux – into the labyrinth of the Global Minotaur.

In the decades that followed, the days when the United States financed Germany and Japan (whether directly, through war financing, or by the exercise of political power) became a distant memory. America began importing as if there were no tomorrow, and its government splurged out, unimpeded by the fear of increasing deficits. So long as foreign investors sent billions of dollars every day to Wall Street, quite voluntarily and for reasons completely related to *their* bottom line, the United States' twin deficits were financed and the world kept revolving haphazardly on its axis.

The Athenians' gruesome payments of tribute to the Cretan Minotaur were imposed by King Minos's military might. In contrast, the tribute of capital that fed the Global Minotaur flooded into the United States voluntarily. Why? How did US policy makers persuade capitalists from all over the world to fund the superpower's twin deficits? What was in it for them? The answer turns on four factors. To stick to the mythological narrative, let's call them the Minotaur's *charismas*.

The Minotaur's four charismas

Reserve currency status

While the Global Plan lasted, it did not matter much which currency one held, since the exchange rates against the dollar were more or less fixed and the exchange rate between the dollar and gold was welded at $35 to an ounce of the gleaming metal. Nevertheless, oil magnates, German industrialists, French winemakers and Japanese bankers preferred to store their cash in dollars simply because of capital controls – that is, restrictions on how much cash one could convert to dollars or other currencies at any one time.

Once Bretton Woods was no longer, the psychological shock occasioned by the idea that currencies would soon be allowed to float freely created a stampede toward the dollar. To this day, whenever a crisis looms, capital flees to the greenback. This is exactly why the Crash of 2008 led to a mass inflow of foreign capital to the dollar, even though the crisis had begun on Wall Street.

Furthermore, the United States is the only country where demand for its currency does not just reflect an increase in the demand for the goods and services it produces. Whenever a Nigerian driver puts petrol in her car, or a Chinese factory purchases Australian coal, the demand for US dollars rises. Why? Because, even if no American companies are involved, primary commodity sales are denominated in dollars. Therefore, every transaction involving oil or coal results in additional demand for the US dollar.

In a 2005 newspaper article, Paul Volcker put it bluntly: '[The] external financing constraints were something that ordinary countries had to worry about, not the unquestioned leader of the free world, whose currency everybody wanted.'[5] The dollar's 'exorbitant privilege' empowers US authorities to run deficits that would have other countries buckle in no time. This is why a crisis that starts in the United States may well act as a magnet for migrating foreign capital.

Rising energy costs

As this point was made earlier, in explaining America's acquiescence to the OPEC-led oil price increases, a brief summary will suffice here: in the early 1970s, the US economy imported 32.5 per cent of its oil, Europe imported almost all of its, and Japan imported every single drop. Increasing energy prices damaged the relative competitiveness of Germany and Japan vis-à-vis the United States. Moreover, the oil trade was intimately linked to US multinationals, and thus the higher oil prices meant a larger revenue base for them, higher profits, and a strengthening of their capacity to diversify internationally. As for non-US producers, the dollar's reserve currency status, coupled with Volcker's huge interest rates, magnetized their petrol dollars to New York where they metamorphosed into shares or US government bonds.

Interestingly, it was not long before Japanese and German industry reacted to the shock by taking innovative paths that transformed their industrial production in ways that clawed back some of the relative gains that the United States had snatched from them by making energy so expensive. For instance, both Japan and Germany shifted their investment plans away from energy-intensive activities toward more high-tech endeavours (e.g. electronics). And even in the sectors that would always be reliant on oil and its by-products (e.g. the car industry), they produced a new generation of small, efficient cars, which competed ruthlessly with American-produced vehicles.

Nevertheless, despite the conflicting effects, the Global Minotaur's brilliance deserves to be marvelled at. Guess what the Germans and Japanese did with the profits from their new, energy-conscious, innovative products: they invested them in, or through, Wall Street!

Cheapened, productive labour

The American Dream may always have been based on a shared fiction. But the reality of more than a century of rising living standards was never in dispute. Things changed in the 1970s.

The fear inspired by the collapse of Bretton Woods, the hike in oil prices and the impending loss of the Vietnam War polarized society and created a playing field on which the strong could do as they pleased, while the weak had to bear their burdens stoically.

With energy prices rising, long queues forming at petrol stations and factories suspending production due to lack of raw materials or electricity, a new setting emerged in which all prior deals were off. Trades unions, incensed with across-the-board price rises, started demanding higher wages for their members. Employers began to imagine a labour market without trades unions. The scene was, in other words, ripe for a confrontation. In this new conflictual environment, corporate America discerned a wonderful opportunity to put a lid on real wages and to strive for simultaneous increases in productivity. Figure 4.1 illustrates their amazing success.

It is clear from the graph that, from 1973 onwards, something spectacular happened in the United States. In a country that prided itself on the fact that, at least since the 1850s, real wages

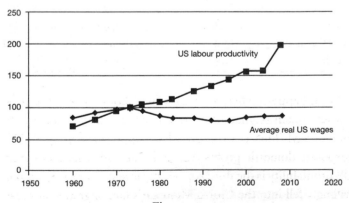

Figure 4.1
Stagnating wages, booming productivity
(indices using 1973 as base year)

had risen steadily, thus giving every generation of workers the hope that their children would be better off than they were, real wages stagnated. To this day, they have not even recovered their 1973 real purchasing power.

Meanwhile, labour productivity accelerated. The employment of new technologies, the intensification of labour processes (often helped by the rising fear of unemployment) and the increasing direct investment from abroad (e.g. German and Japanese firms that sought to boost their profitability by shifting operations to the US) all gave rise to the impressive labour productivity curve. Unsurprisingly, US labour costs per unit of output hardly grew between 1985 and 1990, a period during which America's main competitors saw costs increase by double-digit percentages. Beyond 1990, America's labour costs simply maintained their advantage.

Table 4.1
Average annual rate of change in labour unit costs (in $)

	1985–1990	*1990–1998*
USA	1.6	0.2
Japan	10.8	1.3
West Germany	15.9	0.3
Britain	11.4	1.8

What happens when real wages fall, labour costs per unit of output remain stagnant and productivity booms? Profits reach for the sky! This is precisely what happened after 1973. US corporate domestic profits rose and rose and rose. Increasing US profitability is the third reason why foreign (non-US) capital willingly fell into the Global Minotaur's lap, migrating at great speed and in unprecedented volume from Frankfurt, Riyadh, Tokyo, Paris and Milan to New York.

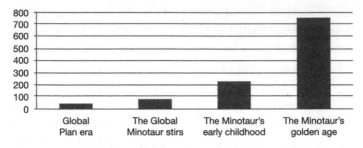

Figure 4.2
Index of average real US profit rates (using 1973 as base year)

Geopolitical might

Power concentrates the minds of the weak. And nuclear power concentrates them even better. The very fact that the United States led the West not only in economic but also in geostrategic terms cannot be neglected when we study the mechanism by which capital readily migrated to nourish the Global Minotaur. Of course, if foreign capital had no expectation of accumulating faster once it made the journey via New York to the US Treasury or to some American company or financial institution, nothing could have enticed it to head for the New World. Nonetheless, geopolitical and military power played a role in shoring up the expectation of such a gain.

Examples of the way in which US policy sought to enlist America's geopolitical might to the Global Minotaur's needs are not difficult to come by. In 1974, Henry Kissinger circulated National Security Study Memorandum 200. Under the cloak of the West's opposition to Soviet encroachments, the Memorandum staked a naked claim, on behalf of the United States and US multinationals, over the mineral wealth of the Third World. Many years later, during a congressional hearing on Afghanistan in 1998, John Maresca, vice president of oil giant Unocal, outlined a rationale for a future US invasion of Afghanistan. His argument turned on Chinese economic development, which had to be, in his view, both abetted and controlled. Maresca implied that, unlike Japan and Europe, China would not willingly liberalize its capital and money markets, and therefore the flow of capital from China to the USA would be impeded. In simpler words, profits made by Chinese, Japanese, European and, of course, US companies operating in China would not be readily transferable to the Global Minotaur, Maresca lamented. So what should be done? The best way to overcome China's recalcitrance, Maresca explained, would be to monopolize the supply of energy in its vicinity.

As if in a display of mutual reinforcement, while American geopolitical power was crucial to the Minotaur's maintenance, the Minotaur often returned the favour. Indeed, a persuasive case can be made that it played a major part in the defeat of America's greatest foes – the Soviet Union and its satellites, as well as those non-aligned Third World regimes that had become too uppity in the 1960s. Key to this triumph was not so much the successful pursuit of the arms race, but rather the humble US interest rates – those very same rates whose phenomenal rise under Paul Volcker had assisted the Global Minotaur's birth.

Arguably, the chain of events that led to the implosion of communism in Poland and Yugoslavia began in the 1970s with the sharp rise in interest rates soon after those countries had accepted offers of substantial loans from Western financial institutions. It was a similar story in Third World countries, where national liberation movements had grabbed power, often against the West's best efforts.

From the early 1960s up until 1972, Western banks, constrained by the Global Plan's low interest rates and tough regulatory regime, cast their gaze far and wide, offering large loans to Third World nations, Soviet satellites (e.g. Poland and Bulgaria), and communist countries that were detached (or semi-detached) from Moscow (Yugoslavia and Romania). The loans were used to underwrite much-needed new infrastructure, education, health systems, fledgling industrial sectors, etc. In this way, by the mid-1970s, most Third World economies (and a number of Eastern European ones) were extremely vulnerable to interest rate rises.

So, when interest rates soared, as part of Volcker's strategic 'disintegration in the world economy', communist regimes in Warsaw, Bucharest and Belgrade began to feel the pinch. Once they realized their grave dependency on the 'capitalist enemy', they gave their all to repay the debts as quickly as possible, imposing particularly harsh austerity measures on their own workforces.[6] The result was mass discontent, major unrest and the first stirrings of organized opposition, e.g. the Polish trades union Solidarity, which was soon to spearhead a chain of events leading to the first collapse of a communist regime.

In the meantime, and for similar reasons, the Third World debt crisis erupted. The IMF happily offered to lend money to governments for the purposes of repaying the Western banks, but at an exorbitant price: the dismantling of much of their public sector (including schools and clinics), the shrinking of the newly founded state institutions, and the wholesale transfer of valuable public assets (e.g. water boards, telecommunications, etc.) to Western companies. It is not at all an exaggeration to suggest that the Third World debt crisis was the colonized world's second historic disaster (after the brutal experience of colonization and the associated slave trade). In fact, it was a disaster from which most Third World countries have never quite recovered.

In short, the interest rate rise that was part and parcel of the Global Minotaur's own rise to prominence proved more effective in destroying the enemies of US foreign policy around the globe than any military operation the US could ever mount.

A most peculiar global surplus recycling mechanism

At the Bretton Woods conference, John Maynard Keynes and Harry Dexter White clashed over the type of GSRM that was best equipped to keep the post-war world economy on a sustainable path (see chapter 3).

Keynes had wanted a formal, institutionalized GSRM that would automatically recycle surpluses, thus curtailing both surpluses and deficits at once. White, on the other hand, insisted on America's right to run large surpluses and to choose, as it pleased, the ways and the means by which these surpluses would be recycled. White, of course, got his way and the Global Plan allowed the United States the privileged role of managing and maintaining the GSRM in accordance with its judgement and interests.

When the United States lost its surplus position, the Global Plan's fate was scaled. As we have seen, the United States turned its new twin deficits to its advantage. Instead of forfeiting its hegemonic role, or trying to reduce its deficits, it did quite the opposite: it enhanced its hegemony by boosting its deficits! And since deficits must somehow be financed, the key to this second post-war phase was to have the rest of the world generate a constant tsunami of New York-bound capital.

The two US deficits worked harmoniously together to accomplish their new task. When the US government reduced taxes or spent enormous amounts of money on missiles (as it did under President Reagan), the budget deficit ballooned. To finance it, it attracted foreign capital, which was only too pleased to buy US Treasury Bills (i.e. IOUs issued by the US Treasury). This capital inflow helped balance out America's increasing trade deficit. Meanwhile, both deficits together drew capital into New York, allowing Wall Street to extend credit further.

This never-ending *haj* by the world's capital to the global financial Mecca nourished America's deficits to such an extent that they soon began to resemble a mythological creature, a Global Minotaur on whose presence the US economy became dependent and whose influence quickly extended to every region of the globe.

The Minotaur's dynamics were synonymous with the global asymmetries on which its new global architecture was erected. To be maintained, they had to keep deepening, accelerating, growing. In this sense, its supremacy required a kind of *permanent negative engineering*: the Minotaur's minders (strategists like Henry Kissinger and Paul Volcker) had to try to rule by unbalancing; to reign by destabilizing; to prevail by unhinging.

These destabilizing moves, which threatened to undermine the international order, were counterbalanced by the Minotaur's most intriguing aspect: the fact that it worked just like a GSRM – a weird, most peculiar, terribly unruly GSRM; but a GSRM nonetheless. In fact, it worked in precisely the opposite way to how the original GSRM had worked under the Global Plan.

Under the Global Plan's GSRM, the United States was the surplus-amassing country with the good sense to recycle part of its surpluses to Western Europe and Japan, thus creating demand for its own exports, but also for the exports of its protégés (Germany and Japan primarily). In sharp contrast, the Global Minotaur worked in reverse: America *absorbed* other people's surplus capital, which it then recycled by buying in their exports.

Conclusion: the Global Minotaur's glittering triumph

In the aftermath of the Crash of 1929, the world understood that, in a time of Crisis, the state (the Fed and the US Treasury) must step in as the *lender of last resort*. In the era of the Global Minotaur, a new dictum was needed: the United States had become the *spender of first resort*. Its trade deficit became the traction engine that pulled world output and trade out of the 1970s mire. Its budget deficit and banking sector acted as a magnet that stimulated the capital inflows necessary to keep Wall Street buoyant and the US deficits satiated. It is no wonder that, when the Minotaur was wounded in 2008, the world ended up in another mire.

While its supremacy held sway, the Global Minotaur performed the duties its minders had planned for it to perfection. Figures 4.3 and 4.4 leave no doubt about the tumultuous changes that the Minotaur inflicted on an unsuspecting world economy. From 1975 onwards, America's twin deficits gathered pace (with the sole exception of a dip during President Clinton's second term). As for its effects on America's relative economic

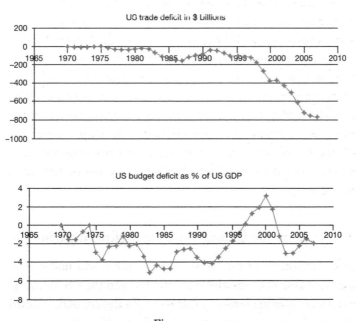

Figure 4.3
The Global Minotaur in two diagrams

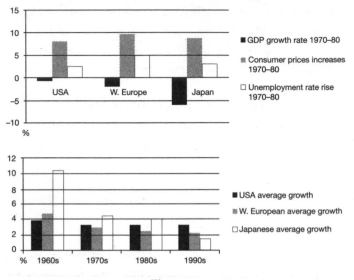

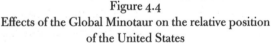

Figure 4.4
Effects of the Global Minotaur on the relative position
of the United States

position, the wilful 'disintegration in the world economy' that
occurred in the 1970s and early 1980s had painful effects for
all: GDP fell all over the world, but, notably, it fell more in
Europe and Japan than in the United States. It was the prelude
to America's revitalized hegemony. For, whereas in the 1960s
US growth trailed behind that of its protégés, in the 1970s and
1980s America caught up. And once the 1990s came, it powered
ahead. The Global Minotaur had worked its legendary magic.

CHAPTER 5

The beast's handmaidens

Minotaur envy

In the run-up to the Crash of 2008, almost everyone sang from the same song sheet in praise of the American economy. European policy makers in Brussels, their Japanese counterparts in Tokyo, Italian ex-communists, Eastern European born-again neo-rightists, academic economists – they all cast an envious gaze across the great oceans and toward the land of the free, convinced that the United States was *the* model to be urgently and unequivocally emulated.

Whole forests were pulped to produce the policy papers heralding yet another 'new era' – one in which American-style unregulated labour and financial markets promised new vistas of prosperity, spreading with the élan of Hollywood's latest blockbuster from Paris to Moscow, from Amsterdam to Athens, from Yokohama to Shanghai.

Ireland, and even Britain, were held up as pioneers on this modern road to Damascus. The proverbial pot of gold was sought at the end of the Anglo-Celtic rainbow, somewhere between a Walmart store and a Wall Street bankers' club, between the City of London and an East End building site on which armies of

Eastern European *Gastarbeiter* constructed new apartments for the platoons of up-and-coming City workers.

Every card-carrying member of the global 'commentariat' was on the same wavelength, convinced that they lived in an age of some *Great Moderation*. Depressingly few seemed willing to notice that the reality was quite the opposite. For under the facade of temperance, the world economy's natural balance was being ravaged by a terrifying Global Minotaur, whose very presence few were willing to acknowledge.

Unable to come to terms with their *Minotaur envy*, the elites pretended there was no beast in the room. Their pretence was so powerful that they hypnotized themselves into believing that, yes, it was possible for *everyone* (Europe, Japan, China, India, etc.) to achieve the same success as the United States had (since the mid-1970s), simply by adopting the American model. As if in a bid to provide yet another testimony to the human capacity for wishful thinking, hordes of otherwise bright people lulled themselves into a remarkable fantasy: that it was possible for *all* major capitalist centres around the world to attract, at once, a massive net flow of capital (in the region of $3–5 billion dollars per working day, which was the sum that the Global Minotaur had managed during its golden years); that it was feasible for *all* major capitalist centres not only to breed their own 'Minitaurs' but also to cajole the rest of the world into nourishing them.

Meanwhile, the Global Minotaur was hollowing out the American economy at the same time as it was strengthening its bottom line. To this purpose, it benefited from the enthusiastic and loyal services of a series of handmaidens. Wall Street was, naturally, the most obedient. But there were others: corporations like Walmart were creating a new business model that added to the rivers of cash, while politicians and economists were providing the institutional and 'scientific' cover that made the whole enterprise appear legitimate, even enlightened. In this chapter I focus on these handmaidens.

Box 5.1
Who were the handmaidens?

The ringleader of the handmaidens was none other than Wall Street. Its first reaction to the Minotaur's capital flows was a takeover and merger frenzy that resulted from the sudden cash inflow both from foreign sources and domestic profits. New financial instruments, mostly hedging devices, soon began to play an influential role.

Beyond Wall Street, a second handmaiden emerged in every state and every city: the ubiquitous Walmart, ushering in a new type of conglomerate that showed the rest of corporate America novel ways of squeezing both labour costs and small-scale suppliers.

Back in Washington (and in other centres of political power), a third handmaiden appeared: the ideology and politics of 'trickle-down' – the idea that the best way to benefit the poor is by piling up new riches on the doorstep of the super-rich.

This particularly ugly handmaiden would have lacked all credibility had it not been for a fourth, pseudo-scientific handmaiden – toxic economic theory. In everyday parlance, this came to be known as *supply-side economics*, but in the great economics departments it functioned as an all-conquering mathematized superstition. Its models, however irrelevant they might have been as depictions of capitalism as it really existed, provided the inspiration for the mathematical formulae that allowed Wall Street to do two things: first, to argue that the finance sector should be liberated from all regulation, and, secondly, to latch on to the real estate sector. Indeed, the toxic derivatives based on sub-prime mortgages (those weapons of mass financial destruction that brought us the Crash of 2008) would never have been possible without the toxic economics that started life in the best universities, at around the same time as the Minotaur was being born.

Takeover fever: Wall Street creates metaphysical values

In a typical year before the Crash of 2008 – even before the crazed frenzy of 2006–08 – the Minotaur was devouring more than 70 per cent of global capital outflows. Japan and Germany were the primary sources until the early 'noughties'. From around 2003, China stepped in as the greatest contributor. Mountains of cash shifted from all over the world to Wall Street, and from there to US corporations and households in the form of equity and loans.

The massive capital inflows, together with the increases in corporate profitability mentioned in the last chapter, caused a great wave of mergers and acquisitions, which naturally produced even better returns for Wall Street operators. Indeed, the 1990s and 2000s saw a manic drive toward 'consolidation' – a euphemism for one conglomerate purchasing, or merging with, another. The purchase of car makers like Daewoo, Saab and Volvo by Ford and General Motors was just the tip of the iceberg. Two periods in the history of capitalism stand out as the pinnacles of merger and acquisition frenzy: the first decade of the twentieth century, when men like Edison and Ford built empires, and the twenty years that preceded 2008. It is no coincidence that both periods led to catastrophic events – 1929 and 2008, respectively.

Reading the 1999 *Economic Report of the President*, we come across the following passage:

> The value of all mergers and acquisitions announced in1997 was almost $1 trillion, and activity in 1998 was over $1.6 trillion... Measured relative to the size of the economy, only the spate of trust formations at the turn of the century comes close to the level of current merger activity. Measured relative to the market value of all U.S. companies, however, the 1980s boom was roughly comparable in size.

Both 'consolidation' waves (of the 1900s and the 1990s) had momentous consequences on Wall Street, effectively multiplying by a considerable factor the capital flows that the banks and other financial institutions were handling. However, the 1990s version was more explosive because of the effects of two new phenomena:

the Minotaur-induced capital flight toward America, and the way in which the so-called *New Economy*, and predominantly the prospects for e-commerce, mesmerized investors.

In 1998, Germany's flagship vehicle maker, Daimler-Benz, was lured to the United States, where it attempted, successfully, to take over Chrysler, the third-largest American auto manufacturer. The price the German company paid for Chrysler, $36 billion, sounded exorbitant – but at the time it seemed like a good price, in view of Wall Street's valuation of the merged company, which amounted to a whopping $130 billion!

Motivated by the psychological exuberance caused by the Minotaur-induced capital inflows, Wall Street's valuations were stratospheric. When internet company AOL (America Online) used its inflated Wall Street capitalization to purchase time-honoured Time Warner, a new company was formed with $350 billion capitalization. While AOL produced only 30 per cent of the merged company's profit stream, it ended up owning 55 per cent of the new firm. The valuations were nothing more than bubbles waiting to burst. And burst they did, just before the Crash of 2008. In 2007, DaimlerChrysler broke up and Daimler sold Chrysler for a sad $500 million (taking a 'haircut' of $35.5 billion on the price it had paid in 1998, lost interest not included). It was a similar story with AOL-Time Warner: by 2007, its Wall Street capitalization had been revised down from $350 billion to $29 billion, and the break-up left both companies reeling.

On the other side of the Atlantic, in the other Anglo-Celtic economy that the Europeans had so much admired before 2008, a similar game was unfolding in the City of London. In 1976, just before the Minotaur took its first wobbly steps, the households with the top 10 per cent of marketable wealth (not including housing) controlled 57 per cent of income. In 2003 they controlled 71 per cent. Mrs Thatcher and her government prided themselves on having introduced what she called an 'entrepreneurial

---

Box 5.2
Wishful thinking – how mergers and acquisitions created fictitious value[1]

Suppose there are two companies selling music: Standard Records is the traditional manufacturer, with a track record of fifty years, while E-Records is an upstart that has been going for only a year and that sells music through the internet (unlike Standard Records, which still relies on its traditional network of outlets). Suppose further that the following statistics capture the fundamentals of the two companies:

Standard Records (50 years old):
Earnings (E) = $700 million per year
Growth = 10% annually for the previous 25 years
Stock market capitalization (K) = $5 billion
K/E = 10:1
E-Records (1 year old):
Earnings (E) = $200 million last year
Projected e-sales share in a year's time = 10% of (an estimated) $1 trillion market = $100 billion
Stock market capitalization (K) = $10 billion
K/E = 50:1

---

culture', a 'shareowners' democracy'. But did they? If we take the British households in the lower 50 per cent income bracket and look at the proportion of the nation's speculative capital that they owned and controlled, in 1976 the figure was 12 per cent. By 2003 it had dropped to 1 per cent. By contrast, the top 1 per cent of the income distribution increased its control over speculative capital from 18 per cent in 1976 to 34 per cent in 2003.

The City of London, attached ever so firmly to Wall Street, could not but emulate the spirit of financialization that first emerged in the United States in response to the large capital inflows from the rest of the world. Two concrete examples well illustrate the change in the logic of economic power during

A prudent person might imagine that Standard Records is probably a safer investment. However, that thought was routinely dismissed as fuddy-duddy, backward looking and insufficiently attuned to E-Records' bright future. So here is how Wall Street thought: suppose E-Records were to utilize its superior stock market value, or capitalization (K), to buy Standard Records. What would the value be of the merged company? Should we just add up the two companies' capitalizations ($10 billion plus $5 billion = $15 billion)? No, that would be too timid. Instead, Wall Street did something cleverer. It added the earnings of the two companies ($700 million + $200 million = $900 million) and multiplied this by E-Records' capitalization to earnings ratio. This small piece of arithmetic yielded a fabulous number: 50:1 times $900 million = $45 billion!

Thus, the new, merged, company was valued at $30 billion more than the sum of the capitalizations of the two merged companies (a sudden leap of 300 per cent). Needless to say, the fees and commissions of the Wall Street institutions that saw the merger through were in line with the marvellously big figure they had miraculously arrived at.

the time of the Minotaur: Debenhams and the Royal Bank of Scotland (RBS). Debenhams, the retail and department store chain, was bought in 2003 by a group of investors. The new owners sold most of the company's fixed assets, pocketed a cool £1 billion and resold it at a time of exuberant expectations, at more or less the same price that they had paid. The institutional funds that bought Debenhams ended up with massive losses.

Even more spectacularly, in October 2007 RBS put in a winning bid of more than €70 billion for ABN-Amro. By the following April, it was clear that RBS had overstretched itself and it tried to raise money to plug the holes exposed by the purchase of ABN-Amro. In July 2008, the parts of the merged company that were associated with ABN-Amro were national-ized by the governments of Holland, Belgium and Luxembourg. The following October, the British government stepped in to salvage RBS. The cost to the British taxpayer? A gallant £50 billion.

In short, the Global Minotaur created capital flows that propelled Wall Street's gains from mergers and acquisitions (and, by osmosis, the City of London's) to the financial strat-osphere. In what seemed to many (wrongly, of course) like a never-ending virtuous circle, these capital flows reinforced the Minotaur, as they satiated the twin US deficits in its belly. And it was not just the mergers and acquisitions flows that became entangled in a mutually reinforcing relationship with the Global Minotaur. Two other capital streams were part and parcel of the same dynamic: the profits of firms adopting the Walmart extrac-tive model and the debts of the average American, for whom borrowed money was the only means of not falling completely out of touch with the American Dream.

Hedging and leverage

Before the Global Minotaur wilfully disintegrated the world economy (to draw on Paul Volcker's sensational phrase of around 1978), *derivatives* were cuddly 'creatures' that actu-ally helped hard-working farmers find a modicum of safety in a viciously uncertain world. The Chicago Commodities Exchange (originally known as the Chicago Butter and Egg Board) allowed long-suffering farmers the opportunity to sell today their next year's harvest at fixed prices, thus affording them a degree of predictability.

All benign instruments can turn malignant as they grow bigger and sharper, and thus derivatives evolved into the Minotaur's grossest handmaiden. At first, they gave us *hedging*. Suppose you want to buy an asset (e.g. a portrait, a house or a pack of shares) currently worth $1 million. However bullish your expectations about its future price, you are worried that it may drop in value. So prudence urges you to buy some insurance – a get-me-out-of-here option to sell at, say, $800 thousand whenever you want (within a certain time frame). Like any form of insurance, if disaster does *not* strike (i.e. the actual price never falls below $800 thousand), the insurance policy will have been a waste of money. But if, say, the shares shed 40 per cent of their value, you are covered for half of that loss.

Hedging has been with us for a long time. But it was the Global Minotaur that gave it a wholly new role, and a terrible reputation after 2008. At a time when the capital flows into Wall Street made its golden boys and girls feel invincible masters and mistresses of the universe, it became common for *options* to be used for purposes exactly the opposite to *hedging*. So, instead of purchasing an option to sell shares (as an insurance in case the shares that they were buying depreciated in value), the smart set bought options to buy even more! Thus, they bought their $1 million shares and, on top of that, they spent another $100 thousand on an option to buy another $1 million (at the current price). If the shares went up by, say, 40 per cent, that would net them a $400 thousand gain from the $1 million shares plus a further $400 thousand from the $100 thousand option. A total profit of $700 thousand.

At that point, the seriously optimistic had a radical thought: why not buy *only* options? Why bother with shares at all? For if they were to spend their $1.1 million only on an option to buy these shares (as opposed to $1 million on the shares and $100 thousand on the option), and the shares went up again by 40 per cent, their profit would be a stunning $4.4 million. And this is what became known as *leverage*: a form of borrowing money to bet big time which increases the stakes of the bet monumentally.

Alas, from 1980 onwards, prudence was for wimps. The Minotaur was generating capital inflows that in turn guaranteed a rising tide in Wall Street that submerged any remaining last islets of caution.

From then on, people 'in the know' flocked to buy new financial 'products' and 'innovations'. There was, of course, no such thing. These 'innovative' contraptions were just new ways of creating *leverage* – a fancy term for good old debt. On this matter, the best line belongs, yet again, to Paul Volcker. After the Crash of 2008, Wall Street's bosses went into damage-control mode, desperately trying to stem the popular demand for stringent regulation of their institutions. Their argument, predictably, was that too much regulation would stifle 'financial innovation', with dire consequences for economic growth (a little like the mafia warning against law enforcement because of its deflationary consequences).

In a plush New York conference setting, on a cold December night in 2009, all the big Wall Street institutional players were assembled to hear Paul Volcker address them. Attendance was high because President Obama had entrusted him with the planning of the new regulatory framework for the banks. Volcker lost no time in lashing out with the words: 'I wish someone would give me one shred of neutral evidence that financial innovation has led to economic growth; one shred of evidence.' One hapless banker retorted that the financial sector in the United States had increased its share of value-added from 2 per cent to 6.5 per cent. Volcker responded with a killer question: 'Is that a reflection of your financial innovation, or just a reflection of what you're paid?' To finish off the banker, he added: 'The only financial innovation I recall in my long career was the invention of the ATM.'

The combination of options to buy, hedging and leveraging is such risky business that, had it been a pharmaceutical, never in a million years would it have secured approval from the US Food and Drug Administration. This is now well understood. Much less well understood is the fact that, without the Global Minotaur guaranteeing a steady torrent of capital into the United States (often via London), these practices would never have taken off as a systemic practice – not even in Wall Street.

An ideology of cheapness for the Age of Excess: the Walmart effect

Walmart is one of the largest conglomerates in the world. With annual earnings in excess of $335 billion, it is second only to oil giant Exxon Mobil. The reason it is singled out here is because Walmart symbolizes a brand new phase of capitalist accumulation – one that is close to the Global Minotaur's logic.

Unlike the first conglomerates, which evolved in the 1900s on the back of impressive inventions and technological innovations, Walmart and its ilk built empires based on next to no technological innovation, except a long string of 'innovations' involving ingenious methods of squeezing their suppliers' prices and generally hacking into the rewards of the labourers involved at all stages in the production and distribution of its wares. Walmart's significance revolves on a simple axis: in the era of the Global Minotaur it traded on the American working class's frustration at having lost the American Dream of ever-increasing living standards and on the related need for lower prices.

Unlike those corporations that focused on building a particular brand (e.g. Coca-Cola or Marlboro), or companies that created a wholly new sector by means of some invention (e.g. Edison with the light bulb, Microsoft with its Windows software, Sony with the Walkman, or Apple with the iPod/iPhone/iTunes package), Walmart did something no one had ever thought of before: it packaged a new *ideology of cheapness* into a brand that was meant to appeal to the financially stressed American working and lower-middle classes.

Take, for example, Vlasic pickles, a well-known everyday brand. Walmart's 'innovation' was to sell these pickles in one gallon (3.8 litre) jars for $2.97. Was this a shrewd retailer's response to market demand? No it was not. Who would want to buy almost four litres of pickles? Few family fridges had the necessary room for such an item. So what was the selling point? It was the *idea* of a huge quantity at an ultra-low price. Walmart's customers, in this sense, were not buying pickles as such. They were buying into the symbolic value of cheapness; into the notion of having appropriated so many pickles for so little money. Indeed, it made them feel as though they were Walmart's accomplices – in association with an icon of American corporate might, they had forced producers to make so much available for so little!

The gigantic jar of cheap pickles in the fridge thus ended up denoting a small victory at a time of wholesale defeat. Whose defeat? That of the average American worker, whose real wages had never recovered since 1973 (as we saw in the previous chapter). Moreover, their working conditions deteriorated as employers everywhere faithfully copied the Walmart model.

Now, it would be wrong to say that Walmart mistreats its employees, for the simple reason that it doesn't have any! At least not according to Walmart, which describes the people who work for it as 'associates'. What this means is that the company does not consider itself to be bound to treat its workforce as living, human, waged labour. Instead it employs Orwellian language to explain its blanket ban on any trades union activity on its premises. The result is a variety of unsavoury allegations: that most Walmart 'associates' work for less than $10 per hour,[2] habitually work overtime with no additional pay, and are often locked inside warehouses while working overnight. These alleged practices have resulted in at least sixty-three lawsuits in forty-two states. Indeed, the company chose to settle all these suits at a cost of $352 million, a large sum but a mere fraction of the wages 'saved'.[3]

The situation in the workshops and fields of the Third World, where goods are grown or produced on behalf of Walmart, is, as one might imagine, bordering on the criminal. Defenders of the type of globalization imposed upon the rest of the world by Walmart and the Global Minotaur will argue that growth has been strong for two decades internationally, a trend that seems set to continue. Surely this is good for the poor. But what this argument misses is the distributive effect of Walmart-type practices on the poor.

Drawing on various reports on global poverty by the United Nations and other sources, a 2006 report tells us that in and around 1980, for every $100 of world growth, the poorest 20 per cent of people received $2.20.[4] Twenty-one years later, by 2001, in the poorer countries both the output and employment related to multinational companies like Walmart had increased substantially. This is the case for the defence: 'We increased their work, boosted their employment,' they contend (with some justification). Yet, at the same time, we now know that, during the same period, an additional $100 of world growth translated into a measly extra 60 cents for the poorest 20 per cent. Furthermore, when one takes into account the disproportionate rise in prices for basic commodities, as well as the diminution in public services following the IMF's structural adjustment programmes (in the wake of the Third World debt crisis of the 1980s), there appears to be very little cause for celebration on behalf of our poverty-challenged fellow humans.

In Robert Greenwald's shocking 2005 documentary *Wal-Mart: The High Cost of Low Price*, a woman working in a Chinese toy

---

Box 5.3
Walmart: a corporation after the Minotaur's heart

The immediate effect of the Walmart 'business model' (which was adopted by many other companies, e.g. Starbucks) was, quite obviously, anti-inflationary. This was essential for the Global Minotaur's continuing rude health, since the flow of foreign capital to the United States was partly predicated upon US inflation trailing that of other, competing, capitalist centres. In Walmart's defence one may argue that it was simply responding to the facts. As the Minotaur was gathering strength, American workers felt their diminishing purchasing power in their bones. Walmart simply responded to this reality by providing them with basic products at prices reflecting their diminishing capacity to pay. Was this not a decent helping hand that American families in danger of slipping into poverty needed?

The facts suggest otherwise: Walmart's overall effect has been quite the opposite. Wherever Walmart expanded, poverty rates rose. Consider, for instance, the 1990s, a period of rapid growth in the United States, courtesy of the Global Minotaur and its astonishing capacity to attract other people's capital to the country. So poverty rates began to decline (only to rise again after 2001, under George W. Bush's administration). During that decade of declining poverty rates, something extraordinary happened: poverty rates not only proved more stubborn in towns where Walmart set up shop, but indeed in many such regions those rates rose, bucking the national trend!

---

factory asks 'Do you know why the toys you buy are so cheap?' and then proceeds breathlessly to answer her own question: 'It's because we work all day, every day and every night.'

Summing up, then, Walmart represents more than corporate oligopoly capitalism. It represents a new guise of corporation, which evolved in response to the circumstances brought on by the Global Minotaur. The Walmart extractive business model reified cheapness and profited from amplifying the feedback between falling prices and the American working class's falling purchasing power. It imported the Third World into American towns and regions and exported jobs to the Third World (through outsourcing), causing the depletion of both the 'human stock' and the natural environment everywhere it went. Wherever we look, even in the most technologically advanced US corporations (e.g. Apple), we cannot fail to recognize the influence of the Walmart model. The Global Minotaur and Walmart rose to prominence at about the same time. It was no coincidence.

Tainted houses, toxic cash: Wall Street generates its own private money

With wages stagnant, and against a background of conspicuous profiteering and a marketing blitz that incessantly depicted the new gadgets and props of a successful life, the banks had an idea: why not use their expanding capital inflows (from abroad, but also from the accumulation of domestic profits) to extend credit to middle- and working-class households in the form of both mortgages and personal loans and credit cards?

Once upon a time, the relatively low paid would risk accepting credit facilities only on the expectation of rising future wages. In the Global Minotaur era, however, there could be no credit expansion on that basis. While the average American worker was bombarded with heroic reports of America's high growth rates, any hopes these figures might have raised were forever crushed by the ruthlessness of her personal, local reality. The sole line of communication with that 'other' world, where incomes rose and living standards improved, was home ownership. At a time when house price rises seemed permanent, bricks and mortar became the only realistic hope of riding the wealth escalator.

Thus, millions of Americans borrowed to buy a home and, almost instantly, borrowed against that home to buy other (mostly imported) goodies. The result was that private debt levels rose even faster than the corporations' profitability throughout the United States and in parts of the world (mostly with a strong Anglo-Celtic ethnic imprint) that had managed to attach themselves to the Minotaur's coat-tails. In America, the rises in unsecured debt levels were stupendous. In the 1970s, personal and credit card debts rose by 238 per cent relative to the 1960s. In the 1980s, the rise relative to the 1970s jumped to 318 per cent. In the 1990s, debt levels rose again (relative to the 1980s), though by 'only' 180 per cent (largely because of the 1991 recession). And in the eight years before the 2008 Crash, we observe a rise (relative to the already indebted 1990s) of 163 per cent.

Perhaps the most widely felt effect of the Global Minotaur's ascendancy was its impact on house prices. Anglo-Celtic countries, with the United States leading the way, saw the largest rises in house price inflation. A combination of the foreign capital inflows, domestic US profits and the increasing availability of bank loans pushed house prices up at breathtaking speed. Between 2002 and 2007, the median house price rose by around 65 per cent in Britain, 44 per cent in Ireland, and by between 30 per cent and 40 per cent in the USA, Canada and Australia.

There is an interesting antinomy in the way popular culture and the financial 'commentariat' treat increasing house prices. Whereas inflation is treated as an enemy of civilization and a scourge, house price rises are almost universally applauded. Homeowners feel good when estate agents tell them that their house is now worth a lot more, even though they know very well that this is akin to monopoly money; that, unless they are prepared to sell up and leave the country (or move into a much smaller house or to a 'worse' area), they will never 'realize' that 'value'. Nevertheless, the rise in the asset's nominal value never fails to make house owners feel more relaxed about borrowing in order to finance consumption. This is precisely what under-pinned the stunning growth rate in places like Britain, Australia and Ireland.

Figure 5.1 exposes neatly the correlation between the housing price inflation rate and consumption growth. The Anglo-Celtic countries where house prices boomed were also the countries where consumption rose fast. Meanwhile, in the two former US protégés, Germany and Japan (the two countries that were financing the Anglo-Celtic deficits through their industrial production, which the Anglo-Celtic countries were, in turn, absorbing), not only did house prices not increase but they actually dropped, at least in the case of Germany.

The graphic correlation shown in the figure between the housing bubble and consumption-driven growth was reinforced by a famous instrument: *securitized derivatives* or *collateralized*

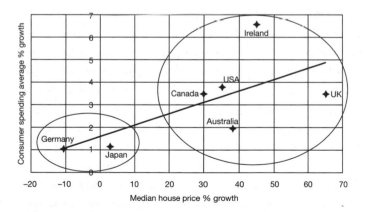

Figure 5.1
Correlation between median house price inflation and the
growth in consumer spending, 2002–07

debt obligations (those CDOs again). How did they link housing debt with consumption-driven growth? To answer this question, it is helpful to begin with a self-evident truth: the banks' main principle has traditionally been *never to lend to anyone unless they do not need the money*. But this principle clashed with the urge to lend to those poor enough to be willing to pay higher interest rates than those who had other alternatives (i.e. the rich). Enter the CDOs.

Their function was to allow banks to lend even to paupers, and at high interest rates, without fear that they would default. Not because some magical formula had been devised to shield the poor from poverty, the job-insecure from unemployment and the bankrupt from bankruptcy, but because the CDOs allowed the banks to *originate and spread*; to lend and then immediately sell the loan on.

The trick was to combine different kinds of loans: safe loans (e.g. taken out by some rich lawyer to buy a holiday home), loans bearing some risk (e.g. money borrowed by a firm with a decent track record) and low-quality (*sub-prime*) loans (e.g. a mortgage taken out by a family that would almost certainly not manage to meet its repayments after the initial low-interest period expired) were all lumped together and then divided into small packages, the CDOs, each containing slices (or tranches) of these different loans, with each slice paying different interest rates and coming with different default risks.

The mathematics that estimated how much money the owner of this CDO was due on the CDO's expiry was so complex that even its creator could not decipher it. However, the mere hint that brilliant mathematical minds had designed their structure, and the solid fact that Wall Street's respected, and feared, credit ratings agencies had given them their seal of approval (which came in the form of triple-A ratings), was enough for banks, individual investors and hedge funds to buy and sell them internationally as if they were high-grade bonds or even cash.

This, as the reader will have gathered by now, is the sad tale of sub-prime mortgages. The story of how Wall Street, not content with processing and building upon the tsunami of foreign capital and domestic corporate profits that the Minotaur was pushing its way, tried to profit also from poor people, by selling them mortgages that they could never really afford. By 2005, more than 22 per cent of US mortgages were of this sub-prime variety. By 2007, the percentage had risen further, to 26 per cent. All of them were inserted into CDOs before the ink had dried on the dotted line.

In raw numbers, between 2005 and 2007 alone, US investment banks issued about $1.1 trillion of CDOs. In terms of value, in 2008 the mortgage-backed bonds came to almost $7 trillion, of which at least $1.3 trillion were based mainly on sub-prime mortgages. The significance of the $7 trillion figure is that it is larger even than the total size of the (arguably gigantic) US debt. But to give an accurate picture of the disaster in the making, it is important to look at these vast numbers in relation to one another, as well as to the level of global income: back in 2003, for every $1 of world income, $1.80 worth of derivatives circulated. Four years later, in 2007, that ratio had risen by 640 per cent: every $1 of world income corresponded to almost $12 worth of derivatives. The world of finance had evidently grown too large to be contained on planet Earth!

It was a heroic time, during which money seemed to be growing on trees. Traditional companies – those that actually produced things – were derided as old-hat. What steel producer, car manufacturer or even electronics company could ever compete with Wall Street's amazing returns? All sorts of companies wanted to join in. Staid corporations like General Motors entered the derivatives racket for this reason. At first it allowed the company's finance arm (whose aim was to arrange loans on behalf of customers who could not afford the full price of the firm's product, e.g. hire purchase for cars) to dip a toe in the derivatives pond. It liked the feeling and the nice greenbacks streaming in. Soon that finance arm ended up as the company's most lucrative section. So the firm ended up relying more and more for its profitability on its financial services, and less and less on its actual, physical product.

Before long, the world economy became addicted to these financial instruments, of which the CDOs were but one example. Soon they began to function not only as 'stores of value' but also as 'means of exchange': they had turned into a very private form of money. Once the Clinton administration released Wall Street from all regulatory restraints (by a decision that is credited to US Treasury Secretary Larry Summers), the global economy was flooded with this *private money*. Its infinite supply kept interest rates down all over the world, fuelling asset bubbles (from Miami and Nevada to Ireland and Spain) and encouraging states in chronic deficit (e.g. Greece) to plug their budgets with cheap, over-the-counter loans.

Notice the irony: in a world ideologically dominated by monetary conservatism, and ringing with long sermons about the perils of printing money, the effective money supply had been turned over to privateers bent on flooding the markets with money of their own making. How did this differ, really, from handing the Fed's printing presses over to the mafia? There is not much difference, is the honest answer.

According to standard conservative economic theory, too much money flooding into the economy, especially during an economic upturn, is a recipe for the catastrophic loss of the market's capacity to send meaningful signals to producers and consumers on what to produce and on how to economize. And yet none of the high priests of fiscal and monetary conservatism batted an eyelid while zillions' worth of toxic private money (over the quantity and worth of which no one had the slightest control) were inundating the globe. For they, just like corporate capitalism in America and elsewhere, had themselves become addicted to the newfangled currency's power.

When the plug was pulled in 2008, and all the private money disappeared from the face of the earth, global capitalism was left with what looked like a massive liquidity crisis. It was as if the lake had evaporated and the fish, large and small, were quivering in the mud. The problem was, however, deeper and larger. The loss of the private money brought the Global Minotaur to its knees. With it came crashing down the only mechanism the world economy had for recycling its surpluses. The upshot is a Crisis from which no liquidity-pumping by the Fed and the other central banks can help us escape.

Toxic theory, Part A: trickle-down politics, supply-side economics

When Ronald Reagan entered the White House in 1981, the fledgling Global Minotaur was already in residence, if not in complete control. Within the United States, its handmaidens[5] were cradling it, preparing it for the bigger and better things to come. With the twin US deficits gradually expanding, the beast's imprint on American society and its influence on the world economy were growing by the day. What the Reagan presidency undoubtedly added to the mix was a political and economic ecology that suited the Minotaur down to the ground.

Reagan's rhetoric struck a chord at the end of a confused decade, during which the pride of the American nation had received the worst sequence of blows in its history: ostensibly held to ransom by a bunch of Middle Eastern oil producers,[6] defeated on the battlefield by the Viet Cong, rooted out of Iran by Khomeini's revolution, passively standing by while the Red Army marched into Afghanistan. American society also felt in its bones the ill effects of new social tensions caused by the disruption to rising real wages. The American public was hungry for a rousing call to arms, for a new 'paradigm' that would restore self-esteem. President Reagan obliged his 'fellow Americans', as he liked to address them: lower taxes, armaments and a return to good old puritan values were his offerings.

The basic idea was neither novel nor complicated: get the government out of Americans' way, let them keep their gains and allow them to get on with their lives. In reality, it constituted a wholesale retreat from the 1929-inspired notion that the market was too capricious to be left to business and consumers; that the US government had to discipline, cajole and shepherd the private sector's progress in order to avert another Crisis, not only at the local but also at the global level. In a sense, Reagan's message was consistent with Volcker's earlier idea that US interests required a 'disintegration in the world economy'.

The only difference was that the old B-movie actor put it more simply: nothing succeeds collectively like unimpeded individual success, was his message. If America seemed in the eyes of many to be stalling, it was because Big Government was holding it back. With a potentially productive private sector straining at the leash of a self-absorbed Leviathan, the only thing that was needed was for the leash to be severed and the Leviathan put in his place. And what was his place, his only legitimate role? Defence of the nation. And that could only be achieved if the American military was allowed to project its power to the four corners of the planet.

Once fully endorsed by the American electorate, Washington embarked upon supply-side economic policies and massive increases in the military budget. Privileging the economy's 'supply side' was code for reducing all impediments to capital accumulation. In practice, it meant large tax breaks for the highest earners, reductions in social spending programmes and the removal of many restraints on Wall Street that were remnants of the Global Plan era. Meanwhile, the fresh military spending proved a boon for the large industrial network connected to the arms industry and the state's defence procurements.

When dissident voices pointed out that tax cuts favoured the rich (especially when combined with cuts in social provisions for the poor), the standard reply came in the form of the so-called *trickle-down effect*: as the rich enrich themselves further (the theory went), their spending and investment will trickle down to the less privileged more effectively than it would through transfers financed by taxing the rich.

Box 5.4
The trickle-up effect

The trickle-down effect was meant to legitimize reductions in tax rates for the rich, by suggesting that their extra cash would eventually trickle down to the poor. All empirical evidence conspires against this hypothesis. Put simply, it never happened. The increasing riches of the conspicuously rich never reached the suffering lower-middle class. In fact, exactly the opposite happened: a quite different effect, the *trickle-up effect*, was occasioned by the securitized derivatives market. As we have seen, securitization of the unsafe debts of the poor (e.g. the conversion of sub-prime mortgages into CDOs) has the effect of making the initial lender indifferent to whether or not the loan can be repaid (for it will already have sold the debt on to someone else). These securitized packages of debt are then sold and resold at tremendous profit (or were, prior to the Crash of 2008). The rich, in an important sense, had discovered another ingenious way of getting richer – by trading on paper assets packaging the dreams, aspirations and eventual desperation of the poorest in society.

The combination of mountainous increases in military spending (of an order of magnitude well above the puny savings achieved through cuts in the social welfare budget) and generous reductions in the taxation of the well-off spattered the US government's accounts with vast quantities of red ink. The irony is truly delicious: the largest post-war expansion in government deficits was effected by an administration whose rhetoric against government profligacy was the strongest in living memory.

The Global Minotaur could not have hoped for better hand-maidens in the White House and the various corridors of power. As the US budget deficit exploded, it accelerated the tsunami of foreign capital that rushed into New York. Eager to buy safe American debt at a time of general uncertainty, the world's surplus was pouring into the US, allowing Wall Street to create even more private money to fuel even greater consumer spending.

The year before Ronald Reagan's presidential victory, Margaret Thatcher had won office in the UK on a similar political manifesto. The difference was that her government inherited an economy that had been on the decline for almost a century. Moreover, it was a social economy in which the working class had managed, especially after the Second World War, to secure considerable power over economic affairs (both through the establishment of a large welfare state and through the nationalization of large industrial sectors, e.g. coal and steel).

The 'commentariat' shaping public opinion hailed Prime Minister Thatcher for having successfully transplanted the American miracle onto European soil. The dominant story was that, if Europe wanted to become competitive again, it ought to follow the Iron Lady's lead in privatizing industries, deregu-lating labour markets and reducing unit labour costs.

The problem with that narrative was that it withstood no close scrutiny. Mrs Thatcher's government never reduced unit labour costs. What she did do was to take a machete to industrial output, 'ridding' Britain of many of its traditional industrial sectors and, in the process, of the bothersome trades unions. This she undoubtedly succeeded in doing. But what effect did the destruction of the trades unions have on British labour costs?

The answer here is more complex than most commentators acknowledge. Together with the mining and steel industries, which bore the brunt of the reforms, millions of full-time jobs disappeared forever. Naturally, the portion of national income that went to workers fell dramatically, and whole areas of Britain were taken over by Third World conditions. But the one thing that did *not* happen was that for which Mrs Thatcher was given credit: real wages per hour did not drop. In fact, and in sharp contrast to the US experience, they rose considerably.[7]

It is now clear that Mrs Thatcher's impressive electoral successes in 1983 and 1987 (Britain's 'first past the post' electoral system notwithstanding) was due to two factors. First, many of the 4.5 million jobless people were too glum and disgruntled to bother to vote. Secondly, the workers who *did* hang on to their jobs saw their real wages rise. In addition, Mrs Thatcher gave them bonuses that roped them into a speculative mood, in tune with the financial frenzy in Wall Street and the City of London.

The bonuses came in two forms: selling the workers (at very low prices) the council houses in which they had been living, and offering them shares in newly privatized companies (like British Telecom, British Gas and the Trustee Savings Bank (TSB)) at far below the estimated market price.[8] Both of these moves encouraged the still-working segments of the working class to consent to an economy that put all its eggs into the basket of speculation – either on house prices or on share prices.

As anticipated, the much-vaunted shareowners' democracy lasted but a few days, as the co-opted workers immediately sold their shares to the conglomerates. They did the same thing with their council houses, in an attempt to move to better neighbourhoods and make some extra cash in the process, since much of the new house's price would be paid for with a mortgage. The newly privatized housing encouraged banks to extend mortgages and credit card facilities to families that had never had them. The concomitant increase in the demand for houses boosted their prices, and that gave the workers the illusion that they were getting richer. On the back of their rising 'assets', the banks tripped over each other to lend workers money to go on holiday, buy a car, upgrade their stereo, etc. In the end, household debt, house prices and consumer spending all went up in perfect unison.

Meanwhile, the City of London's traditional strength in the realm of finance, its deregulation under the Thatcher government (also known as the Big Bang) and the City's links with Wall Street all ensured that a significant portion of the foreign capital flight to the United States passed through the City. That passage gave its institutions access to large sums of money, even if for only a short period of time. Nothing excites bankers more than the challenge of making money for themselves by using transient funds. Together with the proceeds from domestic privatizations of UK industries and of the nation's stock of social housing, as well as the Great British public's mountain of borrowing, these financial streams merged into a potent torrent, which allowed the City of London to prosper.

In conclusion, over the past three decades, much ink has been spilt in assessing the Reagan–Thatcher years. From this book's perspective, suffice it to say that the famous duo's politics proved immensely helpful to the rise of our Global Minotaur. Britain's image as an entrepreneurial society, and all the razzmatazz generated by the cocky estate agents and slick bankers, depended heavily on the City's paper trades and the rising house prices. These twin bubbles developed for the simple reason that London had skilfully situated itself as a strategic refuelling stop on the migration routes that the world's capital took to reach New York.

Toxic theory, Part B: economic models and assorted delusions

The Global Minotaur relied on sympathetic governments standing aside while its mammoth asymmetries were gaining shape. The politics of neoliberalism ushered in by Thatcher and Reagan served it well. But it needed more: a new variant of economic theory that would add a veneer of scientific legitimacy to the actual policies.

We have already discussed the essence of these economic theories (see chapter 1). Whatever their actual content, two were the prerequisites that economic theories had to fulfil to be considered *realistic* and *timely* at a time when the world economy was, as Paul Volcker suggested, in for some wilful disintegration. First, economic theories had to distance themselves from the idea that an economy could be rationally managed. Secondly, they had to feature a model of the economy in which regulatory constraints on capital accumulation and all forms of democratic restraint on unfettered markets appeared not so much inefficient as nonsensical.

Both prerequisites were met by a formalist model (which came in multiple guises, all of them adorned with impressive mathematical complexity)[9] in which capitalism appeared in one of two forms: either as a static system of timeless interlocking markets in a state of permanent equilibrium, or as a dynamic system, steaming ahead along time's arrow, but comprising a single individual (called the *representative agent*) or a single sector. In short, a generation of economists grew up with economic models that could handle *either* complexity *or* time, but never both at once.

The great advantage of these models was that they featured a depiction of capitalism so mathematically complex that practitioners could spend a lifetime delving into their infinitely convoluted formalist structures without ever noticing that, by the way they were constructed, their models could never even really begin to simulate capitalism as it existed.

Now, all models are abstractions, and their purpose is to simplify. In physics, for instance, one begins with many simplifying assumptions (e.g. that there is no friction, or even gravity) in order to get a handle on some basic laws of nature. But then one begins steadily to relax the unrealistic assumptions. At the expense of added complexity, the physicist thus obtains more practicably useful variants of the theory.

Not so in economics. For in economic theory, the process of gradually relaxing restrictive assumptions comes to an abrupt halt before it even gets under way. If the lack of gravity is an example of one of the most restrictive assumptions in physics, the economics equivalent would be that there is no time. Or that all consumers and industries are identical. But unlike physics, which can relax its assumptions to get closer to the truth, economics cannot. Indeed, there is a remarkable theorem in economics proving that solvable economic models cannot handle time and complexity at once.[10]

The practical importance of this impossibility cannot be overstated. Indeed, it explains largely how economic theory ended up as one of the Global Minotaur's most loyal handmaidens. For if no mathematized economic model is possible that depicts the real-time transactions of different people and industries, then economic modelling must be divorced from any theory of crisis.

After all, a crisis is, by nature, a dynamic phenomenon affecting a multi-person (and multi-industry) society that unfolds in real time. Robinson Crusoe may have been unhappy, hungry or have gone through an existentialist crisis, but he could never experience an *economic crisis* (at least not before Friday's arrival). Crises require a failure of coordination between different people and sectors, a collapse in an economy's capacity collectively to utilize its individual resources. Is it not a most peculiar scientific failure that, for all its mind-boggling complexity, mathematical economics cannot even begin to wrap its equations around the idea of a Crisis?

Given that the story of mathematical economics is the story of a dramatic scientific failure, why am I claiming that, as a body of theory, economics ended up as one of the beast's handmaidens? For two reasons. The first is easy to discern: when the panoply of modern economic theory leaves no logical space for Crises and depicts capitalism as a system of interlocking markets in a timeless equilibrium, it serves as the free-market fundamentalist's ideological prop. The second, less obvious, reason has to do with Wall Street's toxic money, whose role as one of the handmaidens has already been well established.

The CDOs that sliced up and then spliced together disparate debts belonging to a heterogeneous multitude of families and businesses were put together on the basis of certain formulae, whose purpose was, supposedly, to calculate their value and their riskiness. These formulae were developed by financial engineers working for Wall Street (e.g. for J. P. Morgan, Bank of America, Goldman Sachs, etc.). To render the formulae solvable, certain assumptions had to be made. First and foremost was the assumption that the probability that one slice of debt within a CDO would go bad was largely unrelated to the probability of a similar default by the other slices in the same CDO. That is, it was assumed that what happened in 2007–08 was...

impossible! That it was unnecessary to factor in the possibility of some crisis, during which Bob lost his house for reasons that increased the chances that Jane would lose her job and eventually also default on her mortgage.[11]

The inescapable question – the one that everyone asked after the Crash – was: why were these CDO valuations believed by numerous smart, self-interested market operators, whose livelihoods depended on the truth of the underlying assumptions? The answer is twofold. First, these market operators were captives of a herd-like behaviour and would have risked losing their jobs if they had gone against the flow.[12] Secondly, during the Global Minotaur's heyday the economics profession had successfully peddled a form of mathematized superstition, which armed the traders with the superhuman – and superinane – confidence needed (perhaps against their better judgement and wishes) to bring down the system that nourished them. A very contemporary tragedy indeed.

Epilogue: the writing on the wall

The demise of the Global Plan and the wilful disintegration of the world economy that followed had their ideological counterpart: the doctrine that our collective attempts to control the world are doomed; that the markets are certain to outflank our best efforts to manage them.

Neoliberals cherished the thought that the 'economy' is too recalcitrant to be planned and is therefore better left to the automated self-adjusting forces of the market. What they missed was that the successor phase to the Global Plan was anything but a case of spontaneous order. Instead, their treasured markets were ruled by the Global Minotaur's iron claws, aided and abetted by a band of merry handmaidens, among them successive US administrations, the effects of economic stagnation on the average American family, shadowy Wall Street operations, and lots of silly economics.[13]

The new creed was underpinned by a gut feeling that market forces resemble the ebb and flow of the great oceans, and that anyone who tries to get in their way is a latter-day King Canute. The great paradox of the time was the incredible optimism that accompanied this species of moral enthusiasm for market solutions. On the one hand commentators believed that nothing good comes of government planning, but at the same time they were convinced that unfettered markets would always perform miracles.

While one can understand the logic of pessimism regarding the effects on our lives of government, its coexistence with a touching, unexamined faith in the market's capacity to deliver success is baffling. How can a radical scepticism about the state be squared with a religious dedication to the notion that market outcomes are, by definition, optimal? What is the mechanism that guarantees the tidy immunity of market outcomes from the vindictiveness of human fate?

From the late 1970s up until 2008, the reason why the world kept growing at a seemingly stable pace was the Global Minotaur. While deregulation, privatization and financialization were running riot, the lack of a discernible Global Plan was tempered by the beast's active role as a surrogate global surplus recycling mechanism, without which the world economy cannot function.

Under the Minotaur, as this book has been arguing, the United States and its satellites (e.g. Britain) were accumulating external national debt, Anglo-American families were amassing retail debt, and Wall Street was generating *and* accumulating toxic private money. Meanwhile, the oil-producing nations, Germany, Japan, South East Asia (especially after the East Asian crisis of 1998) and, latterly, China, were all building up gargantuan currency reserves, which they were pumping into Wall Street and the City of London. In a never-ending cycle, these capital flows financed America's twin deficits in ways that kept surplus production going in Europe and East Asia.

Was it a case of markets performing their miracle? Not really. For this type of precarious GSRM could never have been born out of spontaneously operating markets. It was a mechanism designed and supervised by knowledgeable, proactive US policy makers. While there were quite a few of them, this book pays repeated tribute to one of the smartest of them all: Paul Volcker, the ex Fed chairman, who had been in positions of power from 1971, when the Minotaur was but a gleam in Washington's eye, to well after its 2008 downfall.

In the introductory chapter, I began with the Queen's question to the economists: 'Why had you not seen it coming?' Well, Paul Volcker had. As befits a true statesman who had played a major role in creating the beast, he had what it took to do what others (e.g. the Europeans) had no stomach for: to look the Minotaur, his creation, in the eye and not blink. On 10 April 2005, when no one was interested in 'bad news stories', he had written:

> What holds [the US economic success story] all together is a massive and growing flow of capital from abroad, running to more than $2 billion every working day, and growing...
>
> As a nation we don't consciously borrow or beg. We aren't even offering attractive interest rates, nor do we have to offer our creditors protection against the risk of a declining dollar... We fill our shops and our garages with goods from abroad, and the competition has been a powerful restraint on our internal prices. It's surely helped keep interest rates exceptionally low despite our vanishing savings and rapid growth.
>
> And it's comfortable for our trading partners and for those supplying the capital. Some, such as China, depend heavily on our expanding domestic markets. And for the most part, the

central banks of the emerging world have been willing to hold more and more dollars, which are, after all, the closest thing the world has to a truly international currency.

The difficulty is that this seemingly comfortable pattern can't go on indefinitely. I don't know of any country that has managed to consume and invest 6 per cent more than it produces for long. The United States is absorbing about 80 per cent of the net flow of international capital.[14]

I could not have put it better. If the Global Minotaur requires an introduction, this Paul Volcker quote will do nicely. As further proof that US power brokers were completely aware and wary of the Minotaur's massive hoofprint on the planet's economy, here is what Stephen Roach, chief economist of the investment bank Morgan Stanley, had to say three years earlier, in 2002:

> This saga is...about the unwinding of a more profound asymmetry in the global economy, the rebalancing of a US-centric world... History tells us that such asymmetries are not sustainable... Can a savings-short US economy continue to finance an ever-widening expansion of its military superiority? My answer is a resounding no. The confluence of history, geopolitics, and economics leaves me more convinced than ever that a US-centric world is on an unsustainable path.[15]

In retrospect, we see that the creature's originators (America's top administrators and some of Wall Street's high priests) could discern the writing on the wall. Unlike the clueless handmaidens, they *had* foreseen the Crash. In painful slow motion.

CHAPTER 6

Crash

Tumbling piles

Children learn the dynamics of piles from a young age. They place a cube on top of another cube and keep going until their little tower of cubes topples over, at which point they emit a happy giggle and start afresh. This is not too dissimilar to what happened in 2008. The only difference is that – except for the bankers, who were only too quick to start building a fresh pile (courtesy of the taxpayer) – there were no giggles, and most people remain glum some years after the largest pile of all came crashing down.

The story of how the Crash of 2008 began is now the stuff of legend. Mountains of books have been written on it and stacked on the shelves of university libraries, in airport bookshops, on the stalls of leftist groupings plying their revolutionary wares on street corners, etc. Thus, there is no need to delve into the sequence of events, except to supply a minimalist timeline that serves as a quick reminder of the train of events. The real purpose of this chapter is to remind us of the pace of the plunge, the depth of the abyss and the *aporia* in which the world became entangled. The trick is how to recall the dramatic events while keeping an eye on their deeper causes in the unravelling of the Global Plan and its replacement by the Global Minotaur.

Prior to 2008, as we now know, Wall Street had managed to set up a parallel monetary system, a form of *private money*, underwritten by the capital inflows toward the Global Minotaur. The global economy became hooked on that toxic money, which, by its nature, divided and multiplied unsustainably. So when it turned to ashes, world capitalism crashed. If it were not for the lessons that the central banks had learned from the Crash of 1929, the repercussions would have been unimaginable – as opposed to just frightful.

Chronicle of a Crash foretold: Credit Crunch, bail-outs and the socialization of nearly everything

2007 – *The canaries in the mine*

April – New Century Financial, a mortgage company that had issued a great number of sub-prime mortgages, goes under, with reverberations throughout the sector.

July – Bear Stearns, the respected merchant bank, announces that two of its hedge funds will not be able to pay their investors their dues. The new chairman of the Fed, Ben Bernanke (who had only recently replaced Alan Greenspan) announces that the sub-prime crisis is serious and its cost may rise to $100 billion.

August – French merchant bank BNP-Paribas makes a similar announcement to that of Bear Stearns concerning two of its hedge funds. Its explanation? That it can no longer value its assets. In reality, this is an admission that its coffers are full of CDOs, the demand for which has fallen to precisely zero, thus making it impossible to price them. Almost immediately, European banks stop lending to one another. The European Central Bank (ECB) is forced to throw €95 billion into the financial markets to avert immediate cardiac arrest. Soon it throws a further €109 billion into the markets. At the same time, the Fed, the Bank of Canada, the Reserve Bank of Australia and the Bank of Japan begin to pump undisclosed billions into their financial sectors. On 17 August, Bernanke reduces interest rates slightly, demonstrating a serious lack of appreciation of the scale of the problem.

September – The obvious unwillingness of the banks to lend to one another is revealed when the rate at which they do this lending (the LIBOR, short for the London Inter-bank Offered Rate) exceeds the Bank of England's rate by more than 1 per cent (for the first time since the South East Asian crisis of 1998). At that point, we witness the first run on a bank since 1929. The bank in question is Northern Rock. While it holds no CDOs or sub-prime mortgage accounts, the bank relies heavily on short-term loans from other banks. When this source of credit dries up, it can no longer meet its liquidity needs. When customers suspect this, they try to withdraw their money, at which point the bank collapses, before being brought back to 'life' by the Bank of England at a cost in excess of £15 billion. Rocked by this development, Bernanke drops US interest rates by another small amount, to 4.75 per cent, while the Bank of England pumps £10 billion worth of liquidity into the City of London.

October – The banking crisis extends to the most esteemed Swiss financial institution, UBS, and the world takes notice. UBS announces the resignation of its chairman and CEO, who takes the blame for a loss of $3.4 billion from CDOs containing US sub-prime mortgages. Meanwhile, in the United States, Citigroup at first reveals a loss of $3.1 billion (again on mortgage-backed CDOs) – a figure that rises by another $5.9 billion within a few days. By March of 2008, Citigroup has to admit that the real figure is a stunning loss of $40 billion. Not to be left out of the fracas, merchant bank Merrill Lynch announces a $7.9 billion loss and its CEO falls on his sword.

December – A historic moment arrives when one of the most free market opponents of state intervention ever to have made it to the presidency of the United States, George W. Bush, gives the first indication of the world's biggest government intervention (not excepting that of Lenin after the Russian Revolution). On 6 December, President Bush unveils a plan to help a million American homeowners avoid having their houses confiscated by the banks (i.e. avoid foreclosure, in American parlance). A few days later, the Fed gets together with another five central banks (including the ECB) to extend almost infinite credit to the banks. The aim? To address the *Credit Crunch* – i.e. the complete halt in inter-bank lending.

2008 - The main event

January – The World Bank predicts a global recession, stock markets crash, the Fed drops interest rates to 3.5 per cent, and stock markets rebound in response. Before long, however, MBIA, an insurance company, announces that it has lost $2.3 billion from policies based on bonds containing sub-prime mortgages. These insurance policies suddenly become household names: they are known as credit default swaps, or CDSs.

Box 6.1
Credit default swaps (CDS)

If Mr Spock, of *Star Trek* fame, spotted a CDS and had to describe it to Captain Kirk, he would have said, in his usual expressionless way: 'They are insurance policies, Captain, but not as we know them.' CDSs pay out pre-specified amounts of money if someone else defaults. The difference between a CDS and a simple insurance policy is this: to insure your car against an accident, you must first own it. The CDS 'market' allows one to buy an 'insurance policy' on someone else's car, so that if, say, your neighbour has an accident, then you collect money! To put it bluntly, a CDS is no more than a bet on some nasty event taking place – mainly someone (a person, a company or a nation) defaulting on a debt. When you buy such a CDS on Jill's debt, you are, to all intents and purposes, betting that Jill will fail to pay it back; that she will default. CDSs became popular with hedge fund managers (and remain so to this day) for reasons closely linked to the trade in CDOs.

Take, for example, a trader who invests in a risky CDO. If our investor undertook (in the good old pre-2008 days) to cover $10 million of default losses on this CDO tranche, he could have received an upfront payment of $5 million, plus $500,000 a year! So long as the defaults did not happen, he would make a huge bundle without investing anything! Not bad for a moment's work – until, that is, the defaults start piling up. To hedge against that eventuality, the trader would buy CDSs, which would pay him money if the mortgages in the CDOs he bought defaulted. Thus the combination of CDSs and CDOs made fortunes for traders at a time when defaults on mortgages were rare and uncorrelated. But when the defaults started happening, the issuers of CDSs were badly burnt: they had to pay impossible amounts of cash to those who had bought them. MBIA's bankruptcy was the entree. The American Insurance Group (AIG) was the main course. It was served up when Lehman Brothers failed in September 2008 – its mountainous CDOs were mostly insured by AIG (which had issued CDSs against Lehman's CDOs).

February – The Fed lets it be known that it is worried about the insurance sector, while the G7 (the representatives of the seven leading developed countries) forecast the cost of the sub-prime crisis to be in the region of $400 billion. Meanwhile the British government is forced to nationalize Northern Rock. Wall Street's fifth-largest bank, Bear Stearns (which in 2007 was valued at $20 billion) is wiped out, absorbed by JPMorgan Chase, which pays the paltry sum of $240 million for it, with the taxpayer throwing in a subsidy in the order of $30 billion.

April – It is reported that more than 20 per cent of mortgage 'products' in Britain are being withdrawn from the market, along with the option of taking out a 100 per cent mortgage. Meanwhile, the IMF estimates the cost of the Credit Crunch to be in excess of $1 trillion. The Bank of England replies with a further interest rate cut to 5 per cent and decides to offer £50 billion to banks burdened with problematic mortgages. A little later, the RBS attempts to stave off bankruptcy by trying to raise £12 billion from its shareholders, while at the same time admitting to having lost almost £6 billion in CDOs and the like. Around this time house prices start falling in Britain, Ireland and Spain, precipitating more defaults (as homeowners in trouble can no longer even pay back their mortgages by selling their houses at a price higher than their mortgage debt).

May – Swiss bank UBS is back in the news, with the announce-ment that it has lost $37 billion on duff mortgage-backed CDOs and that it intends to raise almost $16 billion from its shareholders.

June – Barclays Bank follows the RBS and UBS in trying to raise £4.5 billion on the stock exchange.

July – Gloom descends upon the City as the British Chamber of Commerce predicts a fierce recession and the stock exchange falls. On the other side of the Atlantic, the government begins massively to assist America's two largest mortgage providers (Fannie Mae and Freddie Mac). The total bill for that assistance, which takes the form of cash injections and loan guarantees, is $5 trillion (*sic!*), or around a tenth of the planet's annual GDP.

August – House prices continue to fall in the United States, Britain, Ireland and Spain, precipitating more defaults, more stress on financial institutions and more help from the taxpayer. The British government, through its chancellor, admits that the recession cannot be avoided and that it will be more 'profound and long-lasting' than hitherto expected.

September – The City of London stock market crashes, while Wall Street is buffeted by official statistics revealing a spiralling level of unemployment (above 6 per cent and rising). Fannie Mae and Freddie Mac are officially nationalized and Henry Paulson, President Bush's treasury secretary (and a former head of Goldman Sachs), hints at the grave danger for the whole financial system posed by these two firms' debt levels. Before his dire announcement can be digested, Wall Street giant Lehman Brothers confesses to a loss of $3.9 billion during the months June, July and August. This is, of course, the tip of the iceberg. Convinced that the US government will not let it go to the wall and will at least generously subsidize someone to buy it (as it had done with Bear Stearns), Lehman Brothers begins searching for a buyer. Britain's Barclays Bank expresses an interest, on condition that the US taxpayer funds all the potential losses from such a deal. Secretary Paulson, whose antipathy to Lehman's CEO since his days at Goldman Sachs is well documented, says a rare 'No'. Lehman Brothers thus files for bankruptcy, initiating the crisis's most dangerous avalanche.

Monday, 15 September 2008: the day Lehman Brothers dies. Lehman's has been one of the main generators of CDOs. An independent money market fund holds Lehman CDOs and, since it has no reserves, it must stop redeeming its shares. Depositors panic. By Thursday a run on money market funds is in full swing.

In the meantime, Merrill Lynch, which finds itself in a similar position, manages to negotiate its takeover by Bank of America at $50 billion, again with the taxpayer's generous assistance – assistance that is provided by a panicking government, following the dismal effects on the world's financial sector of its refusal to rescue Lehman Brothers.

It never rains but it pours. The bail-out of Merrill Lynch does not halt the domino effect. Indeed, one of the largest dominoes is about to fall: the AIG, which apparently has insured many of Lehman's CDOs against default (by issuing countless CDSs) is unable to meet its obligations under these insurance contracts (held by almost every financial institution around the world). The Fed puts together an $85 billion rescue package. Over the next six months, the total cost to the taxpayer of saving AIG from the wolves rises to an astounding $143 billion. While this drama is playing out in New York and Washington, back in London the government tries to rescue HBOS, the country's largest mortgage lender, by organizing a £12 billion takeover by Lloyds TSB. Three days later, in the United States, Washington Mutual, a significant mortgage lender with a valuation of $307 billion, goes bankrupt, is wound down, and its carcass sold off to JPMorgan Chase.

Sunday, 28 September 2008: Fortis, a giant continental European bank, collapses and is nationalized. On the same day, the US Congress discusses a request from the US Treasury to grant it the right to call upon $700 billion as assistance to the distressed financial sector, so that the latter can 'deal' with its 'bad assets'. The package is labelled the *Paulson Plan*, after President's Bush treasury secretary. In effect, Congress is asked to write a cheque to Paulson for $700 billion, for him to dispense to Wall Street as he pleases, in order to replace the private money that the financial sector created, and which has turned to ashes in 2007/08.

Before the fateful September is out, the British government nationalizes Bradford and Bingley (at a cost of £50 billion in cash and guarantees) and the government of Iceland nationalizes one of the island nation's three banks (an omen for the largest 2008-induced economic meltdown, by per capita impact). Ireland tries to steady its savers' and shareholders' nerves by announcing that the government guarantees *all* savings and *all* bonds held in or issued by *all* banks trading on the Emerald Isle. This is to prove the error of the century, a fateful decision that wipes out Ireland's post-war progress in one day. For in the months that follow, it transpires that the Irish banks have a black hole big enough to consume the country's government budget many times over. Ireland's effective bankruptcy two years later, in December 2010, becomes a foregone conclusion when the state guarantees the private banks' debts.

That same day, 29 September, Belgium, France and Luxembourg put €6.4 billion into another bank, Dexia, to prevent it from shutting up shop. But September is not finished yet. On the last day of the month the big shock comes from the US Congress, which angrily rejects the US Treasury's request for the $700 billion facility with which Paulson has been planning to save Wall Street. The New York stock exchange falls fast and hard, and the world is enveloped in an even denser cloud of uncertainty. Secretary Paulson goes back to the drawing board and returns with a more detailed plan, adding some kickbacks for particular Congress members for good measure. Conditions deteriorate, swap spreads widen, the value of CDSs rises inexorably and banking institutions lose whatever access they have left to overnight or short-term credit. The Fed replies by extending credit to everyone!

October – On 3 October the US Congress succumbs to the pressing reality and passes the $700 billion 'bail-out' package, after its members secure numerous deals for their own constituencies. Three days later, the German government steps in with €50 billion to save one of its own naive banks, Hypo Real Estate. Though painful to a country that has always prided itself on being supremely prudent, the pain comes nowhere close to the agony that Icelanders are about to experience. The Icelandic government declares that it is taking over all three banks, given their manifest inability to continue trading as private lenders. The banks' bankruptcy is bound to bankrupt the whole country, whose economic footprint is far smaller than that of its failed banks. Iceland's failure has repercussions elsewhere – in particular in Britain and Holland, where the Icelandic banks have been especially active. Many of the UK's local authorities have entrusted their accounts to Icelandic banks (in return for high-ish interest rates), and for this reason their failure adds to the malaise.

On 10 October, the British government injects an additional £50 billion into the financial sector and offers up to £200 billion in short-term loans. Moreover, the Fed, the Bank of England, the ECB and the central banks of Canada, Sweden and Switzerland cut their interest rates at the same time: the Fed to a very low 1.5 per cent, the ECB to 3.75 per cent, and the Bank of England to 4.5 per cent. The following morning, the IMF holds its annual meeting in Washington. Europe's leaders leave for Paris the next day, where they announce that no major banking institution will be allowed to fail. But they fail to offer EU guarantees. Every member state is to save its own banks – another fateful decision, whose impact continues to be felt in Europe, and especially in Ireland.

A day later, on 13 October, the British government decides that the banks are in such a state that, despite the huge assistance they have received, they require a great deal more just to stay in business. A new mountain of cash, £37 billion, is handed out to the RBS, Lloyds TSB and HBOS. It is not a move specific to Britain. On 14 October, the US Treasury uses $250 billion to buy chunks of different ailing banks in order to shore them up. President Bush explains that this intervention was approved to 'help preserve free markets'. George Orwell would have been amused: he could hardly have conjured up a better example of naked double-speak.

By the end of October, it is official: both the United States and Britain have entered a recession. The financial crisis has turned into a crisis of the real economy. The Fed immediately reduces interest rates further, from 1.5 per cent to 1 per cent.

November – The Bank of England follows with another interest rate cut, albeit a cowardly one (from 4.5 per cent to 3 per cent), as does the ECB (from 3.75 per cent to 3.25 per cent). The Crash is, meanwhile, spreading further afield, sparking off a crisis in the Ukraine (which prompts the IMF to lend the country $16 billion) and causing the Chinese government to set in train its own stimulus package worth $586 billion over two years – money to be spent on infrastructure projects, some social projects and reductions in corporate taxation.

The eurozone announces that its economy is in recession. The IMF grudgingly lends bankrupt Iceland $2.1 billion, while the US Treasury gives a further $20 billion to Citigroup (whose shares have lost 62 per cent of their value in a few short days). During this frenzy of policy interventions, the British government reduces VAT (from 17.5 per cent to 15 per cent) and the

Fed injects yet another $800 billion into the financial system. Not to be outdone, the European Commission approves a plan to inject €200 billion into Europe's economy. Keynesianism is back on continental soil after decades of neoliberal sermonizing on the evils of having the state pump-prime an ailing economy.

December – The month begins with an announcement by the respected National Bureau of Economic Research that the US economy's recession began as early as December 2007. During the next ten days, France adds its own aid package for its banking sector, worth €26 billion, and the ECB, the Bank of England, and the Banks of Sweden and Denmark, reduce interest rates again. In the United States, the public is shocked when the Bank of America says that its taxpayer-funded take-over of Merrill Lynch will result in 35,000 job losses.

The Fed responds with a new interest rate of between 0.25 per cent and 0 per cent (depending on the particulars of the lender). Desperate times obviously call for desperate measures. Nonetheless, it is a sobering moment when America becomes officially enmeshed in a state that economists had convinced themselves would never be seen again: a typical *liquidity trap*, not seen since 1929.[1] Only this time it is worse. For unlike in 1929, *our* generation's liquidity trap is global. Interest rates have reached rock bottom not only in the United States but throughout the West.

As further evidence that the disease (which began with the CDO market and consumed the world's financial sector) has spread to the real economy, where people actually produce things (as opposed to pushing paper around for ridiculous amounts of cash), President Bush declares that about $17.4 billion of the $700 billion facility will be diverted to America's stricken car makers. Not many days pass before the US Treasury announces that the finance arm of General Motors (which had become ever so 'profitable' during the golden age of financialization) will be given $6 billion to save it from collapse.

By year's end, on 31 December, the New York stock exchange has lost more than 31 per cent of its total value since 1 January 2008.

After 2008 – the never-ending aftermath

In January 2009, newly elected President Obama declares the US economy to be 'very sick' and foreshadows renewed public spending to help it recover. As if to prove the continuity of US administrations, his government continues along the path carved out by Bush and Paulson: it pumps another $20 billion into Bank of America and watches in horror as Citigroup is split in two, in a move intended to help it survive. US unemployment rises to more than 7 per cent and the labour market sheds more jobs than ever before since the Great Depression. US imports fall and, as a result, Japan, Germany and China see their trade surpluses dwindle. These are the first telling wounds to be inflicted on our Global Minotaur.

In Britain, the Bank of England cuts interest rates to 1.5 per cent, the lowest level in its 315-year history, and, as GDP declines by 1.5 per cent, the British government offers loans of £20 billion to small firms to help tide them over. German Chancellor Angela Merkel follows suit, with a €50 billion stimulus package at the same time as the ECB cuts interest rates to 2 per cent. Ireland nationalizes Anglo Irish Bank. Given the guarantee that the government extended to its creditors and depositors (that they would not lose a single euro), the Irish people are saddled with their bankers' almost infinite losses. Ireland will not recover from that treacherous move. Or at least not for another generation.

Still in January 2009, the IMF warns that global economic growth will turn negative for the first time since 1945, and the International Labour Organisation predicts the loss of 51 million jobs worldwide. Both estimates are to prove accurate.

In February 2009, the Bank of England breaks all records by reducing interest rates to 1 per cent. (As these words are being penned, the current interest rate is 0.5 per cent.) Soon after, President Obama signs his $787 billion stimulus Geithner–Summers Plan, which he describes as 'the most sweeping recovery package in our history'.[2] (This is a pivotal moment, to which I shall return in chapter 7.) Meanwhile, AIG continues to issue awful news: a $61.7 billion loss during the last quarter of 2008. Its 'reward'? Another $30 billion from the US Treasury.

In March, the G20 group (which includes the G7, Russia, China, Brazil, India and other emerging nations) pledges to make 'a sustained effort to pull the world economy out of recession'. In this context, the Fed decides that the time for piecemeal intervention has passed and says it will purchase another $1.2 trillion of 'bad debts' (i.e. of Wall Street's now worthless private money).

In April, the G20 meets in London, amidst huge demonstrations, and agrees to make $1.1 trillion available to the global financial system, mainly through the auspices of the IMF, which, soon after, estimates that the Crash has wiped about $4 trillion from the value of financial assets. In London, Chancellor Alistair Darling forecasts that Britain's economy will decline by 3.5 per cent in 2009 and that the budget deficit will reach £175 billion (or more than 10 per cent of GDP). History will prove that he is optimistic!

In May of 2009, Chrysler, the third-largest US car maker, is forced by the government to go into receivership and most of its assets are transferred to Italian car maker Fiat for a song. The news from the financial sector continues to be bleak, and so the

US Treasury organizes another assistance package to the tune of more than $70 billion.

By June it is the turn of General Motors (GM): America's iconic car maker goes bust. Its creditors are then forced to 'consent' to losing 90 per cent of their investments while the company is nationalized (with the government providing an additional $50 billion as working capital). GM's own unions, which have unwittingly become creditors due to the company's failure to cover its workers' pension rights, turn part owners. Socialism, at least on paper, seems alive and well in Detroit!

Over on the other side of the Atlantic, the unemployment rate in Britain continues to rise, reaching 7.1 per cent, which means more than 2.2 million people on the scrapheap. Another indication of the state of the global economy is that, in 2008, global oil consumption fell for the first time since 1993.

The low-down

The above chronicle ends abruptly and arbitrarily around the middle of 2009. It reads like a breathless horror story. Unlike its Hollywood equivalents, however, it features no natural ending, happy or otherwise. It is a never-ending story that began in 2007 and is bound to continue for a long, long time. I had to break off at some point, in order to return to the meaning of it all. I chose June 2009 for no particular reason.

If I wanted to summarize the state of the world after this point, I could do no better than quote the following:

> We are now in the phase where the risk of carrying assets with borrowed money is so great that there is a competitive panic to get liquid. And each individual who succeeds in getting more liquid forces down the price of assets in the process of getting liquid, with the result that the margins of other individuals are impaired and their courage undermined. And so the process

> continues... We have here an extreme example of the disharmony
> of general and particular interest...

These words were penned by John Maynard Keynes in 1932.[3] But they apply even more to our post-2008 world than they did in the aftermath of 1929. For in 1929, total outstanding credit in the United States was 160 per cent of GDP. By 1932, when Keynes scripted these lines, as debts mounted up and GDP fell, it had risen to 260 per cent of GDP. By contrast, the United States, under the Global Minotaur's regime, had entered the Crash of 2008 with total outstanding credit at 365 per cent of GDP. Two years later, in 2010, it had risen to a stupendous 540 per cent of GDP. (And this does not include derivatives, whose nominal outstanding value is at least four times GDP.)

However appallingly impressive the numbers may be, they fail to convey the reality. On the eve of the Crash of 2008, after three decades of serving the Global Minotaur's world, the average American worker earned a real wage that was still below the level of the early 1970s. Though they worked longer hours than ever before and had achieved remarkable productivity gains, workers had no tangible benefits to show. And then, all of a sudden, in or shortly after 2008, they were literally turned into the streets in their millions.

Almost 4 million Americans lost their jobs. According to the US Mortgage Bankers Association, it is estimated that one in 200 homes was repossessed by the banks. Every three months, from 2008 to 2011, some 250,000 families had to pack up and leave their homes in shame. On average, one child in every US classroom is at risk of losing her or his family home because the parents cannot afford to meet their mortgage repayments. Adding to this tale of woe, the US-based Homeownership Preservation Foundation tells us (based on a survey of 60,000 homeowners) that more than 40 per cent of American households are falling deeper and deeper into debt every year (even though the American economy as a whole is *de-leveraging*, i.e. reducing its debt).

Anyone who wishes to grasp the discontent that permeates Main Street (as average America is depicted) is advised to contrast the wholesale angst experienced by American families with the imagery of a revivified Wall Street (Main Street's binary opposite). On the one hand, the multitudes who worked hard and for decreasing returns were rewarded, during the Minotaur's reign, with bitterly hard labour, and then after the Minotaur's fall from grace, they were scrapped like discarded appliances. On the other hand, the small minority who produced worthless paper assets and brought the world to its knees with their immense pay packets (and equally colossal egos) received more than $10 trillion worth of tax-propelled assistance. Is it any wonder that the Tea Party is finding it easy to recruit from among those disgruntled enough to believe that the 'system' is rotten to the core?

Meanwhile, in Europe the crisis is gathering pace, threatening the common currency's very existence (an interesting crisis to which I return in chapter 8). Beyond the United States and Europe, it is often said that the emerging countries (i.e. the parts of the Third World that started growing in the late 1990s) were relatively unscathed by the Crash of 2008. While it is true that China successfully used simple Keynesian methods to delay the crisis, spending more than $350 billion on infrastructure works in one year (and close to twice that by 2010), a study by Beijing University shows that poverty rates have actually increased, the rate of private expenditure has fallen (with public investment accounting for the continuing growth) and even consumption has declined markedly (as a proportion of GDP). Whether this type of Keynesian growth is sustainable without the Global Minotaur is our era's next big question.

Countries like Brazil and Argentina, which export large quantities of primary commodities to China, weathered 2008 better than others. India, too, seems to have managed to generate sufficient domestic demand. Nevertheless, it would be remiss not to take into consideration the fact that the Third World had been in a deep crisis, caused by escalating food prices, for at least a year before the Crash of 2008. Between 2006 and 2008, average world prices for rice rose by 217 per cent, wheat by 136 per cent, corn by 125 per cent and soya beans by 107 per cent. The causes of this price rise were multiple, but were also intertwined with the Global Minotaur.

Financialization and the ballistic rise of options, derivatives, securitization, etc. led at the Chicago Futures Exchange to new forms of speculation over food output. In fact, a brisk trade in CDOs, comprising not mortgages but the future price of wheat, rice and soya beans, gathered steam in the run-up to 2008. The rise in demand for bio-fuels played a role, too, as they displaced normal crops with crops whose harvest would end up in 4x4 monsters loitering around Los Angeles, Sydney and London. So did the many natural disasters (e.g. devastating floods in Pakistan and Australia, consuming bushfires in Russia and Australia – most likely the manifestations of global warming) that served to inflate food prices further.

A fuller picture emerges when we add the drive by US multinationals like Cargill and Monsanto to commodify seeds in India and elsewhere, the thousands of suicides of Indian farmers caught up in these multinationals' poisonous webs, and the effects of the demise of social services at the behest of the IMF's structural adjustment programmes, etc. In that picture, the Crash of 2008 seems to have made an already bad situation (for the vast majority of people) far worse.[4]

Tellingly, when the G20 met in London in April 2009 and decided to bolster the IMF's fund by $1.1 trillion, the stated purpose was to assist economies worldwide to cope with the Crash. But those who looked more closely saw, in the fine print, a specific clause: the money would be used exclusively to assist the global financial sector. Indian farmers on the verge of suicide need not apply. Nor should capitalists interested in investing in the real economy.

Epilogue: the slide into 'bankruptocracy'

The Crash of 2008 seriously wounded the Global Minotaur. Since 2008–09, the Crisis has eased. But it has not gone away. The beast is down and no one any longer fulfils its crucial function of keeping America's twin deficits running and absorbing the world's surpluses. Thus, the Crisis is constantly metamorphosing, taking its toll differently in different places. This is no longer a financial crisis. It is not even an economic crisis. It has become a political crisis.

In the United States, unemployment continues at an unsustainable (especially for America) 10 per cent level. Europe's unemployment is up there, too. Both entities, the dollar-zone and the eurozone, have, in the meantime, been rendered ungovernable by their squabbling elites. In the United States, the Obama administration, following the Republicans' victory in the November mid-term elections of 2010, is effectively bamboozled. With the government no longer able to pump-prime the economy with fiscal stimuli, the lonely task of tilting at the slow-burning Crisis has fallen on Ben Bernanke's Fed. So the Fed, unhappily, is still desperately trying to increase the quantity of money circulating in the American economy by buying hundreds of billions of dollars' worth of paper assets (*quantitative easing* is the name of the game).[5] Bernanke knows that this is far from an ideal situation, but is left with no choice at a time of stalemate between the White House and Congress.

In Europe, the Crisis has set in train centrifugal forces that are tearing the eurozone apart, setting the surplus economies, with Germany at the helm, against the stragglers, whose structural deficits cannot be cured, no matter how much belt-tightening goes on. Unable to coordinate policy at some central level, Europe dithers, its economies stagnate, the productive fibre degenerates and, consequently, the dream of political union, which was pushed along so brilliantly by post-war US administrators on the basis of enhanced growth prospects, fades.

Three years after the Crash of 1929, the election of President Roosevelt brought to power a government hell-bent on grappling with the Crisis by political means. The banking sector had collapsed and the new authorities seized the day. Wide-ranging regulatory controls were introduced, and, for a while, the political will to deal with the Crisis decisively, rationally and at all costs met with little resistance from the exhausted rentiers and bankers – men whose antipathy toward political solutions is always in direct proportion to the extent to which they believe their power will be curtailed.

Alas, today, three years after our very own 1929, the balance of power is exactly the reverse: political authority waned within a year or two of the Crash because it expended all its capital *unconditionally* shoring up the almost-defunct financial sector. In a typical zombie-movie setting, the un-dead banks drew massive strength from our state system and then immediately turned against it! Both in America and in Europe, politicians are quaking in terror of the very banks which, only yesterday, they had saved.[6] Thus, the very financial sectors that were at the heart of the problem are now held in awe by our politicians. Not only does this make it impossible to implement sensible policies to deal with the ongoing Crisis, but it also stifles all rational public debate on what really happened.

If evidence of this state of zombie terror were needed, consider the report on the Crash of 2008, delivered on 27 January 2011 by the Financial Crisis Inquiry Commission.[7] Two years of research and intensive deliberation led to the lame conclusion that the Crash was due to excessive risk-taking and inadequate regulation. And, as if the spectacular lameness of this conclusion were not sad enough, the Republican minority members issued their own verdict: it was the state's fault! How come? The two state-controlled mortgage providers, Fannie Mae and Freddie Mac, had encouraged too many poor Americans to take out sub-prime mortgages: another case of the state making a mess of things by stepping into a market about which it understood nothing. The evident truth that Fannie Mae and Freddie Mac were the tail wagged by the Wall Street dog; that they only joined in the frenzy of CDO production late in the day; that the private money-generation machine was a global phenomenon designed and directed by Wall Street's private banks; that Europe saw exactly the same pattern form in the complete absence of Fannie Mae and Freddie Mac – none of that counts. The only thing that matters is that the truth does not get in the way of Wall Street's resurgence.

A similar cloud of silliness permeates Europe's post-Crash official debates. A visiting extraterrestrial reading the serious European press would come to the conclusion that Europe's crisis happened because some peripheral states borrowed and spent too much. Because little Greece, uppity Ireland and the languid Iberians tried to live beyond their means by having their governments debt-finance living standards over and above those that their production efforts could sustain. Setting aside the irony of this accusation, especially when it comes from US financiers (whose pre-2008 Minotaur-reliance would put to shame anyone else's attempts to live off other people's capital), the problem with this type of narrative is that it is simply not true. While Greece was, indeed, running a large deficit, Ireland was a paragon of fiscal virtue. Spain was even running a *surplus* when the Crash of 2008 hit, and Portugal was no worse than Germany in its deficit and debt performance. But who cares about the truth when lies are so much more fun, not to mention useful to those who are desperate to shift the spotlight from the real locus of the Crisis – the banking sector?

Once upon a time, the Left–Right divide dominated political and economic debate. In the red corner, the Left argued that economic life was too important to leave to market forces, and that society was better off with centrally planned economic activity. In the blue corner, free-marketeers countered that the best way of serving the social good was to allow a Darwinian market-based process to weed out the least efficient economic practices, so that the successful ones could prevail. In 1991, the red corner met with a calamitous defeat, from which it never really recovered. In 2008, unbeknownst to most, it was the blue corner's turn. For since then, in view of the post-2008 developments on both sides of the Atlantic, nothing seems to succeed like grand failure.

If anything, the Darwinian process has been turned on its head. The more unsuccessful a private organization is, and the more catastrophic its losses, the greater its ensuing power, courtesy of taxpayer financing. In short, socialism died during the Global Minotaur's Golden Age, and capitalism was quietly bumped off the moment the beast ceased to rule over the world economy. In its place, we have a new social system: *bankruptocracy* – rule by bankrupted banks (if I were allowed to indulge in Greek, I would call it *ptocho-trapezocracy*).[8]

To sum up, future generations will study the story of the Crash of 2008 in a bid to understand a crucial ingredient of their own present. In it they will find important clues to a new type of regime that changed the texture and dynamic of global capitalism for ever. Whether my chosen term, *bankruptocracy*, will catch on is neither here nor there. What matters is that 2008 marked a significant discontinuity: that life after it will not resemble life before it. In the context of this book's narrative, the new post-2008 era is marked by a grand absence and a looming presence: absent is the Global Minotaur, which gave us the world prior to 2008 and which led us to the Crash of 2008; present are its resurgent handmaidens, which, since 2008, have returned with a vengeance. A world in which the Minotaur's handmaidens are running riot, liberated from the beast's whims, is the world of our near future.

CHAPTER 7

The handmaidens strike back

With a little help from my friends: the Geithner–Summers Plan

If Crises are the laboratories of the future, the chief experimenters who try out different 'treatments' play a central role in the outcome. Following the Crash of 2008 such experiments shaped its aftermath – what I called *bankruptocracy*. No better example can be found of these audacious experimental methods than the famous Geithner–Summers Plan.

The Geithner–Summers Plan started life in February 2009 and constituted President Obama's $1 trillion package to save the banks from the worthless CDOs in which they were drowning. The problem with an asset that no one wants to buy is that it has no price. The honest thing would have been to force the banks to write the CDOs off as bad investments. But if they had done that, their losses would have greatly exceeded their assets, and all banks would have had to file for bankruptcy.

One solution would have been to have the taxpayer, or the Fed, 'buy' these 'assets' at made-up prices, which would be just high enough to prevent across-the-board bank failures. This was what

---

Box 7.1

Failure pays

Nothing is so persistent as privilege's determination to reproduce itself. During the Global Minotaur's days, Larry Summers (President Clinton's secretary of the treasury) gave the green light to the complete deregulation of Wall Street. At the time, Timothy Geithner was his under-secretary. So, when President Obama came to power eight years later, who was to be summoned to clean up the mess they had had a major hand in creating? Summers and Geithner, of course! The explanation? Who else could be trusted with such a big job and all the privileges it brought? Once capitalism grows sufficiently complex, failure pays. Every crisis boosts the power of incumbents, because to the public they seem to be the only good candidates to mop up the mess. The trouble is that the 'solutions' implemented by the original creators of the problem create even more centralized and complex power – which, in turn, further boosts the culprits' indispensability …

Secretary Paulson had in mind, though he never secured enough money from Congress to implement it. So, after the change of government, the ball landed in the court of Geithner and Summers. And they decided that they would try something new – a brilliant idea that would create a marketplace for these defunct CDOs and save the taxpayer the cost of bailing the banks out again.

Their idea was simple: To set up, in partnership with banks, hedge funds, pension funds, etc. – a *simulated market* for the toxic CDOs that would yield *simulated prices*, which could then be used to rewrite the banks' accounts. Here is how it was meant to work.

Suppose Bank B owns a CDO (let's call it c) that B bought for $100. Of this, $40 was B's own money and the remaining $60 was leverage (i.e. a sum that B somehow borrowed in order to purchase c). B's problem is that, after 2008, it cannot sell c for more than $5. Given that its vaults are full of such

CDOs, if it sells each below $60, it will have to file for bankruptcy, as the sale will not even yield enough to pay its debt of $60 per CDO (i.e. a case of negative equity). Thus, *B* does nothing, holds on to *c* and faces a slow death by a thousand cuts, as investors, deterred by *B*'s inability to rid itself of the toxic CDOs, dump *B*'s shares, the value of which on the stock exchange falls and falls and falls. Every penny the state throws at it to keep it alive, *B* hoards in desperation. Thus, the great bail-out sums given to the banks never find their way to businesses, which need loans to buy machinery, or to customers who want to finance the purchase of a new home. And this makes a bad recession worse.

Now enter the Geithner–Summers Plan, which creates an account (let's call it *A*) that could be used by some hedge or pension fund (call it *H*) to bid for *c*. Account *A* amounts to a total of, say, $60 (the lowest amount that *B* will accept in return for *c*) as follows: hedge fund *H* contributes $5 to *A*, as does the US Treasury. The $50 difference comes in the form of a loan from the Fed.[1] The next step involves the hedge or pension fund, our *H*, participating in a government-organized auction for *B*'s *c* – an auction in which the highest bidder wins *c*.

By definition, this auction must have a reserve (or minimum) price of at least $60 (i.e. the minimum *B* must sell *c* for if it is to avoid bankruptcy). Suppose that *H* bids $60 and wins. Then *B* gets its $60, which it returns to its creditor (recall that *B* had borrowed $60 to buy *c* in the first place). While *B* loses its own equity in *c*, it lives to profit another day. As for hedge fund *H*, its payout depends on how much it can sell *c* for. Let's look now at two scenarios – one that is good for *H* and one that is bad.

In the good scenario case, hedge fund *H* discovers that, a few weeks after it purchased *c* for $60 (to which it contributed only $5), its value has risen to, say, $80, as the simulated market begins to take off and speculators join in. Of that $80, *H* owes

$50 to the Fed and must share the remaining equity ($30) with its partner, the US Treasury. This leaves H with $15. Not bad. A $5 investment has become a $15 revenue. And if H purchases a million of these CDOs, its net gain will be a cool $10 million.

In the case of the bad scenario, H stands to lose its investment (the $5) but nothing beyond that. Suppose, for instance, that it can only sell CDO c (which it bought for $60 using account A) for $30. Then H will still owe $50 to the Fed on a revenue of only $30. Normally, it would be $20 out of pocket (as would the US Treasury). However, the $50 loan by the Fed to H is what is known as a *non-recourse loan*. This means that the Fed keeps the money from H's sale of c but has no way of getting the rest of its money (the $20 of outstanding loans) back from H.

In short, if things work out well, the fund managers stand to make a net gain of $10 from a $5 investment (a 200 per cent return); if things do not work out well, they will only lose their initial $5. Thus, the Geithner–Summers Plan was portrayed as a brilliant scheme by which the government encouraged hedge and pension fund managers to take *some* risk in the context of a government-designed and -administered game that *might* work and leave everyone a winner – the banks (which would have rid themselves of the hated CDOs), the hedge and pension funds (which would have a cool 200 per cent rate of return) and the government (which would recoup its bail-out money).

It all sounds impressive. Until one asks the question: what smart fund manager would rate the probability of the good scenario materializing at better than around a third?[2] Who would think that there is more than a chance of one in three that the duff CDO would sell for more than $60, given that now no one wants to touch the toxic CDO for more than $5? Who would participate in this simulated market? Committing some $1 trillion to a programme founded on pure, unsubstantiated optimism seems quite odd.

Were Tim Geithner and Larry Summers, two of the smartest people in the US administration, foolhardy? Of course not.[3] Their plan was brilliant – but not for the stated purpose. While that stated purpose was to motivate hedge and pension funds to buy the banks' burnt-out toxic money (the CDOs), as we just saw, no prudent hedge or pension fund manager would play any part in it. So, did Geithner and Summers not know that? Of course they did. Who, then, did they count on to bid for the banks' toxic derivatives, if the hedge and pension funds were certain to stay away? The ground-shattering answer is: the banks themselves!

Here is what was really intended (and, unsurprisingly, happened). Consider Bank B again. It is desperate to get CDO c off its balance sheet. The Geithner–Summers Plan then comes along. Bank B immediately sets up its own hedge fund, H', using some of the money that the Fed and the US Treasury has already lent it in a previous bail-out. H' then takes part in the Plan, helps create a new account, A', comprising $100 (of which H' contributes $7, the US Treasury chips in another $7 and the Fed loans $86) and then immediately bids $100 for its very own c. In this manner, it has rid itself of the $100 toxic CDO once and for all at a cost of only $7, which was itself a government handout![4]

It was a devilish plan for allowing the banks to get away with figurative murder. However, the significance of the subterfuge in the Geithner–Summers Plan goes well beyond its ethical or even fiscal implications. The Paulson Plan that preceded it was a crude but honest attempt to hand cash over to the banks, no questions asked. In contrast, Geithner and Summers tried something different: allowing Wall Street to imagine that its cherished financialization could rise, phoenix-like, from the ashes on the strength of a government-sanctioned plan to create new derivatives – new forms of private money underwritten by taxpayers' public money.

In essence, the administration allowed the Global Minotaur's staunchest and ugliest handmaiden to make a mighty comeback *after* the beast's fall from grace. It was only one move of many that politicians made along a path which, ironically, led them to their own disempowerment. By strengthening the hand of the bankrupt banks, they deprived themselves of any serious room for effective policy making. Once Wall Street's powers had been restored, politics lost its capacity to rein in the ongoing Crisis.

Europe's version of the Geithner–Summers Plan

Europe's Crisis (which is dealt with in detail in the next chapter) has its own special peculiarities. However, it is instructive to take a quick look at the incredible hold that the toxic derivatives had over the imaginations of European institutions. On a continent that was, purportedly, scornful of American-sourced CDOs, it is fascinating to find that, when the EU decided to create a loan facility for its fiscally stressed member states (e.g. Ireland, Portugal, Spain), it found its inspiration in the structure of the derided CDOs.

In May 2010, the EU created a so-called *Special Purpose Vehicle* (SPV). Its purpose was to borrow on behalf of solvent eurozone countries and lend to the rest, who had been frozen out of the money markets. This would avoid defaults on state debts, which would have decimated the banks, since they had loaned large amounts to these selfsame states.

The SPV, later named the *European Financial Stability Facility* (EFSF), was meant to be a temporary fund. As the euro crisis deepened, though, it was decided that it would evolve, by 2013, into a permanent institution called the *European Financial Stability Mechanism*. The idea was to borrow, on behalf of the eurozone, €440 billion, which would be lent to the illiquid, and possibly insolvent, member states.[5]

Two features of the EFSF make it a fascinating example of 'bankruptocracy'. The first feature (which we examine in detail in the next chapter) is that the EFSF is raising money to bail out not Ireland, Portugal, etc., but Europe's failing banks. The second feature, which is more pertinent here, is that the EFSF is borrowing money by issuing toxic eurobonds – bonds that are structured in an identical manner to the errant CDOs of yesteryear.

Recall how Wall Street's CDOs bundled together slices of different mortgages (prime and sub-prime), each bearing different interest rates and default risks. Recall, too, that the mix was truly toxic (or explosive), because if one slice within a given CDO went bad (e.g. Jack defaulted on his loan), that increased the risk of a default by the next slice (e.g. Jill would default, because the chances that she would lose her job increased when Jack lost his job and home).

So it was with those EFSF bonds issued, for example, for lending to the Irish state, which, in December 2010, teetered on the verge of bankruptcy, having failed to find the money to fulfil its promises and repay its private banks' debts. The EFSF loans for Ireland were raised from the money markets by the EFSF on the strength of guarantees issued by the remaining fifteen eurozone states, in proportion to their GDP (Greece had already been frozen out of the marketplace in May 2010). The total sum raised was then cut up into small 'packets', each containing a slice that was guaranteed by Germany, another slice guaranteed by France, another by Portugal, etc. Now, given that each country had different degrees of creditworthiness, each was charged a different interest rate. Lastly, these 'packets' were sold off as bonds, mostly to Asian investors and Europe's own (quasi-bankrupted) banks.

Now, let's imagine what might happen if Portugal, too, is forced to exit the money markets, just as Greece and Ireland were before it. One reason why this may well happen (if it has not already happened by the time you read this) is the very fact that Portugal, already on the brink, has been forced to borrow, at high interest rates, on Ireland's behalf! Speculators may well buy CDSs that will pay them if Portugal defaults, and the rise in the price of these CDSs may push the interest rates that Portugal must pay for new loans to a level that is unsustainable. Thus, Portugal goes to the EFSF cap in hand!

The EFSF will then have to issue new debts, on behalf of the remaining eurozone countries, to help Portugal. Thus, with Portugal out of the group, a greater burden will be shared by the fourteen countries remaining to guarantee the EFSF's bonds. How will markets react? By focusing immediately on the new 'marginal' country: the one that is currently borrowing at the highest interest rates within the EFSF in order to loan the money to Greece, Ireland and, now, Portugal. So Spain's interest rates will rise until Madrid is also pushed out of the markets. Then there will be thirteen countries left to borrow on the EFSF's behalf and the markets will focus on the newest 'marginal' country. And so on, until the band of nations within the EFSF is so small that they cannot bear the burden of total debt (even if they wished to).

In the next chapter I employ the metaphor of a group of stricken mountaineers, bound together by a single rope, who fall off the mountain face one after the other until the strongest members also fall, unable to withstand the weight of all the rest. Seen through this prism, the EFSF's brief begins to look desperate. Its bonds have bundled together different kinds of guarantees (offered by each individual state) in ways that remain woefully opaque. This is precisely how the CDOs came to life prior to 2008, complete with two fatal flaws.

First, structuring the EFSF bonds like the CDOs that caused such problems for the world economy seems, at the very least, careless. One immediate repercussion of the reliance on the CDO structure is that the EFSF must borrow €440 billion, but only hand over loans worth at most €250 billion. The remaining €190 billion must sit idly by gathering dust! Why? Because investors know that the bonds they are buying are toxic and will only buy them if the EFSF keeps a lot of money on hold to repay them in case of default by Portugal or some other eurozone member state. It is, in short, a highly inefficient way of pooling debts.

Secondly, this type of political intervention, just like the Geithner–Summers Plan in the United States, not only absolves the *principle* of CDOs (and by extension its Wall Street progenitors) but, more importantly, allows banks, insurance companies, hedge funds, etc. to create new forms of private money. As though the Crash of 2008 had never happened! We have already seen how, in the United States, the Geithner–Summers Plan created new derivatives and thus pumped new private money, underwritten by good old public money, into Wall Street. In Europe, something equally sinister has occurred.

When it became clear that EFSF-style interventions to bail out countries like Greece and Ireland would be financed by toxic eurobonds (and given that the markets were not convinced for a single moment that they would, in the end, deal effectively with these states' solvency issues), banks and hedge funds seized with both hands the opportunity to turn the uncertainty about the euro into another betting spree. And this is precisely what they did: they took out bets, in the form of CDSs, against European member-state bonds (e.g. Greece's, Ireland's, Spain's, Italy's). In the end, both the toxic EFSF eurobonds and this voluminous output of fresh CDSs constitute a new round of unsustainable private money generation. When the latest pile of private money turns to ashes, too – as it certainly will – what next for Europe?

Biting the hand that saved them: the ugliest handmaiden at its boldest

The very essence of the Geithner–Summers Plan, both in its original and its European incarnations, was a vindication of Wall Street's private money formation. Rather than resoundingly declaring 'never again!', our political leaders have effectively signalled to the banks that it is business as usual. Moreover, it is business as usual *with public funds*. Karl Marx once mused that history repeats itself, only the second time as farce. So, whereas prior to 2008 Wall Street created its synthetic financial products on its own (perhaps with the government turning a blind eye), following the 2008 meltdown it has done so with massive government (American and European) subsidies.

In summary, as early as in February of 2009, the Obama administration filled Wall Street's sails by engineering a new marketplace for the old derivatives (which were replete with poor people's mortgage debts). The medium of exchange in this new marketplace was a mixture of the old (refloated) derivatives and new ones (based not on poor people's mortgages but on the taxes of those who could not avoid paying them – often the very same poor people). Thus, many of the banks' toxic assets were moved off their accounts, while the production of new private toxic money took another turn. A year and a half later, the Europeans, not to be outdone, followed suit with EFSF-style debt issues and bank bail-outs, making their own contribution to a new wave of highly toxic financial 'products'.

Once the banks' balance sheets were cleansed of most of the toxic CDOs, Wall Street used some of the proceeds, and some of the bail-out money from the various waves of assistance received from the state, to pay the government back. Of course, when I say they paid the government loans back, that is a gross exaggeration. What they returned was only a tiny fraction of what the US Treasury and the Fed had given them. For the vast bulk of the bail-outs came in the form of gargantuan, but unreported, guarantees. And these were never repaid. Nor was the gigantic cost of the Geithner–Summers Plan reimbursed. Moreover, the banks never even acknowledged the hundreds of billions of dollars' worth of their shares and other assets purchased by the Fed under the table in a show of solidarity with Wall Street (otherwise known as quantitative easing). That none of that will ever be repaid either is a foregone conclusion.

In short, first the banks were empowered (by the taxpayer) to return to their racket of creating private toxic money, and then they repaid a smidgeon of their debts to the government – a sum just high enough to legitimize the fresh bonuses of their managers. Once the bonuses started flowing again and the stock exchange recovered, the press began to wax lyrical about the end of the recession. The economy, we were told, was growing again. The press, commentators, economists, Wall Street experts – almost everyone – seemed to be heaving a collective sigh of relief that the end of the world had been averted. Although most serious voices speak the language of caution, and some worry loudly about a double-dip recession, conventional wisdom has it that we are out of the woods. And yet unemployment is as high as ever, house foreclosures or repossessions continue unabated, and real wages remain static.

In political terms, our governments have well and truly capitulated to the failed banks. And, as is usually the case with capitulations to sinister characters, no one thanked the capitulator. Indeed, the Geithner–Summers Plan increased the banks' blackmailing power vis-à-vis the state. While President Obama's administration was busily accepting the Wall Street mantra about no full-blown nationalizations (i.e. the bogus argument that recapitalizing banks by means of temporary nationalizations, as in Sweden in 1993, would quash the public's confidence in the financial system, thus creating more instability, which might in turn jeopardize any eventual recovery), Wall Street's banks were already plotting against the administration, intent on using their renewed financial vigour to promote Obama's political opponents (who offered them promises of offensively light regulation).

This twist assumed added significance in January 2010, when the US Supreme Court, by a 5-4 vote, overturned the Tillman Act of 1907, which President Teddy Roosevelt had passed in a bid to ban corporations from using their cash to buy political influence. On that fateful Thursday, the floodgates of Wall Street money were flung open as the court ruled that the managers of a corporation can decide, without consulting with anyone, to write out a cheque to the politician who offers them the best deal, especially regarding regulation of the financial sector in the aftermath of 2008.

In reacting to this 'betrayal', President Obama boxed clever: he empowered Paul Volcker (who is still going strong in his eighties) to author the regulatory legislation under which Wall Street would have had to labour in the future – and to write it in such a manner as to tighten the authorities' grip over Wall Street in important ways. Volcker, in his new capacity as head of the Economic Recovery Advisory Board (ERAB), came up with the Volcker Rule, which the administration promised to push through Congress. The Volcker Rule revived the New Dealers' Glass–Steagall Act, which Larry Summers had done away with in the 1990s. It would have prohibited banks from dabbling in derivatives and other exotic financial products. Volcker's basic idea was that banks which accept deposits and are insured by the state against failure ought not to be allowed to participate in either the stock market or the derivatives trade. Though an attempt was made to pass the Volcker Rule, in the end Wall Street won the day.

Having to face one of the Global Minotaur's early prophets, and its minder during its 1980s adolescence (recall Volcker's role as outlined in chapter 4), gave Wall Street bankers a few sleepless nights. But those did not last long. By January 2011, Volcker had been retired, as had the ERAB. It is clear that the brief moment when Wall Street was weak enough to be forced into significant concessions had passed. The Minotaur's most unsightly hand-maiden had been emancipated. The question that now remains is: how will it manage without the Global Minotaur? We shall leave such speculation to the end of the book.

The return of predatory governance, vacuous economics and the curious tragedy of market fundamentalism

Free market fundamentalism, at the levels both of political ideas and of economic theory, has already featured as one of our Minotaur's handmaidens (see chapter 5, Toxic theory, parts A and B). In a sense, it functioned in ways not much different from the way in which Marxism was employed under the Soviet regime: more honoured in the breach than in the observance. In both cases, lofty ideals, underpinned by fascinating economic treatises, were utilized for baser purposes: to legitimize a partic-ular social group's usurpation of power and wealth.

Conquering the state apparatus on behalf of the high and mighty was a well-established pattern in America before 1929 (recall chapter 2). The Crash of 1929 was the nemesis that history unleashed on a society that had allowed itself to be preyed upon by a predator state – one initially captured by the robber barons, then by the new corporate magnates and then, soon after, by Wall Street.[6]

After the New Deal and the Second World War engendered the Global Plan, a new socio-economic realignment saw to a more inclusive compact between the corporations, government and working Americans. That lasted a couple of decades – a time that almost everyone still remembers as capitalism's Golden Age.[7] However, when the Global Plan collapsed in 1971, and both the American and the world economies were wilfully 'disintegrated' to pave the way for the Global Minotaur, the post-war compact broke down.

This was no accident. Its dismantling, as we have seen, was a prerequisite for attracting to the United States the capital inflows that would keep the twin deficits forever on the rise. Its implosion was a *requirement* for the domination of the Global Minotaur. But who really benefited from the beast? The top earners, the parts of American society that worked in or around the financial institutions, the fossil fuel industry, the industrial sectors attached to the military-industrial complex (mainly the electronics, IT-related, aeronautical and mechanical engineering sectors). It also benefited those lucky enough to own a part of Walmart-type, highly exploitative firms. The Minotaur worked for them. And free market fundamentalism was its ideological handmaiden.

As for the actual ideals underpinning free market fundamentalism, their fate was identical to that of Marxism in Moscow: they became the first victims of its political champions' rise to power. Indeed, when, in 1981, Ronald Reagan entered the White House, he spoke the language of supply-side economics, balanced budgets, the withering of big government (ironically, an expression first coined by Marx), etc. However, after a few months of toying with such policies, and once unemployment skyrocketed in 1981, Reagan performed an abrupt U-turn (just as Lenin had done by adopting his New Economic Policy the moment he discovered that socializing the factories did not work as well as planned). Instead of shrinking government and balancing the budget, the president put his foot on the accelerator. The twin deficits ballooned and, as a result of his unbridled Keynesian practices, unemployment shrank and the Global Minotaur was on its merry way.

With the Crash of 2008, three things changed. First, the Minotaur was left lying wounded in its labyrinth, too unwell to keep consuming enough of the surplus outputs of Europe, Japan, China and South East Asia to prevent their economies from stalling. Secondly, the financial markets collapsed and the private money they had created was gone, dust carried away by the Crisis's powerful winds. Thirdly, politicians were either emboldened to rein in the Minotaur's handmaidens or were replaced by fresh stock who promised to do so.

Of these three effects of 2008, only the first is still with us. Both in America and in Europe, the politicians who wanted to stand on their own two feet and face down the fallen Minotaur's handmaidens hesitated. While they were dithering, other (less scrupulous) politicians sprang into action. Their first step was to take the freshly minted public money that was pouring into the banks to keep them alive and use it to allow Wall Street and the rest of the world's banks to start pumping out new forms of toxic private money. Once that racket had been re-established sufficiently to restore the banks' political power, those politicians who wanted to make a difference realized that it was too late. And so they recoiled, preferring to live to fight another day than to put up a futile fight.

Epilogue: the worst of both worlds

What happens when the bullying master is taken ill and the handmaidens take over? That depends on the handmaidens. Unfortunately, those we are saddled with rule in a way that preserves the worst aspects of the Global Minotaur's rule (the inequities, the boorishness and the instability) without offering

the important function it used to fulfil – to keep generating sufficient overall demand for Europe's and Asia's surplus output by
recycling the world's surpluses.

Up until 2008, while international trade imbalances were
growing unstoppably, the Global Minotaur attracted sufficient
capital from across the world to recycle other people's surpluses,
and therefore to keep them re-materializing year in and year out.
In addition, Wall Street, on the back of these inflows, generated
its private money, which subsequently provided the world with
the mammoth liquidity that allowed a steady increase in aggregate surpluses. An unsteady and unsustainable racket it may
have been, but at least while it lasted there was a certain logic
to it.

Nowadays, the Minotaur can no longer perform this
balancing act. The American economy is running at far below
full capacity, unemployment is eating into demand for goods,
houses and services, and Wall Street, while in full recovery
mode thanks to the captured political personnel, finds it impossible to generate enough of the private money of yesteryear to
fuel another consumer and investment boom – the boom that
Europe, Japan and even China *must* have if they are to return to
a sustainable growth path.[8]

We are, essentially, ruled by the Minotaur's handmaidens
without benefiting from the beast's stabilizing influences. If
the pre-2008 period was unsustainable, the post-2008 period
is replete with tensions that threaten future generations with a
tumult, the likes of which the mind cannot even envisage.

CHAPTER 8

The Minotaur's global legacy: the dimming sun, the wounded tigers, a flighty Europa and an anxious dragon

The dimming sun: Japan's lost decades

As a pillar of the Global Plan, and under the loving patronage of the United States, Japan's export-led post-war growth was nothing short of miraculous. It came in two phases: by the late 1950s, Japan was already exporting light industrial goods, while importing heavy industrial goods from the United States plus raw materials from elsewhere. Very quickly it graduated to a more mature pattern of trade, exporting heavy industrial goods and limiting its imports to scarce raw materials.

Japanese wages rose throughout the post-war period, but never as fast as growth and productivity. The surpluses that this gap occasioned were guided by the Tokyo government to building infrastructure for the benefit of the private sector (e.g. transport), research and development, training, etc., and, to a much lesser extent, toward a social safety net for the population at large.

Production was based on large-scale capital investments yielding impressive economies of scale. It took place within highly concentrated oligopolistic structures known as *keiretsu* (e.g. Mitsui, Mitsubishi and Sumitomo). The *keiretsu* were vertical conglomerates – hierarchical organizations that included their own large bank, factories, plus an intricate sub-contracting system that involved countless small and medium-sized enterprises (SMEs) or *chusho-kigyo*. Though the SMEs accounted for up to 80 per cent of total employment, their contribution to overall productivity was quite low, at less than half the average level of the larger firms.

The Japanese economic miracle was built on this combination of large, interconnected conglomerates, the many small businesses that revolved around them, and a government that looked after the infrastructural and financial needs of both. From this perspective, it is easy to understand Japan's reliance on foreign demand. With so much emphasis on investment and production, with wages trailing productivity and with minimal social spending, the Japanese economy could consume but a fraction of its output. This is why, after the Global Plan's passing, the Global Minotaur was so important to Japan's economy. And why, with the Minotaur bleeding on the floor, Japan is currently so seriously destabilized.

Of course, Japan embarked on its path of long decline in the 1990s. Commentators shine their searchlights on its banking sector for clues as to what went wrong. Free market aficionados thought they had spotted the problem the moment they discovered that Japanese banks are largely controlled by the state. However, the trouble with that idea is that not only is the state-dependence of the banks a problem for Japan's economy, but it is also the reason for its success. Indeed, the long-standing alliance of government and banks afforded the authorities leverage over investment, the result being a relatively easy implementation of the 'national policy' of industrialization in the post-war period. The Japanese miracle would not have been possible without that tight embrace. It allowed government to discourage Japanese firms from financialization, while the Ministry of Finance performed that task on their behalf and in association with the Bank of Japan. Industry was instructed to mind its core business (of making 'things' well), while government and each bank affiliated to each *keiretsu* were responsible for the flow and circulation of capital into and around these industrial groups.

During the Global Plan, and under America's tutelage, authoritarian de facto one-party rule (by the almost invincible Liberal Democratic Party) ensured that the Japanese state was semi-detached from civil society. Its policy makers had a major part to play in the unfolding drama that followed the Global Plan's replacement after 1971 by the Global Minotaur. In particular, the Japanese social economy faced a major overhaul in response to the dollar's initial devaluation. Japanese officials quickly reacted to the prospect of collapsing exports to the United States in two ways. First, they found new technological solutions to maintain competitiveness. Secondly, they exported capital to the United States in the form of foreign direct investment, purchases of US Treasury Bills, and placements on the New York stock exchange. In short, to keep its oligopolistic industry going, Japan chose to nourish the Global Minotaur, exactly as the US authorities had anticipated.

The tacit US–Japanese accord was simple: Japan would continue to recycle its trade surpluses by purchasing US debt and investing in America; in return, it would be granted continued privileged access to America's domestic market, thus providing Japanese industry with the overall demand that Japanese society was incapable of producing. However, there was a snag: when one buys foreign assets, at some point these assets start to generate income, which must eventually be repatriated. Japan thus ran the risk of ceasing to be able to remain a net capital exporter and of turning into a rentier nation. This prospect was at odds with the post-oil crisis Japanese growth strategy, which was to concentrate on high-value-added, low-energy-using industries like electronics, integrated circuits, computers and mechatronics (industrial robots).

On 22 September 1985, the United States, Japan, West Germany, France and Britain signed the Plaza Accord. The agreement's stated purpose was to devalue the US dollar in an attempt to reduce America's trade deficit (and, by extension, its budget deficit), in other words to rein in the Global Minotaur. Today, many commentators recall the Plaza Accord as a model of an agreement that America should be imposing on the Chinese, in order to reverse China's large trade surplus with the United States. While it is true that the Plaza Accord did succeed in devaluing the dollar vis-à-vis the yen by more than 50 per cent (within two years of its signing), these commentators overlook the Accord's real purpose. Its aim was, at least in part, to prevent Japan from becoming a rentier nation, a development that would jeopardize both Japan's own long-term plans and the Global Minotaur, whose wont was to remain the undisputed global rentier.[1]

The yen's post-1985 climb forced the Japanese economy into a major, sustained slowdown. As Japanese exports became dearer in the United States, in an attempt to maintain the rate of investment the Bank of Japan pumped a lot of liquidity into the *keiretsu* system. The result was the largest build-up of excess liquidity in modern history. The side effect was massive speculative activity in Japanese real estate. And when, in the early 1990s, the authorities tried to deflate the real estate bubble by increasing interest rates somewhat, house and office prices crashed. The nation's banks ended up with huge loans on their books that no one could repay.

It is often argued that Japan's authorities neglected to force the banks to come clean regarding these bad loans. While this is accurate, it ignores the fact that the banks were intimately connected, via the *keiretsu* structure, to an intricate network of firms, small and huge. Had the state allowed the banks to write off their bad debts, the nation's banking sector would have gone to the wall and the Japanese industrial miracle would have ended there and then. Instead, the government and the Bank of Japan injected as much liquidity as was required into the banks. Lamentably, most of these injections were absorbed by the black holes within the banks (the non-performing loans) without generating substantial new investment.

For the first time since the mid-1930s, an advanced capitalist economy had been caught in a recessionary liquidity trap. Despite the monetary authorities' best efforts to boost investment by pushing interest rates down to almost zero and pumping liquidity into the banks, Japan's zombie banks could not deliver the hoped-for investments. The government tried one fiscal stimulus after the other. Roads were built, bridges were erected, railway projects criss-crossed the nation's islands. Even though this activity helped keep the factories going, the 'malaise' could not be remedied.

Interestingly, before 2008, the Japanese 'malaise' actively boosted the Global Minotaur. Japan's next-to-zero interest rates resulted in the accelerated migration of capital from Tokyo to New York, in search of better returns. To the already large amounts of capital that the government of Japan was investing in US government debt, and the equally large amounts of capital that Japanese firms were diverting to the United States in the form of foreign direct investment (e.g. the purchasing of American shares, of whole firms or the setting up by Sony, Toyota, Honda, etc. of production facilities on US soil), a third capital flow was now added: the so-called *carry trade* by financial speculators, who would borrow in Japan at rock-bottom interest rates and then shift the money to the United States, where it would be lent for much higher returns. This carry trade expanded significantly the Minotaur's inflows, thus speeding up the financialization process that was to be, paradoxically, the Minotaur's undoing.

And it was not just the induced crisis in Japan that contributed to the Minotaur's rapid expansion. Financialization, coupled with repeated attempts to tie domestic currencies to the US dollar (the so-called *dollar peg*), led to a long chain of financial crises whose ultimate effect was a real economic meltdown in each link of the chain. The chain began in 1994 with the Mexican peso crisis, then moved to South East Asia (with the collapse of the Thai baht, the South Korean won and the Indonesian rupiah), proceeded to Russia and soon ended up back in Latin America (with Argentina being its most tragic victim). All these crises began with a large inflow of cheap foreign capital that led to bubbles in the real estate markets. However, once they burst, a violent outflow of capital, plus a friendly visit by the good people of the IMF, turned these economies into the financial equivalent of scorched earth.

So, quite naturally, when these nations eventually rose from their ashes, they saved and saved and saved, so as to preclude any repetition of that nightmare. And what happened to these savings? They flocked to New York, fuelling further the Minotaur's continuing rise. Paradoxically, the 'never again' spirit that emerged from the wreck of the Latin American and South East Asian crises proved that the peripheral financial crises that criss-crossed the globe in a chain between 1994 and 2002 were part of an elaborate dress rehearsal for the Crash of 2008.

After 2008, and the Global Minotaur's forced abdication, the United States and Europe discovered to their horror that the Japanese liquidity trap had spread to them. At that point, all the chastisement that the Japanese authorities had received from American and European commentators for not having taken tough action against their zombie banks was quietly forgotten. Indeed, Europe and the United States followed the same recipes that delivered Japan's lost decades. Zombie banks became a feature of the whole wide West. Moreover, unlike Japan's zombie banks, which remain politically weak, America's and Europe's zombie banks rule the roost in the new socio-economic configuration that I call *bankruptocracy*.

Wounded tigers: Japan, America and the South East Asian crisis

Ever since the Korean and, more significantly, the Vietnam wars caused advanced capitalism to take root in South East Asia, Japan has played the hegemonic role in the region (see chapter 3). Japan lent the South East Asian tigers the necessary technology and provided the initial growth spurt. However, it would be false to argue that Japan was to South East Asia what the United States was to Germany and Japan under either the Global Plan or the Global Minotaur. The difference is that Japan neither enjoyed substantial trade surpluses vis-à-vis the South East Asian countries (as the United States had with Europe and Japan under the Global Plan) nor went through a period of absorbing South East Asia's trade surpluses (as America did with Europe's and Japan's under the Global Minotaur). Instead, South East Asia was always in a structural, long-term trade deficit with Japan, having to rely on net export revenues from America and Europe for its growth.

During the Global Minotaur's best years, especially during 1985–95, the decline in the value of the dollar was accompanied by a shift in Japan's foreign direct investment towards Asia. In a few years, the Japanese *keiretsu* had spread their wings over Korea, Malaysia, Indonesia and Taiwan by exporting capital goods used both in production and in the building of new infra-structure. This development was always part of the intention behind the 1985 Plaza Accord, a part compensation for Tokyo's acquiescence to American imperatives. The American government, the IMF, the World Bank – indeed the whole gamut of advanced Western capitalism – leant on the South East Asian governments, pushing relentlessly for a complete liberalization of their capital markets. The idea was, simply, to facilitate Japanese investment in South East Asia, but also to spread Wall Street's reach and profiteering in that part of the world (where fast growth meant returns were higher than in the West).

South East Asia buckled under the pressure. Foreign capital streamed in, pushing real estate and share prices up and causing those countries' trade deficits vis-à-vis Japan to rise. And as the Japanese were always incapable of generating sufficient overall demand for their own output, the pressure to find export markets for South East Asian output *outside Japan* grew even stronger. At that point, once again, the United States came to the rescue. For unlike Japan (which could produce everything except the demand required to absorb its shiny, wonderful industrial products), America, under the Minotaur's gaze, had mastered the art of creating immense levels of demand for other people's goods. Thus the United States became *the* export market for the area as a whole, inclusive of Japan, while South Korea and Taiwan imported mostly from Japan. This process created, perhaps for the first time, the Japanese *vital space* that the Global Plan's designers had imagined in the late 1940s, but that was never implemented after Chairman Mao's unexpected victory in China.

After the Plaza Accord, the flood of Japanese liquidity and foreign investments spread rapidly into South East Asia. These capital inflows into the tiger economies came on top of the increasing revenues from net exports to the United States. Soon they spearheaded a real estate bubble. Toward the end of the 1990s, that bubble burst and foreign capital departed much faster than it had poured in, plunging these countries into a terrible nightmare. Building sites were abandoned, currencies were devalued precipitously, investment dried up, unemployment heightened social tensions, poverty began to rise again and, worst of all, the IMF was called in. Its loans were conditional on policies that were designed for countries with an unproductive, corrupt public sector. The tragedy was that these policies were completely ill-suited to the tiger economies, whose problem was not too much social spending or corruption, but over-extended financial institutions and a liquidity crisis.

After a hideous period of utterly unnecessary austerity imposed by the IMF's fundamentalist 'austerian' logic, the South East Asian tigers gradually recovered – partly because of the Minotaur's continuing rude health and partly because of the large devaluations of the local currencies. Their governments came out of the late 1990s crisis with one cast-iron commitment in mind: never again would they call in the IMF. Never again would they allow Wall Street and assorted foreign bankers to destroy their hard-earned progress.

From that day on, South East Asia made a point of accumulating dollar reserves for a rainy day. Those reserves were then merged with the New York-bound tsunami of capital that kept the Minotaur vibrant, insolent and ultimately dominant.

After the Crash of 2008, the yen revalued substantially, dealing a further blow to Japan's plans for export-led growth. The tigers, on the other hand, kept their currencies tied to the dollar. The conventional wisdom is that, at a time of crisis, capital flows back to the largest economies in search of safe havens and that this is why the dollar and the yen rose in 2008. But that leaves unanswered the question of why the yen rose so fast against the dollar (and thus against the South East Asian currencies). The explanation is that, with interest rates in Europe and America competing against Japanese interest rates in a frantic race to zero, Japanese privately owned capital no longer had a good reason to stay abroad. Thus, a mass repatriation of Japanese capital (the part of it that did not 'burn up' during the Crash) pushed the yen up, placing Japanese industry at a disadvantage in relation to both the United States and South East Asia.

The long-term effect of this repatriation of Japanese savings is of global importance. On the one hand, it has deepened Japan's stagnation, through the appreciation of the yen; on the other hand, the end of the yen carry trade has translated into an upward push for world interest rates at a time when the global economy is wrestling with powerful recessionary forces. The tragic tsunami of 11 March 2011 will intensify this very process of capital inflows into Japan while, at the same time, reducing economic activity in the short run and boosting it in the medium term (as the massive reconstruction gathers pace). Meanwhile, in the midst of all this unsettling volatility, the ongoing repatriation of Japanese capital is the real reason why China has been resisting Western attempts to make its currency convertible and un-peg it from the US dollar: the dragon has learned its lessons from the tigers' bitter experience.

For East Asia, the only silver lining in the Crash of 2008 is that South East Asia has strengthened its position relative to Japan, even though it faces great uncertainty in terms of the demand for its exports. Its struggle to maintain net exports to the rest of the world will prove particularly challenging, especially as it must proceed under the long shadow of the Great Dragon to the north.

Summing up, Japanese capitalism's Achilles heel was that, unlike the United States, it never managed to cultivate a hegemonic position in relation to South East Asia. While Korea, Taiwan, Malaysia, Singapore, etc. relied on Japan for technology and capital goods, they could not look to it as a source of demand. The whole area remained tied to the Global Minotaur and its whimsical ways. China grew into a superpower in this context. It is determined not to get caught either in a Japanese type of malaise or in a trap like the one in which the South East Asian tigers found themselves in the late 1990s.

Germany's Europe

It is now appropriate to turn to the Global Plan's second pillar, Germany, and its mixed fortunes during the Age of the Minotaur and beyond. There is an important difference between it and Japan. In trying to shield its own export-led growth from the post-1971 dollar devaluation, Germany had something that Japan lacked: access to its own *vital space*, a space that the United States had previously laboured so hard to create on Germany's behalf – the European Common Market, today's European Union. The role of German exports to the rest of Europe remained as the Global Plan's American architects had envisioned: to support a strong Deutschmark and, at the same time, to be central to the industrial development of the rest of Europe. Indeed, German exports were not just Volkswagens and refrigerators, but also capital goods essential to the normal functioning of every aspect of Europe's productive apparatus.

Nevertheless, Germany was not Europe's locomotive. From 1973 onwards, the developmental model of continental Europe has rested on the combined effect of maintaining a powerful capital goods industry, linked through Germany's global corporations. However, the overall demand that keeps these corporations going was always scarcer in Germany than in the neighbouring countries where they had extended their operations. Like Japan, Germany, too, showed a magnificent capacity for efficiently producing the most desirable and innovative industrial products. Equally, it, too, failed miserably to generate endogenously the requisite demand for them. But, unlike Japan,

Germany had the advantage of its European periphery, or vital space, which provided a significant portion of demand for its industrial output, thus making Germany less dependent (than Japan) on the Minotaur.

Much ink has been expended in recent years in discussing Europe's fundamental heterogeneity. But how could it be otherwise? Is the dollar-zone homogeneous? Does Germany itself consist of equally developed and dynamic *Länder*? Of course not. Broadly speaking, the pre-enlargement EU comprises three different species of economy: persistent surplus-generating countries (Germany, Holland, the Flemish part of Belgium, Austria and the Scandinavian countries), persistent deficit-inducing countries (Italy, Greece, Spain and Portugal) and France, a country in a category of its own.[2] The reason why France is an outlier has to do with the fact that, while it consistently fails to join the group of surplus nations, it nevertheless enjoys two major strengths: the calibre of its political institutions, which (perhaps due to its Napoleonic past) were the nearest Europe got to a policy-making civil service that might rival that of Washington; and its large banking sector, which is more advanced than that of the surplus countries. Because of the gravitas of its banks, France had achieved a central position in the facilitation of trade and capital flows within the European economy.

From 1985 onwards, the Global Minotaur's drive to expand the American trade deficit translated into a major improvement in Germany's trade balance. This rubbed off on the rest of the EU, which saw its collective trade position go into surplus. This was the environment in which the forces that would create the common currency, the euro, gathered pace. Each grouping had different reasons for wanting a currency link-up.

From the 1970s onwards, Germany was keen to shore up its position in the European scheme of things, as a net major exporter of both consumer and capital goods and a net importer of overall demand. Key to its success was the policy of keeping its growth rate below that of the rest of Europe, while, at the same time, maintaining investment at a much higher level than that of its neighbours. The aim of this policy was simple: to accumulate more and more trade surpluses from within its European vital space in order to feed the Minotaur across the Atlantic, so as, in turn, to financialize its own export expansion within the United States and, later, China.

The one spanner in the works of this German strategy was the threat of competitive currency devaluations, which Italy (and other countries) was using with good effect to limit its trade deficits vis-à-vis Germany. Ideally, from a German perspective, Berlin would keep its cherished Deutschmark but also create a European monetary mechanism that would keep currency fluctuations within certain bounds. That mechanism came to be known as the *European Exchange Rate Mechanism* (ERM), a short-lived arrangement that collapsed after a massive speculative attack in the early 1990s. It was at that moment that Germany bit the bullet and acquiesced to a common currency: a permanent currency union that would stop the speculators from speculating against the incidence and range of currency fluctuations.

The rest of the Europeans all had their own reasons for wanting a common currency. The elites in the deficit countries had grown particularly tired of devaluations. Plain and simple. The fact that the Deutschmark value of their bank accounts and their beautiful summer villas was subject to large and unexpected falls bothered them. And as their working classes were also tired of watching inflation eat into their hard-won wage rises, the Greek and Italian elites found it easy to convince them to share the dream of a common currency. Of course, there was a hefty price to pay. In order to lower inflation to the 3 per cent limit that was a prerequisite for entering the eurozone, deficit countries had to induce

effective stagnation in the productive sectors of their own economies. The shortfall in wage income was, nevertheless, ameliorated
by the rise in lending, which was made cheaper as interest rates
fell. Just as in the United States in the 1970s and 1980s, when
working people were forced to accept lower real wages in return
for shiny credit cards, the underprivileged in Europe's deficit
countries were obliged to take on more debt.

However, the key to the euro project was none other than
Europe's glorious outlier, France. France's elite had three
reasons for seeking a lock-in between the franc and the
Deutschmark. First, it would strengthen the political elite's
bargaining position vis-à-vis the powerful French trades
unions, in view of the moderate wage rises across the Rhine
that German trades unions negotiated with employers and the
federal government. Secondly, it would shore up its already
important banking sector. And thirdly, it would offer the political elites an opportunity to dominate Europe in the one realm
where French expertise outstripped German: the construction
of transnational political institutions.

The Deutschmark's new clothes

The formation of the euro engendered deepening stagnation in
the deficit countries plus France. It also enabled Germany and
the surplus eurozone nations to achieve exceptional surpluses.
These became the financial means by which German corporations internationalized their activities in the United States, China
and Eastern Europe. Thus Germany and the other surplus
countries became the Global Minotaur's European opposite –
its *simulacrum*.[3] As the Minotaur created demand for the rest
of the world, the simulacrum drained the rest of Europe of it. It
maintained Germany's global dynamism by exporting stagnation into its own European backyard.

At the aggregate level, the eurozone was making good progress. Total incomes were rising but, underneath the surface, the industrial sectors of France and the deficit countries entered a slow-burning recession. It was the price that stragglers and ambitious France had to pay for hooking their currencies up to the Deutschmark. Their reward? Cheaper loans and debt-driven consumerism.

Before the Crash of 2008, Europe's Minotaur envy (see the start of chapter 5) manifested itself in long treatises on the sluggishness of continental growth and the superiority of the Anglo-Celtic model. In reality, the lethargic European growth rates, which did decline during every single one of the previous four decades, had nothing to do with inflexible labour markets, an arthritic financial system or overgenerous social security. They were due, simply, to the way in which most of Europe was falling under the spell of German surpluses. The only relief Europe's deficit countries had during the Global Minotaur's halcyon days came from net exports to the United States. But when 2008 struck, even that silver lining vanished.[4]

The institutional guise of the simulacrum came in the form of the famous Maastricht Treaty, which set the rules governing eurozone membership. It stipulated *budget deficits* for member states capped at 3 per cent of GDP, *debt-to-GDP* ratios below 60 per cent, *monetary policy* that was to be decided upon and implemented by the 'independent', inflation-busting ECB, and last but by no means least a *no-transfers clause* (or no 'bail-outs', in post-2008 parlance). This last element meant that, if member states ever got into fiscal trouble, they should expect no assistance from the euro's institutions (the ECB, Eurogroup, etc.) or from fellow eurozone members.

The Maastricht Treaty was sold to the European public and elites as reasonable measures to shield the euro from *free riding*. The metaphor most often used was that of a joint bank account from which each account holder could withdraw money, irrespective of whether he or she had contributed, and without prior agreement. Such an account would soon be depleted, the story went. The equivalent for the eurozone would be member state profligacy that undermined the common currency's credibility and value.

Although a mechanism preventing such free riding is necessary for any currency union, it is certainly not sufficient. Something was missing. Was that 'something' left out accidentally, or was there a hidden agenda? I think the latter. In fact, it was the same agenda that lay behind Harry Dexter White's rejection of Keynes' International Currency Union proposal at Bretton Woods, in 1944 (see chapter 3). Just as the Americans insisted on preserving their right to run large surpluses under the Global Plan, so Germany demanded that the Maastricht Treaty should not include any explicit surplus recycling mechanism. The objective? To use the creation of the eurozone as a mechanism by which to cast in stone the 'obligation' of the deficit countries (plus France) to provide Germany with net effective demand for its exports.

The great difference between American hegemony worldwide and German dominance within the EU was that the United States understood well the importance of recycling surpluses. The Americans' only difference with Keynes was that they did not want the surplus recycling mechanism to be formally instituted. So, under the Global Plan, they made a habit of supporting Germany and Japan with generous capital injections. And when the Global Plan died an ignominious death, the Global Minotaur that took over recycled with glee, albeit by reversing the flows of capital and trade surpluses in favour of Wall Street. So long as that ecumenical beast kept going, the eurozone's faulty architecture held out.

When the Crash of 2008 wounded the Minotaur, the euro cracked. Greece was its weakest link, but the problem was

---

Box 8.1
Europa's flight

It is tempting to stretch this book's central metaphor to include the myth of *Europa*. According to the same mythology that gave us the Minotaur, Europa was a fair Phoenician princess to whom Zeus took a fancy. Having metamorphosed into a white bull, he lured her into riding him and, before she had a chance to jump off, he dashed into the Aegean Sea and carried her off to Crete. King Minos was the product of their union. Which makes Europa the Minotaur's step-grandmother (see the Minotaur's birth story in chapter 1).

Another wrinkle to this story is that, before returning to his wife, the goddess Hera, Zeus bestowed certain gifts upon Europa. One of these gifts was Laelaps, a hound that always caught its prey. (Another was a javelin that never missed its target.) Some generations later, Laelaps was enlisted in the task of hunting down the Teumessian fox – a fearsome animal designed by the gods never to be caught. The impossibility of the match between Laelaps and the Teumessian fox taxed Zeus's mind so much that he decided to turn them both into stone and cast them into the night sky. While racking their brains as they search for policy fixes to the euro's troubles, Europe's policy makers may be amused to recall this metaphor for impossible tasks.

---

deeply ingrained in the whole design and, in particular, in the lack of a surplus recycling mechanism. But before saying more on this, we should take a few steps back, to the moment when the two post-war Germanies became one.

German reunification and its global significance

The steady disintegration of the Soviet Union, which began unexpectedly in the late 1980s, soon led to the demolition of the Berlin Wall. German Chancellor Helmut Kohl moved quickly to seize this opportunity to annex East Germany. Conventional

wisdom has it that the inordinate cost of Germany's reunification is responsible for the country's economic ills and for its
stagnation in the 1990s. This is not my reading.

While it is undoubtedly true that reunification strained
Germany's public finances (to the tune of approximately $1.3
billion), and even led it to flout the very Maastricht Treaty that
it had insisted upon, reunification also helped reduce German
labour's bargaining power. What the oil crises, Walmart and
some aggressive corporate moves had achieved in the United
States in the 1970s, reunification brought to Germany in the
1990s. It is also worth noting that East Germany was not the
only part of the former Soviet empire whose collapse boosted
German capital. From Poland to Slovakia and from Hungary
to the Ukraine, dirt-cheap labour became available to German
companies.

More generally, Germany's response to the cost blowout
of reunification was the pursuit of *competitive wage deflation*.
Indeed, while the eurozone was being prepared, Germany,
courtesy of reunification, was locking into its labour markets
substantially decreased wages (in relation to the wages elsewhere
in the eurozone). Almost in a bid to copy the Global Minotaur's
domestic strategy, the German simulacrum promoted a strategy
of restraining wage growth to a rate significantly below productivity growth. Once the euro was introduced, and German
industry was shielded from the competitive currency deprecia-
tion of countries like Italy, its gains from the fall in wages became
permanent.

Moreover, Germany's system of collective wage bargaining,
based on a corporatist *cum* neo-mercantilist entente between
German capital and the German trades unions, enabled the gap
between productivity and wage growth to be more favourable to
capital than in the rest of Europe. Essentially, low growth reinforced German export competitiveness on the back of continual

real wage deflation and vigorous investment. After 2004, as the Global Minotaur began to soar, Germany's trade surplus took off in sympathy, capital accumulation rose, unemployment fell to 2 million (having risen to almost double that) and German corporate profits rose by 37 per cent.

However, even though the picture seemed quite rosy for the German elites, something rotten was taking over its banking sector – a nasty virus that the Minotaur simulacrum had wilfully contracted from the Global Minotaur itself. And when the Crash of 2008 happened in New York and London, that virus was energized in earnest.[5] It was to be the beginning of the euro's existentialist crisis.

First as history, then as farce: Europe's bank bail-outs

Despite European gloating that the Crash of 2008 was an Anglo-Celtic crisis, and that its own banks had not been taken over by financialization's equivalent of gold fever, the truth soon came out. German banks were caught with an average *leverage ratio* of €52 borrowed to every €1 of their own funds – a ratio worse even than that racked up by Wall Street or London's City. Even the most conservative and stolid state banks, the *Landesbanken*, proved bottomless pits for the German taxpayer. It was a similar story in France, where the banks had to admit that they had at least €33 billion invested in CDOs. To this sad sum, we must add the European banks' exposure to the indebted eurozone states[6] (€849 billion), to Eastern Europe (more than €150 billion), to Latin America (more than €300 billion) and to bad Icelandic debts (around €70 billion).

The ECB, the European Commission (the EU's effective 'government') and the member states rushed in to do for the European banks what the US administration had done for Wall Street. Only there were two profound differences. The first was that the euro is nothing like the dollar: while the dollar remains the world's reserve currency, the Fed and the US Treasury can write blank cheques, safe in the knowledge that it will make very little difference to the value of the dollar, at least in the medium term. Indeed, IMF data shows that the dollar's share of global reserves was 62 per cent at the end of 2009 and has since risen in response to Europe's post-2010 debt crisis.

The second difference relates to the eurozone's problematic architecture, and especially the way that, though its member states are bound by a common currency, their public debts are strictly separate, banks are the responsibility of member states alone, and there is no surplus recycling mechanism to prevent structural fault lines from developing. To put it simply, imagine what would have happened in 2008 if, in the 'dollar-zone', each state (e.g. California or Nevada) had to bail out the banks registered on its soil and there was no way of financing public deficits from Washington!

Within this institutionally problematic framework, the ECB and the European Commission struggled to contain the banking crisis. Between 2008 and 2009, they 'socialized' the banks' losses and turned them into public debt. Meanwhile, the economy of Europe went into recession, as expected. In one year (2008–09) Germany's GDP fell by 5 per cent, France's by 2.6 per cent, Holland's by 4 per cent, Sweden's by 5.2 per cent, Ireland's by 7.1 per cent, Finland's by 7.8 per cent, Denmark's by 4.9 per cent and Spain's by 3.5 per cent.

Suddenly, hedge funds and banks alike had an epiphany. Why not use some of the public money they had been given to *bet* that, sooner or later, the strain on public finances (caused by the recession on the one hand, which depressed the governments' tax take, and the huge increase in public debt on the other, for which the banks were themselves responsible) would cause one or more of the eurozone's states to default?

The more they thought that thought, the gladder they became. The fact that euro membership prevented the most heavily indebted countries (Greece *et al.*) from devaluing their currencies (meaning that they bore the brunt of the combination of debt and recession) led the bankers to train their sights on those countries. So they decided to start betting, small amounts initially, that the weakest link in that chain, Greece, would default. As London's famous bookmakers could not handle multi-billion-pound bets, the banks and hedge funds turned to the trusted CDSs, insurance policies that pay out pre-specified amounts of money if someone else defaults (see chapter 6 for a full description of CDSs).

Of course, as the volume of trade in this newest form of private money increased, so the crisis worsened. There were two reasons for this. First, the rise in the price of CDSs taken out against Greece or Ireland pushed up the interest rates that Athens and Dublin had to pay to borrow, thus pushing them further into the red (and toward effective bankruptcy). Secondly, the more money that was spent on these CDSs, the more capital was siphoned off both from corporations seeking loans to invest in productive activities and from states trying to refinance their burgeoning debt.

In short, the European variant of the banks' bail-out gave the financial sector the opportunity to mint private money all over again. Once more, just as the private money created by Wall Street before 2008 was unsustainable and was bound to turn into thin ash, the onward march of the new private money was to lead, with mathematical precision, to another meltdown. This time it was the *public debt crisis* (also known as the *sovereign debt crisis*), the first stirrings of which were felt at the beginning of 2010 in Athens, Greece.

Greeks bearing debts

In October 2009, the freshly elected socialist government of Greece announced that the country's true deficit was in excess of 12 per cent of national income (rather than the projected 6.5 per cent, already more than double the Maastricht limit). Almost immediately, the CDSs predicated upon a Greek default exploded, as did the interest rate the Greek state had to pay to borrow in order to refinance its €300 billion debt. By January 2010, it had become clear that, without institutional help, the Greek government would have to default.

Informally, the Greek government sought the assistance of the eurozone. German Chancellor Angela Merkel issued her famous *nein*-cubed: *nein* to a bail-out for Greece; *nein* to interest rate relief; *nein* to a Greek default. That triple *nein* was unique in the history of public (or even private) finance. Imagine if, on 15 September 2008, Secretary Paulson had said to Lehman Brothers: 'No, I am not going to bail you out' (which he did say); 'No, I shall not organize very low interest rate loans for you' (which he also probably said); and 'No, you cannot file for bankruptcy' (which he would *never* have said). That last 'no' is inconceivable. And yet that is precisely what the Greek government was told. The German government could fathom neither the idea of assisting Greece nor the idea that Greece would default on so much debt held by the French and German banks (about €75 billion and €53 billion, respectively).

For five agonizing months, the Greek state had to borrow at usurious rates, getting deeper and deeper into insolvency, pretending that it could weather the storm. Mrs Merkel seemed prepared to let Greece twist in the wind until the very last moment. That moment came in early May 2010, when the world's bond markets went into something close to the Credit Crunch of 2008. The Greek debt crisis had panicked investors and caused them not to buy *anyone's* bonds, fearing a cascading default similar to that of 2008. So, on 2 May 2010, the eurozone, the ECB and the IMF agreed to extend a €110 billion loan to Greece at an interest rate high enough to make it very unlikely that the Greek public purse would be able to repay this new loan as well as the existing ones.

Understandably unconvinced that tossing new, expensive loans to an insolvent government that was presiding over an economy in deep recession would somehow magically render it solvent, investors continued to bet on a default by Greece (and by other vulnerable eurozone states). So, a few days later, the EU announced the creation of the European Financial Stability Facility (the EFSF, whose toxic structure was discussed in chapter 7), supposedly a war chest of €750 billion that would be on standby, just in case another eurozone member needed assistance with its public debt repayments.

The markets, after a few days of calmness, took a good look at the EFSF and decided it was merely a stop-gap measure. Thus the euro crisis continued with a vengeance. The reason was, of course, that expensive new loans do not address the deficit states' descent into bankruptcy, and they certainly do nothing for the faulty architecture, the noxious simulacrum, whose destructive potential was released the moment the Global Minotaur was wiped out by the Crash of 2008.

If I am right, and the euro crisis is a systemic failure that began as a banking crisis, then Europe's medicine is worse than the disease. It is like sending a weak swimmer out to sea to save a drowning bather: all you can expect is the sad sight of the two weak swimmers hanging onto one another for dear life, both sinking fast to the bottom of the sea.

The two swimmers are, of course, the eurozone's deficit states and Europe's banking system. Overburdened as the banks are with almost worthless paper debts issued by states like Greece and Ireland, they constitute black holes into which the ECB keeps pumping oceans of liquidity, which of course only yields a tiny trickle of extra loans to business. Meanwhile, the ECB, the surplus countries and the IMF steadfastly refuse to discuss the banking crisis, concentrating their energies solely on imposing massive austerity on the deficit states. In a never-ending circle, the imposed austerity worsens the recession afflicting these deficit states, and thus inflames the bankers' already grave doubts about whether they will ever be paid back by Greece, Ireland, etc. And so the crisis reproduces itself.

Tumbling mountaineers and the euro crisis

The domino effect, with one deficit-stricken country falling upon the next, until none is left standing, is the common metaphor used to describe the eurozone crisis. I think there is a better one: a group of disparate mountaineers, perched on a steep cliff face, tied to one another by a single rope. Some are more agile, others less fit, but all are bound together in a forced state of solidarity. Suddenly an earthquake hits (the Crash of 2008) and one of them (let's call her Helen) is dislodged, her fall arrested only by the shared rope. Under the strain of the stricken member's weight as she dangles in mid-air, and with loosened rocks falling from above, the next weakest (or 'marginal') mountaineer struggles to hang on; eventually, Paddy has to let go, too. The strain on the remaining mountaineers increases greatly, and the next 'marginal' member now teeters on the verge of another mini free-fall that will cause another sharp tug on the remaining string of 'saviours'.

This is precisely why the euro crisis has not been dealt with. The EFSF structure was compared (in chapter 7) to the structure of Wall Street's toxic CDOs. As each country leaves the bond markets and seeks shelter in the EFSF, the next 'marginal' country faces higher interest rates, and the average country's burden also rises. This is a dynamic from hell. It is like watching a tragic accident happen in slow motion. Only the reality of the euro crisis is, in fact, much worse. For there is another aspect of it that the mountaineering analogy does not capture: the banking crisis, which intensifies with each 'transition' of a country to the 'receiving' end of the EFSF.

Indeed, as the tragedy on the cliff face deepens, the drama in the banking arena intensifies, too. Budget deficits grow, austerity causes more banking anxiety as it speeds the shrinkage of the deficit economies, and, in a vicious feedback effect, this parallel drama dislodges the next 'marginal' country from the cliff face.

Most puzzlingly, this is a crisis that Europe could resolve in a few weeks. How? And, if I am right, why is Europe dithering?

Why is Europe dithering when the crisis could be resolved simply and quickly?

I shall start by explaining how the twin crises facing the euro-zone – the one involving the indebted states and the other afflicting the banking sector – could be resolved without delay. Europe's approach has failed because it has both ignored the way the debt crisis and the banking crisis reinforce one another and also turned a blind eye to the deeper cause of the crisis: the lack of a surplus recycling mechanism at the heart of the euro-zone. Here are three simple steps in which effective remedies could be put in place.

The first step would be for the ECB to make the continuation of its generous assistance to the banks conditional on having the banks write off a significant portion of the deficit countries' debts to them.[7] (The ECB has ample bargaining power to effect this, as it is constantly keeping Europe's effectively bankrupt banks liquid.)

Step two would have the ECB take on its books, with immediate effect, a portion of the public debt of *all* member states, equal in face value to the debt that the Maastricht Treaty allows them to have (i.e. up to 60 per cent of GDP). The transfer would be financed by ECB-issued bonds that are the ECB's *own liability*, rather than being guaranteed by member states. Member states thus continue to service their debts, but, at least for the Maastricht-compliant part of the debt, they pay the lower interest rates secured by the ECB bond issue.

Finally, the third step brings into play another venerable EU institution, the European Investment Bank (EIB). The EIB has double the capacity to invest in profitable projects than does the World Bank. Unfortunately, it is underutilized because, under existing rules, member states must advance a proportion of the investment. Given the awful state in which they find themselves, the eurozone's deficit states cannot afford to do this. But by granting member states the right to finance their contribution to the EIB-financed investment projects by means of bonds issued for this purpose by the ECB (see step two above), the EIB can become the surplus recycling mechanism that the eurozone currently lacks. Its role would be to borrow, with the ECB's assistance, surpluses from European and non-European surplus countries and invest them in Europe's deficit regions.

Summing up, the first two steps would make the debt crisis go away, and the third would underpin the eurozone by providing its missing link – the mechanism that it never had and the lack of which caused the euro crisis in response to the Crash of 2008.

But if I am right about all this, why does Europe not take up this suggestion, or something along these lines? The answer lies in the preceding pages, but it is perhaps time to spell it out. If the euro crisis were to be resolved quickly and painlessly, Germany (and the other surplus eurozone countries) would forfeit the immense bargaining power that the simmering crisis hands the German government vis-à-vis France and the deficit countries.

To put the same point differently, the surplus countries now have one foot inside the eurozone and one foot outside it. On the one hand, they have bound the rest of the eurozone to them by means of a common currency, thus securing large intra-eurozone surpluses. On the other hand, they know that the ongoing crisis affects the deficit countries dispro-portionately and, so long as the surplus countries retain the option of getting out of the eurozone, their bargaining power in Europe's forums is immense. For instance, whenever the German chancellor wants to take some item off the agenda, she does so unopposed. But were the crisis to end tomorrow in a manner that prevents the surplus countries from ever leaving the eurozone, then Germany's chancellor would be just one of almost two dozen heads of government around a large table.

Now notice how the second step of my proposed euro crisis solution would stop Germany from ever leaving the eurozone: once the ECB, a common institution, acquires large debts (by issuing its own bonds), it becomes impossible to allocate this common debt among different member states.[8] Thus, it is impossible for anyone to leave. Furthermore, if the third step is adopted, and Europe is equipped with the missing surplus recycling mechanism, Germany's simulacrum will be well and truly debased.

So it seems that the euro crisis is wholly unnecessary from an economic viewpoint, but that it serves the interests of main-taining within Europe the role that Germany developed for itself during the reign of the Global Minotaur. And now that the Minotaur is *kaput*, Europe is in crisis and Germany is in denial.

The dragon soars, then plunges into angst

On 4 December 2010, Wikileaks posted an official cable relating a conversation (some time around 28 March 2009) between US Secretary of State Hillary Clinton and Australian Prime Minister Kevin Rudd. In it we read: 'The Secretary also noted the challenges posed by China's economic rise, asking, "How do you deal toughly with your banker?"'

The reader may, understandably, protest that there is a startling omission in this book: while it purports to address the future of the world economy, there has been little mention of China. Undoubtedly, the swashbuckling re-emergence of what was, historically, one of the world's leading powers is the big story of our times. Its bearing upon the future will be as significant as that of the United States in the twentieth century. Of this I have no doubt. Nevertheless, neither the nature of China's rise nor its future impact can be understood without a good grasp of the world as shaped by the Global Minotaur. For, come to think of it, the soaring dragon not only grew up in an environment shaped by the Global Minotaur, but must also mature in an unstable world occasioned by the latter's demise.

Deng Xiao Ping's new course for China was modelled on Japan and the South East Asian tigers. The guiding principle behind the Chinese plan for growth was that of a dual economy, in which special economic zones would dot China with small Singapores or Hong Kongs – islands of intense capitalist activity in a sea of unlimited labour power. Meanwhile, the centre would direct investment (very much along the lines of the Japanese model), but would also negotiate technology transfers and foreign direct investment directly with Western and Japanese multinational corporations. As for China's global positioning, it would resemble that of South East Asia, in seeking sources of demand for its export-led growth from the United States and Europe.

It can be safely suggested that China owes its élan to the Global Minotaur. American, European and Japanese multinationals played a crucial role in setting up shop in China and using its low costs to export to the rest of the world, and especially to the United States. At the same time, cheap Chinese imports to the United States have helped Walmart-style American companies squeeze prices to unbelievably low levels, assisting in the drive to minimize relative US wage and energy inflation, a key requirement (as we saw in chapter 4) for the continuing capital flows into the United States that kept the Minotaur happy and joyous.

As China learned the ropes, becoming one of the Minotaur's favourite feeders, its leaders became keen observers of US policies that had the potential to affect China's growth path. In particular, they learned important lessons from the 1985 Plaza Accord (which, as we saw, condemned Japan to an untenable position) and from the 1998 South East Asia crisis, which was caused by America's successful bid to rid the tigers of financial regulation and expose their financial markets to the vagaries of Wall Street, the City and the European banks.

A widely accepted current hypothesis is that, because of these experiences, the Chinese are resisting America's asphyxiating pressure to revalue the Chinese currency (the *renminbi*, or RMB). Seemingly, following the Crash of 2008, the United States is pushing hard for an RMB revaluation, for the same reasons that it pushed the Japanese in the 1980s to sign the Plaza Accord. The conventional view here is that the US government, in its haste to do something about the low level of demand in its domestic market, is trying to do what all governments do in a recessionary climate: drum up demand abroad, usually by devaluing the currency (or, equivalently, by enticing foreigners to revalue theirs). Once again, I do not believe that the standard explanation is the whole story.

While American firms that have their base predominantly in the United States push for an appreciation of the RMB (for the reasons given above), it is not at all clear that the heralded currency wars between China and the United States are of the traditional type just outlined. There are two reasons for remaining sceptical on this issue. First, it is not at all clear that US policy makers have accepted that the Global Minotaur is finished, and that the strategy of expanding (or at least not shrinking) the US twin deficits must be abandoned. Secondly, some of the largest, best-endowed and most dynamic American corporations would be hit hard if the RMB were to revalue. For they already produce a good deal of their output within China, before exporting it to the rest of the world. An RMB appreciation would cut into their profit margins. Every iPad, each HP computer and even American cars (many of which use Chinese-manufactured parts) would have to increase in price. Indeed, while the American government is lobbying Beijing to revalue the RMB, countless Western multinationals are threatening to withdraw from China (and relocate to India or even Africa) if the RMB is allowed to rise significantly against the US dollar.

Besides the US–Chinese nexus, China's startling growth has left an indelible mark on the rest of the developing nations. Some have been devastated by the competition, but others have been liberated from a relationship of dependence on the West and its multinational corporations. Mexico was among the first to suffer from China's rise. Because it had chosen to invest much energy in becoming a low-wage manufacturer on the periphery of the United States (and a member, with the US and Canada, of the North American Free Trade Agreement (NAFTA)), China's emergence was a nightmare for Mexican manufacturers. However, it was a godsend for other countries – ranging from Australia (which in effect put its vast mineral resources at the disposal of Chinese firms) to Argentina, and from Brazil to Angola (which in 2007 received more funding, as direct investment, mainly into its oil industry, than the IMF had lent the whole world).

Latin America is possibly the one continent that has been changed forever by China's emergence as the Global Minotaur's major feeder. Argentina and Brazil turned their fields into production units supplying 1.3 billion Chinese consumers with foodstuffs, and also dug up their soil in search of minerals that would feed China's hungry factories. Cheap Chinese labour and China's market access to the West (courtesy of World Trade Organization membership) allows Chinese manufacturers to undercut their Mexican and other Latin American competitors in the manufacture of low-value-added sectors, such as shoes, toys and textiles. This two-pronged effect is causing Latin America to deindustrialize and return to the status of a primary goods producer.

These developments have a global reach. For if Brazil and Argentina turn their eyes toward Asia, as they have already started doing, they may abandon their long-term struggle to break into the food markets of the United States and Europe, from which they have been barred by severe protectionist measures in favour of American, German and French farmers. Already, Latin America's shifting trade patterns are affecting the orientation of a region that was, until very recently, thought of as the United States' backyard.

Latin America's governments are choosing not to resist their countries' transformation into China's primary goods producers. They may not like deindustrialization much, but it is preferable to the prospect of another crisis like that of 1998–2002, and another visit from an IMF seeking to exact more pounds of flesh from their people.

Returning to Secretary Clinton's remark above, it is clear what she meant by referring to China as America's banker. As we see in Figure 8.1, the United States has, since 2000, shifted its reliance for financing its budget deficit from Europe and Japan to

China. But what exactly was Mrs Clinton referring to when she hinted at 'dealing toughly' with China? Did she mean, yet again, pressurizing Beijing to revalue its currency? And was the reason the stated purpose of limiting the US trade deficit with China?

Possibly. However, an even more pressing reason is to preserve the profits of US multinationals, which, in the 1980s and beyond, set up production facilities in countries like Mexico and Brazil, and which are now under threat from severe Chinese competition.[9]

Box 8.2: America's bankers

Figure 8.1 looks at four distinct years and deconstructs the owner-ship of US assets (public and private) by non-US government or government-controlled financial institutions. It is clear that since 2003 America's old protégés, Europe and Japan, have been fading as its financial supporters. The Chinese state is, mean-while, pushing its contribution through the roof. In this sense, the Minotaur's recent travails have posed a serious threat to the US assets that China already owns.

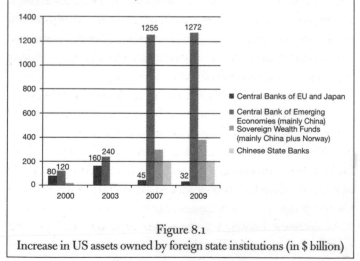

Figure 8.1

Increase in US assets owned by foreign state institutions (in $ billion)

America's conundrum in the face of stupendous Chinese growth is that the Crash of 2008 stopped the Minotaur from quick-marching the Chinese to its tune. Up until then, the Chinese had depended on the Minotaur for their trade surpluses, and were thus forced to reinvest them in the United States, either in buying US government debt or in the private sector. With the Minotaur no longer capable of absorbing increasing quantities of Chinese goods at anything like the pre-2008 rate (especially now that China has shifted production to high-tech, big-item products, like superfast railways), China does not automatically need to send all of its capital to New York.

This leaves China with only one reason for investing hugely in US assets: the fact that it has already invested hugely in US assets and does not want to see its people's accumulated hard labour lose much of its worth if the United States were to be hit by a public debt crisis. At the same time, and despite its public proclamations, the US government does not have the backing of a large segment of American corporations to pursue a Plaza-type agreement that would see the RMB rise against the dollar. Unable to expand its deficits (as it did when the Minotaur was exploding with youthful vigour) and lacking the clout to do to China what it did to Japan in 1985, the United States is finding it hard to decide how to deal with China.

China, too, unable to secure sufficient demand for its industries in the absence of a roaring Minotaur, is in a bind and has ended up responding in surprising ways. For instance, Brazil's central bank revealed that, whereas in 2009 China's foreign direct investment in the Latin American country was only $300 million, in 2010 it rose to $17 billion. Why? What is China up to?

As everyone knows, for some time now, Brazil, Argentina, etc. have been enriched by the dragon's purchases of iron ore, soya beans, oil, meat, etc. But when the Global Minotaur was grievously wounded in 2008, and these economies continued to grow on the back of their primary exports to China, their currencies shot up in relation to the dollar. There were three immediate effects of this.

First, Latin American high growth rates attracted a new carry trade, this time from the United States, whose growth rate and interest rates hovered around zero, thus motivating a capital flight away from America.

Secondly, new Chinese industrial imports flooded into Brazil and Argentina as their prices fell because the local currencies strengthened against the dollar (and, by pegged association, the RMB).

Thirdly, to perpetuate this cycle, China increased its investments in Latin America. Now, this third development is of some significance. Up until recently, China would invest in Africa and elsewhere in projects, the ultimate purpose of which was to secure raw materials for its domestic industries. With these new investments in countries like Brazil, China seems to be pursuing a new strategy of creating something like its own Global Plan! It is directing part of its outbound capital flows to countries other than the United States, in an effort to stimulate demand for Chinese goods there, in those other places.

The broader significance of China's relationship to the rest of the emerging nations comes in the form of clues as to how China will seek to address the gaping hole left in the overall demand for its exports by the Minotaur's 2008 misfortune. What is clear is that China, the United States and the rest of the emerging nations will, from now on, engage in a triangular game of chicken. With no dominant party in sight, and no clear objectives on the part of any of them, the prospects of a new, efficient (formal or informal) global surplus recycling mechanism seem slim and distant. Which means that the Minotaur's legacy is a rather bleak one for the world economy.

Epilogue: between the West's bankruptocracy and the East's fragile strength

Judging by the mood in the centres of power, what we used to call the 'Third World' is having a good crisis. The 'emerging economies' are growing at the expense of Europe and the United States, the two loci of long-established capitalism, which, regrettably, have spawned the new socio-economic 'system' of bankruptocracy.

The Global Minotaur's 2008 moment has raised the prospect of a worldwide realignment. And yet, the Minotaur is still in the room, threatening to wreak havoc. Wounded it may be, perhaps mortally, but its imprint is still all over our world. When it was hurt, and Wall Street's near-collapse sapped its energy, America's abandoned protégés failed to rise to the occasion.

Europe entered a crisis of its own making – one that is endangering sixty years of European integration. South East Asia has found itself more dependent than before on a powerful neighbour, even if this time it is not Japan, but China. Japan itself, which had its own recession well before the Minotaur's infirmity, seems to have made its peace with stagnation.

Of all the major non-US economic powerhouses, only China is dynamic enough to aspire to the Minotaur's throne. But China knows it cannot yet fill that illustrious role, unable as it is to create demand even for its own output. Its most recent efforts to create its own Global Plan, in particular in relation to Latin America, stirred up tensions with its potential protégés (e.g. Brazil), reminding us that America's own Global Plan only came to pass with minimal resistance because, at the time of its design and implementation, the rest of the world lay in ruins.

Some think that China only needs to wait, certain that, in the fullness of time, it will prevail. The Chinese leadership is less sure. It understands intimately the scarcity of total demand in the post-Minotaur world. It knows that Germany, Japan and China are all fully reliant for their very survival on maintaining aggressive, expanding surpluses. But this also requires someone to absorb those surpluses as deficits.

That someone used to be the Global Minotaur. Now it is gone, and nothing seems likely to replace it. To buy time, the Chinese government is stimulating its growing economy and keeps it shielded from currency revaluations, in the hope that vibrant growth can continue. But it sees the omens, and they are not good. On the one hand, China's consumption-to-GDP ratio is falling – a sure sign that the domestic market cannot generate enough demand for China's gigantic factories. On the other hand, its fiscal injections are causing real estate bubbles. If these go unchecked, they may burst and thus cause a catastrophic domestic unravelling. But how do you deflate a bubble without choking off growth? That was the multi-trillion dollar question that Alan Greenspan failed to answer. It is not clear that the Chinese authorities can.

CHAPTER 9

A world without the Minotaur

Almost two years have passed since the first edition of this book was written.[1] Its prognosis for our tormented beast was not good. Have events since confirmed that the Global Minotaur's wounds were too deep to allow it to continue to perform its miraculous global surplus recycling? Is this still the best explanation available as to why the American, the European and, indeed, the global economies are stuttering, and why generalized insecurity has become the 'new norm'?

To be worthy of serious consideration, a theory of what went wrong with the global economy must not only offer a logical explanation of the past but must also describe the future developments that would *falsify* it. Would the argument that was the kernel of this book's first edition pass such a test in the light of the last two years? Before addressing the question, it may be helpful to restate clearly (and with the help of a diagram) the book's overarching 'Global Minotaur Hypothesis'. Once the reader is reminded of the hypothesis, a series of 'facts' that would have falsified it will follow. As I hope to show in the remainder of the chapter, the original explanatory thrust, the Global Minotaur Hypothesis, survives the empirical test of falsifiability rather well. And, in so doing, it illuminates usefully the current policy debates unfolding on the drama's three parallel stages: America, Europe and China.

The Global Minotaur Hypothesis: a summary[2]

Since the 1970s, the United States began absorbing a large portion of the rest of the world's surplus industrial products. America's net imports were, naturally, the net exports of surplus countries like Germany, Japan and China; their main source of demand. In turn, the profits earned by the surplus nations' entrepreneurs were returned, daily, to Wall Street, in search of a higher pay-off. Wall Street would then use this influx of foreign capital for three purposes: (a) to provide credit to American consumers, (b) as direct investment into US corporations and, of course, (c) to buy US Treasury Bills (i.e. to fund American government deficits).

Central to this global surplus recycling mechanism (GSRM), which I have likened to a Global Minotaur, were the two gargantuan deficits of the United States: the *trade deficit* and the federal government *budget deficit*. Without them, the book argues, the global circular flow of goods and capital (see diagram below) would not have 'closed', destabilizing the global economy.

This recycling system broke down because Wall Street took advantage of its central position in it to build colossal pyramids of *private money* on the back of the net profits flowing into the United States from the rest of the world. The process of private money minting by Wall Street's banks, also known as *financialisation*, added much energy to the recycling scheme, as it oozed oodles of new financial vitality, thus fuelling an ever-accelerating level of demand within the United States, in Europe (whose banks soon jumped onto

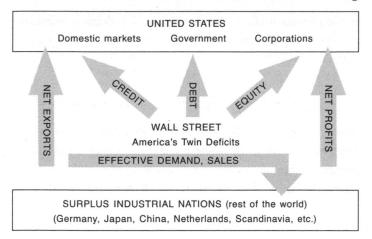

Figure 9.1
The Global Minotaur's global surplus recycling mechanism

the private money-minting bandwagon) and Asia. Alas, it also brought about its demise.

When, in the fall of 2008, Wall Street's pyramids of private money auto-combusted, and turned into ashes, Wall Street's capacity to continue 'closing' the global recycling loop vanished. America's banking sector could no longer harness the United States' twin (trade and budget) deficits for the purposes of financing enough demand within America to keep the net exports of the rest of the world going (a financing process that, until the autumn of 2008, tapped the rest of the world's surplus profits which these net exports produced). From that dark moment onwards, the world economy would find it impossible to regain its poise – at least not without an alternative global surplus recycling mechanism that replaces the wounded Global Minotaur.

This was, in brief, the central hypothesis of the book's first edition. Did it stand the test of history?

The Minotaur is dead! Long live America's deficits!

Had the global economy found its feet without some GSRM to replace the Minotaur, there would have been no new edition of this book (since an apology for the first one would have sufficed). Similarly, if the eurozone had bounced back, on the strength of its austerian policies, or if China had discovered some inner force by which to arrest the declining rate at which its people consumed, the book's central pillar would have lain in ruins. Sadly, this is not what transpired: the world continues its journey in the uncharted waters of a dark ocean whipped up continually by the evil winds of dread and fear.

The fact that recovery has not spread its soothing wings over us is, of course, no proof that the 'Global Minotaur Hypothesis' holds. To reach the conclusion that the last two years have kept it alive and potentially insightful, we need to state carefully and in some detail its predictions and then to compare those with the facts. So, let us begin: what observations would we have to make regarding the past two years or so to conclude that the Global Minotaur Hypothesis was flawed?[3]

Suppose we observed that, despite the Crisis, America's deficits remain high but that they continue to absorb the net exports of both goods and capital from the rest of the world, and at a pace not too dissimilar to that of the pre-2008 era. If this is what we observed in 2009 and beyond, then the Global Minotaur Hypothesis would be refuted: for it would then be impossible to claim (a) that the Global Minotaur is kaput, and (b) that its demise must be blamed for the world's economic continuing woes.

So, let's look at the facts: The first observation worth noting is that America's twin deficits are alive and kicking.

At the height of the Minotaur's reign, in 2005, the US federal government posted a deficit of $574 billion. In the same year American consumers and firms absorbed a staggering $781 billion of net imports from the rest of the world. Almost 70 per cent of the profits that the non-American producers of these goods made returned to Wall Street. Once in the bankers' hands, they were turbocharged (through so-called 'financial engineering') and, thereby, financed the US deficits, with the residual being exported to the four corners of the globe (where it helped build a variety of bubbles).

Following the 2008 catastrophe, America's deficits diverged massively. As all sorts of incomes (from labour, capital and rent) collapsed, asset values fell through the floor, home foreclosures and the ranks of the unemployed burgeoned, it was inevitable that Americans would reduce drastically their consumption of imported goods. Indeed, in 2009 the trade deficit fell from $781 billion in 2005 to $506 billion. However, in the same year, the US federal deficit shot up (from $574 billion in 2005) to $1,400 billion, as government strove to prop up Wall Street and stimulate Main Street. By 2011 the trade deficit had recovered to, more or less, its 2005 level (reaching $738 billion) while the budget deficit stabilised at the historically gigantic $1,228 billion mark.

Granted that the Crisis did not dent America's deficits (indeed, it boosted their sum), the pertinent question is this: did the United States manage, post-2008, to continue re-cycling other people's surplus goods and profits at a pace that, judging from the pre-2008 period, is necessary to keep world total demand for produced goods buoyant? The answer that surfaces upon close inspection of official statistics is unambiguously negative. In brief, the facts confirm the hypothesis that the Global Minotaur is now defunct. Two pieces of data confirm this.

First, America has lost its capacity to recycle the rest of the world's net exports at the pre-2008 pace. More precisely, in 2011 America was generating 23.7 *per cent less demand* for the rest of the world's net exports than it would have been without the Crash of 2008. (See Figure 9.2 where it is evident that in 2011 the United States was absorbing almost 24 per cent less of the main exporters' net exports than their underlying trend value.)

Secondly, and at the same time, America was failing to attract (through Wall Street) the level of capital flows necessary to maintain the pre-2008 pace of investment into its private sector. In particular, by 2011 the United States had lost *56.48 per cent of the assets held by foreigners* compared to the (trend) level that would have been had the Crash of 2008 not happened (see Figure 9.3). The main, and indeed crucial, reason for this precipitous decline was that foreign net capital flows ending up as loans to US corporations fell drastically from around $500 billion in 2006 to –$50 billion in 2011 (see Figure 9.4).

In conclusion, a crystal clear picture is emerging: the Crisis did not alter the deficit position of the United States. The federal budget deficit more or less doubled while America's trade deficit, after an initial fall, stabilised at the same level. *However, the US deficits are no longer capable of maintaining the mechanism that keeps the global flows of goods and profits balanced at a planetary level.* Whereas until 2008 America was able to draw into the country mountains of net imports of goods, and a similar volume of capital flows (so that the two balanced out), this is no longer happening post-2008. American markets are sucking 24 per cent fewer net imports (thus generating only 66 per cent of the demand that the rest of the world was used to before the Crash) and are attracting into the American private sector 57% less capital than they would have had Wall Street not collapsed in 2008.

In short, of the mighty Global Minotaur, the only reminder that remains is the still accelerating flow of foreign capital into America's public debt (see Figure 9.5), evidence that the world is in disarray and money is desperately seeking safe haven in the bosom of the reserve currency in this age of tumult. But as long as the Rest of the World is reducing its injection of capital into America's corporate sector and real estate, while America is reducing its imports of their net exports, we can be certain that the beast is dead and nothing has taken its place with a capacity to re-start the essential process of surplus recycling. Thus the sad cry: *The Global Minotaur is dead! Long live America's deficits!*

The Minotaur's death in pictures

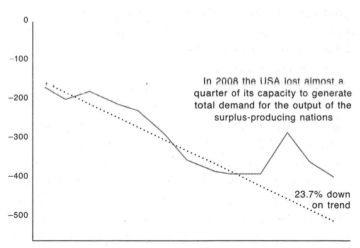

Figure 9.2   US goods trade deficit with major surplus countries, including the eurozone's surplus member states, China, Hong Kong, Japan and Korea (US$ bn)

Source: US Bureau of Economic Analysis.

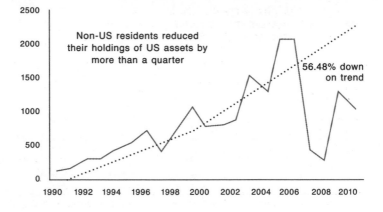

Figure 9.3   Foreign assets in the US except derivatives
(US$ bn)

Source: US Bureau of Economic Analysis.

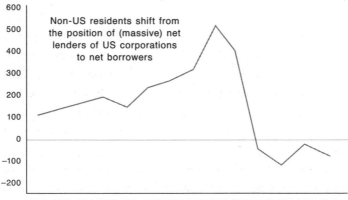

Figure 9.4   Corporate bond purchases (net)
by non-US residents (US$ bn)

Source: US Bureau of Economic Analysis.

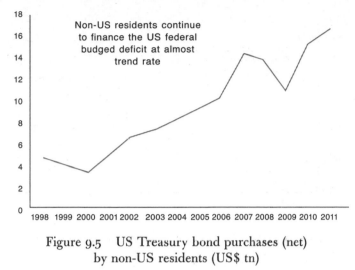

Figure 9.5   US Treasury bond purchases (net)
by non-US residents (US$ tn)

Source: US Bureau of Economic Analysis.

America after the Minotaur

Once Wall Street lost its ability to harness America's twin
deficits for the purposes of recycling the rest of the world's
surplus goods and profits, the American economy had to
settle at a much reduced level of economic activity. This
would not be a bad thing per se if it were not for the fact
that the accumulated debts (e.g. unpaid mortgages and many
bad loans that one bank had made to another) remain as if
nothing had happened.

A lower level of economic activity would have, indeed,
been fine as long as employment had picked up quickly and
the lower wages were able, in conjunction with lower prices,
to preserve a level of consumption consistent with calm but
steady recovery. Alas, the success of the banking sector in ensuring that monetary policy was tuned towards *their* interests,
just like in the good old (pre-2008) times, guaranteed that

endogenous growth was out of the reach of American society. When taken together with (a) Europe's suicidal dallying with Herbert Hoover-like austerity[4] (at a time when half of the continent is in the clasps of its own Great Depression), and (b) China's structural failure to stimulate domestic demand, it is no great wonder that the Crisis remains with us.

Chapters 7 and 8 described vividly the *rise of bankrupt-ocracy*; the way in which bank failures armed the failed bankers with remarkable extractive, predatory political power; a power to extract a larger part of a shrinking national income at rates proportional to their banks' black holes. We have already seen (see Chapter 7) the manner in which the American public was betrayed and misled by the Geithner–Summers Plan; how the Fed's strategy was no more than an overt campaign unconditionally to refloat Wall Street;[5] the half-hearted stimulus package introduced by the Treasury which, when the rapid contraction of state spending is taken into account, amounted to no more than a trickle of funding entirely inadequate to arrest the fall in aggregate demand for goods and services within America.

Very quickly, the Obama administration lost political momentum. The obscene sight of those who had played a major role in setting the scene for the Crash (men like Larry Summers, Tim Geithner, Ben Bernanke) effectively return-ing to the scene of the crime as 'saviours', wielding trillions of freshly minted or borrowed dollars to lavish upon their banker 'mates', was enough to turn off even the hardiest of Mr Obama's supporters. The result was predictable: as often happens during a deflationary period (think of the 1930s, for example), those who gain politically do not come from the revolutionary Left; they come from the loony Right. In the United States it was the Tea Party that grew on the back of a disdain for bankers,[6] a denunciation of the Fed, a clarion call for 'honest', metal-backed money,[7] and a revulsion towards all government.

Ironically, the rise of the Tea Party increased the interventions of the Fed that the movement denounced. The reason was simple: once the Obama administration had lost its way, and could not pass any meaningful bills through Congress that might have stimulated the economy, only one lever was left with which anyone could steer America's macroeconomy – the Fed's monetary policy. And since interest rates were dwelling in the nether world of the first liquidity trap to hit the United States since the 1930s[8] (recall Chapter 2 here), the Fed decided that *quantitative easing* or QE – the strategy that Chapter 8 describes in the context of the 1990s' 'lost Japanese decade' – was all that was left separating America from a repugnant depression.

Did Mr Bernanke have good reason to act? Most certainly so! From 1990 to 2008 aggregate demand in America[9] hovered around a narrow band (between 98 per cent and 104 per cent) of its long-term trend level. In 2009 it fell off a cliff, and to this day has not recovered. Presently, aggregate demand remains 14 per cent down compared to where it would have been (its trend level) without the Crisis. This is a huge gap which, taken together with (a) the debt under which households are labouring and (b) the banks' reluctance to lend, guarantees not just high unemployment but also that many Americans will soon fall through society's cracks, becoming permanently unemployable.

When Mr Bernanke adopted QE, in a bid to put some oomph back into American aggregate demand, he inadvertently offered the Tea Party, and later the Republican mainstream, an excellent target: it was a wonderful opportunity to portray QE as the devil's attempt to corrupt the nation's soul; to debase its currency; to give a nation addicted to the debt drug another dose that sinks it deeper into dependency on Mephistopheles' cruellest instrument – the printing presses, which can provide only temporary relief at the expense of medium-term hyper-inflation.

Of course none of that is true. While QE can be branded ineffectual, for reasons outlined below, the assertion that the Fed's QE will push America into another 1970s-like period of ever accelerating prices is ludicrous. Yet truth is not the currency in which the recalcitrant Right trades: terrifying impressions (that can be employed further to boost private appropriation of publically produced wealth) are!

Quantitative easing as the most complex form of wishful thinking

At the time of writing, the third round of quantitative easing, QE3, was in the air. It is worthwhile taking a look at what it means, because a great number of false accounts circulate whose profound error is particularly instructive regarding the nature of our Crisis.

According to the Fed's own announcement, every month (until further notice) America's central bank will be buying $40 billion of paper titles backed by mortgages (so-called mortgage backed securities, or MBS). Who will the Fed buy these MBS titles from? From private banks and other financial institutions, of course. And how will the Fed pay for them? Simply by crediting electronically the accounts that those institutions have at the Fed with the sums necessary to take these pieces of paper (the MBS) off their books. However, this new balance of dollars in the banks' Fed account *cannot* be lent to customers or business. They can only be swapped with other paper assets held by other banks. This is crucial for understanding why QE is *not* the same as money printing.

Despite the technical nature of the 'transactions' involved, it is worthwhile taking a close look at it.

When the Fed buys $1,000 worth of MBS paper from Bank X, $1,000 is taken out of the bank's 'assets' column in the Bank X's balance sheet and is replaced by $1,000 spending money held at a 'reserve account' Bank X keeps with the Fed. The said account is called 'reserve' because of the conditions the Fed attaches to its uses. To be precise, the Fed stipulates that this $1,000 can only be lent to other banks or used to buy other paper titles from other banks. Thus, the only way that the Fed's purchase of this $1,000 'worth' of MBS can find itself in the economy is if Bank X wants to buy some other piece of paper from another bank, say Bank Y. But even if it does, the money will enter the real economy only if that piece of paper title is new – for example, if Bank Y had just lent $1,000 to some customer and passed this loan on to Bank X. If the paper title concerned is old, pre-QE, debt, all that QE would accomplish is that a paper title worth $1,000 would pass from the books of one bank to the books of another. The $1,000 would simply never enter the circular flow of income.

This is precisely why QE cannot fuel inflation. Indeed, it is the reason why the 2012 US inflation rate is lower than it was two years ago – despite the massive volumes of QE1 and QE2 that preceded. So, what was the logic behind QE? Mr Bernanke's stated purpose is that the Fed's purchases of MBS will increase their price, setting off the following chain reaction:

- increased MBS prices will push down the interest rates people demand from them before purchasing MBS paper (since they will now sport more attractive price-growth potential);

- the lower interest rates associated with MBS paper will translate into lower interest rates for new mortgages;
- the lower interest rates on mortgages will boost the demand for new homes;
- the extra demand for housing will push up house prices;
- the increasing house prices will reduce the number of American families whose home is worth less than the mortgage that they have on it, turning them into mortgage slaves.

If all this transpires, the next hope is that a reduction in the incidence of mortgage bondage in American society ('negative equity' in the parlance of financiers) will cause more families to spend more readily, many to sell up and move to an area where they can find work more easily, others to slow down the rate at which they pay down existing debt (and spend some more) and, importantly, shift investors from MBS paper purchases to corporate bonds (i.e. more lending directly to corporations). This is, dear reader, Mr Bernanke's heroic theory of how his QE3 will deliver the nation from recession.

What's wrong with it? There is one simple omission: that for QE's virtuous wheel to start turning, a multiple coincidence of impossible beliefs *must* exist:

- Jack and Jill, who are Bank Y's customers, must trust that the real-estate market has bottomed out in the medium term and that their job is secure, so as to dare ask Bank Y for a mortgage.
- Bank Y must be willing to take the risk of stretching its already large 'assets' column by lending to Jack and Jill to buy a house in the hope that some other bank, Bank X, will buy that iffy mortgage from it using its QE-funded 'reserve account' at the Fed.

- Firms that are thinking of employing people like Jack and Jill (in the medium to long term) must believe that Bank X will indeed buy Jack and Jill's mortgage from Bank Y and, moreover, that this sort of transaction will increase demand for their products, thus justifying more hires.

To cut a long story short, a great deal of believing must occur before QE delivers on its promise to boost employment and help the real-estate market recover. Alas, given the prevailing state of self-confirming pessimism, to expect that these beliefs will flood into the different agents' minds at once is to believe in miracles.

To recap, ever since America became ungovernable (with the White House and Congress at loggerheads), the Fed was the only branch of government with any capacity to act upon the recession. QE helped to some extent to slow it down, if only because someone was doing something 'big'. It was like cortisone that diminished the pain and lessened the symptoms without, however, providing a cure. As long as it did nothing directly to reduce the size of the debts people faced, or to increase the wages the low levels of which were (from the 1970s onwards) a fundamental root cause of the problem (recall Chapter 4), QE was never going to work.

While QE's side effects may be nowhere near as toxic as the Fed's ardent rightist opponents make them out to be, nonetheless they are real: mainly, QE gives bankers an incentive to lend overseas, just as Japan's QE in the 1990s led to the carry trade that boosted the capital flows into the United States. As a result the exchange rate of developing currencies (Brazil being a case in point) appreciates fast, resulting in higher commodity (particularly food) prices, which worsen the circumstances of less-well-off Americans and threaten developing nations with rapid capital inflows;

this (as South East Asia, Ireland and Spain can testify) can quickly turn into an exodus that leaves nothing standing behind in its wake.

Perhaps America's greatest tragedy, as these words are written, is that the public debate is ensnared in a cul-de-sac. By focusing on QE, on the pros and cons of a new gold standard, on the unsustainability of the federal debt, on whether the solution lies perhaps in a large reduction in living standards, Americans are thrown off the key point: the cause of their distress is the fact that, for the first time since World War II, the United States has lost its capacity to recycle the planet's surpluses. Without an alternative mechanism for achieving this recycling, America's (and the world's) capacity to recover is severely circumscribed.

Europe after the Minotaur

Bankruptocracy, as the previous chapter argued, is as much a European predicament as it is an American 'invention'. The difference between the experience of the two continents is that at least Americans did not have to labour under the enormous design faults of the eurozone. Imagine their chagrin if the citizens of hard-hit states (e.g. Nevada or Ohio) had to worry about a death embrace between the debt of their state and the losses of the banks who happened to operate within the state! Additionally, Americans were spared the need to contend with a central bank utterly shackled by inner divisions and the German central bank's (the Bundesbank's) penchant for treating the worst-hit parts of the Union (the eurozone, that is) as alien lands that had to be fiscally waterboarded until they ceased to obey the laws of macroeconomics![10]

In the past two years, the debate in Europe has focused exclusively on issues that sound technical and minor, especially when projected against the background of Europe's extraordinarily rich history. Will there be 'conditionality' attached to the recently announced purchases of Italian and Spanish bonds by the European Central Bank? Will the bonds that the ECB purchases be treated on something financiers refer to as a *pari passu* basis (in relation to bonds held by private institutions)? Will the ECB supervise all of Europe's banks, or just the 'systemic' ones?

These are questions that ought to be of no genuine interest to anyone other than those with a morbid interest in the interface between public finance and monetary policy. And yet these questions (and the manner in which they will be answered) will probably prove as important for the future of Europe as the Treaties of Westphalia, Versailles or even Rome. For these are the issues that will determine whether Europe holds together or succumbs to the vicious centrifugal forces that were unleashed by the Crash of 2008.

Even so, they are not issues that are worth expounding upon here. All they do is to reflect a tragic, underlying reality that can be described in simple lay terms without the use of any jargon whatsoever: *Europe is disintegrating because its architecture was simply not sound enough to sustain the shockwaves caused by our Minotaur's death throes.* The previous chapter dedicated several sections to describing the eurozone's construction and all its faults; the manner in which Europe's version of bankruptocracy sprang up. In particular, the section on Europe's 'tumbling mountaineers' captures nicely the domino effect which began with Greece and ended up (after this book's first edition saw the light of day) engulfing two proud and immensely productive large European nations: Spain and Italy.

On the basis of Chapter 8's analysis, it is quite obvious that the insolvency of Madrid and Rome had nothing to do with fiscal profligacy (recall that Spain had a lower debt than Germany in 2008 and Italy has consistently smaller budget deficits) and everything to do with the way in which the euro-zone's macroeconomy relied significantly for the demand of its net exports on the Global Minotaur. Once the latter keeled over in 2008, and Wall Street's private cash disappeared, two effects brought Europe to its knees.

One was the sequential death-embrace of bankrupt banks and insolvent states (beginning with Greece, moving to Ireland, to Portugal and continuing until Italy and Spain were torn asunder). The other was the Minotaur's simulacrum (see the previous chapter for this metaphorical sketch of the German economy) and its determination to hang on to its option of exiting the eurozone at will, therefore denying each and every rational plan for mending the currency union in a sustainable manner.

Has anything of analytical significance occurred in Europe since Chapter 8 was penned two years ago? I can think of three moves that Europe's leadership made that are worth a mention as they prevented the eurozone's final collapse, keeping it in a state of slow-burning disintegration:

1. The European Central Bank's decision, between December 2011 and February 2012, to print around 1 trillion euros and lend this to the eurozone's insolvent banks in exchange for worthless collateral. In so doing, some of that money (no more than 30 per cent) was then lent by the banks to the fiscally stricken member states (e.g. Italy). This operation (known as LTRO) bought the eurozone another eight to nine months.

2. The partial write-off of Greece's debt, in March of 2012. Alas, this write-off, a formal default by any standards, was unique in economic history in that it left the indebted

nation with a heavier debt burden at the end of 2012 than that which it was shouldering at the end of 2011![11]

3. Following an admission, in August 2012, by the president of the European Central Bank that the eurozone was disintegrating,[12] the ECB announced that it would be prepared to buy unspecified Italian and Spanish second-hand bonds in order to keep the interest rates paid by these two countries manageable. However, as the price for carrying the German government with him, the ECB's president, Mr Mario Draghi, also announced that these 'operations' (which are now known as outright monetary operations, or OMT) would be conditional on further austerity, vouched for by inspectors. Thus, surreptitiously, Europe's central bank sacrificed, on the altar of keeping on Germany's 'right side', its most prized principle: central bank independence.[13]

Many a reader may protest that I left out of my short list of significant changes the June 2012 Summit Agreement according to which Europe's leaders, at the insistence of the Italian and Spanish prime ministers, agreed to separate the continent's banking crisis from the debt crisis. How would that separation be achieved? By unifying the banking systems of the eurozone countries, infusing them with capital from the 'centre' and desisting from counting these capital injections as part of the national debt of the countries in which the banks are domiciled. This agreement, if it were implemented fully, would have been an important step towards arresting the euro crisis's triumphant march. But it will not be! Days after it was reached, Germany's leadership began a clever and determined campaign to pull the plug. I have no doubt that this – the most significant agreement to date – is dead in the water, and thus not worth the ink in which it is printed.

The telling question thus becomes: why such resistance, particularly from Germany, to every idea that would end the euro crisis? The standard answer is that Germany does not wish to pay for the debts of the periphery and will resist all federal-like moves (e.g. a banking or a fiscal union) until it is convinced that its partners will behave responsibly with their German-backed finances. While this captures well the mindset of many Northern Europeans, it is beside the point. Consider the following mental experiment, which, I believe, helps us unveil a deeper motive.

Picture the scene when a sheepish finance minister enters the chancellor's Berlin office bearing a control panel featuring one yellow and one red button, and telling her that she must choose to press one or the other. This is how he explains what each button will do:

> *The Red Button* If you press it, Chancellor, the euro crisis ends immediately, with a general rise in growth throughout Europe, a sudden collapse of debt for each member state to below its Maastricht limit, no pain for Greek citizens (or for the Italians, Portuguese, etc.), no guarantees for the periphery's debts (states or banks) to be provided by German and Dutch taxpayers, interest rate spreads below 3 per cent throughout the eurozone, a diminution in the eurozone's internal imbalances, and a wholesale rise in aggregate investment.

> *The Yellow Button* If you press it, Chancellor, the situation in the eurozone remains more or less as it is for a decade. The euro crisis continues to bubble along, albeit in a controlled fashion. While the probability of a break-up, which will be a calamity for Germany, remains non-trivial, the chances are that, if you push the yellow button, the eurozone will not break up (with a little help from the European Central Bank), German interest rates will remain extremely low, the euro will be nicely depressed ('nicely'

from the perspective of German exporters), the periphery's spreads will be sky-high (but not explosive), Italy and Spain will enter deeper into a debt-deflationary spiral that sees to a reduction of their national income by 15 per cent over the next three years, France shall slip steadily into quasi-insolvency, GDP per capita will rise slowly in the surplus countries and fall precipitously in the periphery. As for the first 'fallen' nations (Greece, Ireland and Portugal), they shall become little Latvias, or indeed Kosovos: devastated lands (after the loss of between 25 per cent and 40 per cent of national income, a massive exodus of their skilled labour) on which our people will holiday and buy cheap real estate. In aggregate, if you choose the yellow button, Chancellor, eurozone unemployment will remain well above UK and US levels, investment will be anaemic, growth negative and poverty on the up and up.

Which button do you think, dear reader, the chancellor would want to push? And, a quite separate question, which of the two buttons would the median German voter want her (or him, in years to come) to push?

Of course, this is both a hypothetical and an empirical question and no one can answer it definitively. However, the answer is not as straightforward as it would be in America or Britain. Whereas the yellow button would hold no attraction for the American president or the British prime minister, for the German chancellor the yellow button is a far more powerful option. Even if the chancellor wanted to opt for the red button, she would be terrorised by the reaction of the German electorate were she to do so. Letting the Greeks and the Italians, the Spaniards and the Portuguese, off the hook of their Great Depression so 'easily' would be unlikely to win many votes east of the Rhine and north of the Alps.

For two years now, the German public has become convinced that Germany has escaped the worst of the Crisis

because of the German people's virtuous embracing of thrifti-
ness and hard work; in contrast to the spendthrift Southerners,
who, like the fickle grasshopper, made no provision for when
the winds of finance would turn cold and nasty. This mindset
goes hand in hand with a moral righteousness which implants
into good people's hearts and minds a penchant for exacting
punishment on the grasshoppers – even if punishing them
also punishes themselves (to some extent). It also goes hand
in hand with a radical misunderstanding of what kept the
eurozone healthy and Germany in surplus prior to 2008: that
is, the Global Minotaur whose demand-generation antics were
for decades allowing countries like Germany and the Netherlands to remain net exporters of capital and consumer goods
within and without the eurozone (while importing US-sourced
demand for their goods from the eurozone's periphery).

Interestingly, one of the great secrets of the post-2008
period is that the Minotaur's death adversely affected aggregate demand in the eurozone's surplus countries (Germany,
the Netherlands, Austria and Finland) *more* than it did the
deficit member states (like Italy, Spain, Ireland, Portugal
and Greece) – see Figure 9.6. While the sudden withdrawal
of capital from the deficit countries brought about their insolvency, countries like Germany saw their 'fundamentals'
more grievously affected by the Crash of 2008. This fact, in
conjunction with the terrible squeeze on German wages (discussed in the previous chapter), explains the deeper causes
of the animosity in places like Germany that so very easily
translates into anger against the Greeks and assorted Mediter-
raneans – feelings that are then reciprocated, thus giving the
wheel of intra-European animosities another spin, favouring
the rise of xenophobia, even Nazism (in countries like Greece
quite incredibly), and thus leading to a wholesale readiness to
push all the yellow, as opposed to the red, buttons in sight.

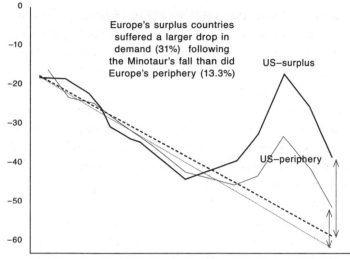

Figure 9.6   US goods trade deficit with the eurozone's
periphery (Italy, Spain, Ireland, Greece and Portugal)
and with the eurozone's surplus countries
(Germany, Austria, the Netherlands and Finland)

Source: US Bureau of Economic Analysis.

To recap, the Minotaur's surplus recycling was essential
to the maintenance of the eurozone's faulty edifice. Once it
vanished from the scene, the European common currency
area would either be redesigned or it would enter a long,
painful period of disintegration. An unwillingness by the
surplus countries to accept that, in the post-Minotaur world,
some other form of surplus recycling is necessary (and that
some of their own surpluses must also be subject to such
recycling) is the reason why Europe is looking like a case of
alchemy-in-reverse: for whereas the alchemist strove to turn
lead into gold, Europe's reverse alchemists began with gold
(an integration project that was the pride of its elites) but will
soon end up with the institutional equivalent of lead.

China after the Minotaur

The final chapter of the first edition of this book looked at the soaring dragon waiting in the wings, purportedly to take over from the Global Minotaur. In that conclusion, written back in January 2011, I wrote:

> To buy time, the Chinese government is stimulating its growing economy and keeps it shielded from currency revaluations, in the hope that vibrant growth can continue. But they see the omens. And they are not good. On the one hand, China's consumption-to-GDP ratio is falling; a sure sign that the domestic market cannot generate enough demand for China's gigantic factories. On the other hand, their fiscal injections are causing real estate bubbles. If these are unchecked, they may burst and thus cause a catastrophic domestic unwinding. But how do you deflate a bubble without choking off growth? That was the multi-trillion dollar question that Alan Greenspan failed to answer. It is not clear that the Chinese authorities can.

In the period that followed after those lines were written, events have confirmed the projected pattern. Figure 9.7 reveals that the falling rate of Chinese consumption is continuing unabated. In 2011, of every one dollar of income produced, only 29 cents entered China's markets. With net exports making a small annual contribution to domestic demand (even though they contribute greatly to the country's capacity to invest and thus boost productivity), the onus falls increasingly on investment to meet the demand shortfall. However, as suggested in the above paragraph, this emphasis on investment is a double-edged sword, as it threatens to let the genie out of the bottle in real-estate markets, where bubbles have been looming threateningly for a while now.

Indeed, in 2011 the Chinese authorities tightened up the administrative conditions for providing new housing loans,

Figure 9.7

Composition of Chinese aggregate demand (% of GDP)

	1990	1995	2000	2005	2009	2011
Private consumption	49	44	45	40	34	29
Investment	35	42	36	42	48	58
Government consumption	12	13	17	12	11	10
Net exports	4	1	2	6	7	3

Source: National Bureau of Statistics of China.

in the hope that such a move would leave productive investments unaffected while curtailing the funding of more white elephants and empty apartment blocks (which Chinese middle-class professionals buy, having borrowed heavily, but leave empty in the hope of selling them for more later on – a standard bubble-in-the-making).

Unfortunately, while demand for housing fell, the telltale signs soon appeared that the government's intervention was about to deflate not just the housing bubble but also industrial output. What telltale signs? The level of electricity output plateaued in early 2012. The last time that had happened, in 2008/9, the growth rate of industrial production declined sharply soon after, causing Beijing to stimulate the economy at a level that further suppressed the consumption ratio. To avoid this, the government is now relaxing its constraints on mortgage provision, accepting the renewed risk of a bubble in housing.

In summary, just as in Europe's surplus countries, so too in China, the one-fourth reduction in global aggregate demand occasioned by the Global Minotaur's passing has impeded any meaningful recovery. Indeed, it has made the world we live in more precarious because the remedies attempted (stimulus in China, QE in the United States, austerity in Europe) increase the probability that the Crisis will spawn nasty little appendages. For until and unless a global recycling mechanism rises from the Minotaur's ashes to replace him, the world will remain an insecure, depressing place.

Postscript

History's actors

We are an Empire now, and when we act, we create our
own reality. And while you are studying that reality –
judiciously as you will – we will act again, creating other
new realities, which you can study too, and that's how
things will sort out. We are history's actors ... and you,
all of you, will be left to just study what we do.[1]

With these words, a high-ranking US official captured nicely
the essence of America's post-war magnificent audacity. Not
once, but twice, the United States smashed pre-existing realities to fashion new ones. The first time, it had no choice.
World War II had thrust America into the role of an unwilling
reality-fashioner. It responded brilliantly, with a *Global Plan*
that delivered global capitalism's finest hour. And when its
Global Plan reached its sell-by date, the United States spent
no time dithering, or 'studying' the existing reality.

Instead, it actively sought to disintegrate the degenerating
reality, to cause a major, worldwide crisis that would spawn
a newer, hyper-vibrant reality: the *Global Minotaur*. It was
the second time in its history that America had reshaped the

world not so much in its image but in a manner that converted a creeping weakness into majestic hegemony.

The key to America's success was the recognition of the indispensability of a global surplus recycling mechanism (GSRM). Hegemony differs from domination, or from vulgar exploitation, in that the true hegemon understands that its power must be replenished not through further extraction from its subjects but from investment into their capacities to generate surpluses. To take from its subjects, the hegemon must master the art of giving in return. To maintain power, it needs to bolster its surpluses; but to do this, it must redirect large parts of it to its underlings.

All through the two distinct post-war global realities that it singlehandedly created, America took great care to put in place serviceable GSRMs over which it expected to have total control. During the Global Plan era, it assumed it would be the surplus trader. Its hegemony thus revolved around the recycling of large parts of its surplus capital (earned on the back of its trade surpluses) to Japan and Europe which, as planned, it was benefiting from, since the Japanese and the Europeans were using these transfers to buy American-produced, or -controlled, goods and services.

When the United States found itself, unwittingly, in a large trade and budget deficit, it moved on. It caused a global earthquake as a prelude to the Age of the Global Minotaur; my allegory for a massive GSRM which reversed the flow of global trade and capital flows. America henceforth was to provide foreign industrial centres with sufficient demand for their output in return for around 80 per cent of their capital flows. That this violent transition took at least a decade of terrible disintegration, debt crises, wholesale instability and global stagflation was, to America's elites, a reasonable price to pay; no more than a transition cost that the world's social economy and America's working families were billed for by our history's actors – the astute officials of successive American administrations.

Self-restraint and the dangers of success

Self-restraint, as the philosophers know, is a rare and bewildering virtue. It is also a virtue that tends to come unstuck the more powerful we become. In this it resembles the relationship between trust and success: the stronger the bonds of trust between us, the greater our collective and individual success. But success breeds greed, and greed is a solvent of trust. Similarly with self-restraint: having it can help one succeed. But then success poses a threat to one's self-restraint.

This *paradox of success*, as it pertains to self-restraint, proved the undoing of both of the global 'realities' that the United States created after World War II. The first time, it was the US government that fell prey to its negative engineering. The second time, it was America's private sector, and in particular its financial sector. To see how these two failures were snatched from the jaws of success, let us consider two questions, one concerning 1971, the other 2008.

What tripped up the Global Plan, causing it to lose its footing and to collapse in 1971? The answer: the US government's inability to exercise self-restraint vis-à-vis its own capacity to exploit its original exorbitant privilege; its ability, as custodian of the world's reserve currency, to print *global public money* at will.

And what was it that wounded the Global Minotaur mortally in 2008? Again, it was an American failure at self-restraint. Only this time it was not the US government's failure (even if a case can be made that it happened on the US government's watch) but that of the private sector in general and of the banks in particular: the American financial sector failed spectacularly to exercise self-restraint vis-à-vis its capacity to exploit its newfangled exorbitant privilege; its ability, as custodian of global financialisation, to print *global private money* at will.

Can the Minotaur survive?

In the book's first edition, I expressed serious doubts that the Minotaur can survive. Two years later all hope of a resurrection has evaporated. The Crash of 2008 has knocked so much of the financial stuffing out of the American economy, as well as depleting New York-based financialisation of its overall energy, that the Minotaur's magnetic power over foreign capital cannot recover. Wall Street may have been fully resurrected, reporting profits that would not look out of sorts back in the heady days of 2006; the US government is attracting more foreign capital than ever before; the banks that were too big to fail have grown even bigger (at least in relative terms). Yet the capitalisation of Wall Street is now too thin to attract the tsunami of foreign capital that kept the Minotaur in rude health. Indeed, in 2012 bankers were complaining loudly that, despite a return to obscene levels of profit-taking, they were failing to provide their investors with 'sufficiently' high returns due to the new regulations introduced by government.

In reality, what lies behind the bankers' squeals against the new reality is that their banks can no longer single-handedly recycle the world's surpluses. What is more, the new regime that has been established after 2008–09, in the United States and in Europe – the 'system' I have labelled *bankruptocracy* – is too introverted and insufficiently attractive to act as a drawing card for the necessary capital inflows. No, the Global

Minotaur is today at the stage the Global Plan had found itself in after 1971: a state of irreversible degeneration.

A world economy stunned

Despite the welcome rise of the 'emerging economies', we still live in a world dominated by the West. Post-Minotaur, this means that our lives are ruled over by the Global Minotaur's surviving handmaidens: Wall Street, Walmart, Germany's provincial mercantilism, the European Union's absurd pretence that a currency union can prosper without a surplus recycling mechanism, the growing inequities within the United States, within Europe, within China, and so on. A world without the Minotaur but ruled by its handmaidens is an illogical, absurd place.

The best example of its absurdity is the way in which public debate deals with so-called *global imbalances*: the systematically increasing trade surplus of some countries (Germany and China are good examples), which are mirrored in increasing trade deficits in others.[2] All commentators are now in agreement that increasing global imbalances were a cause of the eventual rupture in 2008. One would, consequently, be forgiven for imagining that a reduction in global imbalances would have been welcomed. Alas, the opposite is true.

After 2008, because of America's deep recession, its trade deficit shrank and the global imbalances thus diminished. Similarly, in the eurozone a devastated periphery abruptly turned away from imports, and therefore the internal trade imbalances are shrinking there too. Nevertheless, such rebalancing is further destabilising the world economy as the drop in trade deficits (within and across regions) goes hand in hand with *greater* imbalances in the realm of capital movements.

Worse still, the rebalancing of trade accounts is accompanied by a worldwide increase in both the mountains of unpayable debts and of idle savings (that are too scared to turn into long-term, productive investments).

It is, indeed, a strange world that one moment exorcises global imbalances but suffers the next when they diminish. Of course the puzzle dissolves the moment we begin to think of these matters in terms of the Global Minotaur parable; of a terrible beast that, nevertheless, stabilised an unstable world by filling the gap of an official GSRM that went missing in 1971. And now that the beast is gone, our world is in a state of permanent instability, chronic uncertainty and a never-ending slump.

The missing mechanism

Global capitalism cannot be stabilised on the basis of more investment, better gadgets, faster railways, smarter innovations. This is the error of vulgar Keynesians who think that if only the state spent and invested wisely, all would be well. Similarly, global capitalism will not regain its lost poise if central banks focus on price stability, and the task of rebalancing the world economy is left to the magical machinations of supply and demand. This is the even more menacing error of libertarians. The stability of global, but also regional, capitalism requires a global surplus recycling mechanism – a mechanism that markets, however globalised, free and well-functioning they might be, cannot provide.

So, the question is: if America cannot supply the missing GSRM, and Europe is too busy disintegrating, who can? China? Alas no. China is evidently working hard, and with considerable success, in creating a Chinese version of partial globalisation; one that puts Beijing at the centre of a vast network of trade and investment deals with India, Africa, Latin America, but also involving European, American and Japanese multinationals. China will try to keep US, European and Japanese officials at bay and, before long, promote its own currency, the renminbi (RMB), as the main means of exchange within those networks. However, these networks are condemned to be embedded in a wider world economy that China cannot rebalance due to a radical incapacity to generate sufficient demand for it.

And now what? In search of history's next actors

Without a GSRM materialising soon, the future is better left uncontemplated. For, on the one hand, we shall have a West caught in the poisonous webs of the dead Minotaur's handmaidens, unable to rise to the challenges of our post-2008 world, stagnating, losing its grip on reality, failing to match its outcomes to its capacities or to create new 'realities'. On the other hand, there will be the emerging economies, bristling with people ready to transcend constraints, to spawn new 'realities', to expand existing horizons. Such a two-speed world is highly inflammable, predicated as it is upon the clash between those speeding ahead economically and the others who stagnate while maintaining a virtual monopoly over military power, over the world's reserve currency, and over the planet's transnational institutions (the UN Security Council, NATO, the OECD, the IMF and the World Bank).

So, if a GSRM is *sine qua non* for a stable globalised social economy, and without it we run the risk of returning to a pre-World War II form of radical precariousness (with the added risks emanating from modern means of mass annihilation), is there a brighter, an alternative, future?

One bright scenario would see the formation of a grand coalition of emerging countries that forges a de facto GSRM on the basis of planned investment and trade transfers between them. For instance, instead of China simply stepping on Brazilian toes, and purchasing Brazilian productive assets without the consent of Brazilian officials, imagine a system whereby China's investments are channelled on the basis of some agreement with Brazil's government that involves capital inflows into Brazil analogous to Brazil's sale of primary goods to China as well as Chinese technology transfers to Brazil. Such agreements between Brazil, China, Argentina, India, Turkey and selected African countries could act as a GSRM that would promote stable growth. The fact that it would leave our Western bankruptocracies out on a limb would be the icing on the cake.

A second, even brighter, scenario would be for the West to have an epiphany and, at long last, embrace John Maynard Keynes's suggestion of an International Currency Union; the very suggestion America rejected in the Bretton Woods conference of 1944. Is this far-fetched? Very much so. But then again, the Crash of 2008 did concentrate some intelligent minds. Before his fall from grace, Dominique Strauss-Kahn, the former managing director of the IMF, was asked by a BBC journalist about his thoughts on how the global economy ought to be reconfigured in the aftermath of the 2008 events. His astonishing answer was:

> Never in the past has an institution like the IMF been as necessary as it has been today... Keynes, sixty years ago, already foresaw what was needed; but it was too early. Now is the time to do it. And I think we are ready to do it![3]

Clearly, the 'it' which Strauss-Kahn was referring to was none other than the creation of a multilateral GSRM, just like

John Maynard Keynes had proposed in 1944, at the Bretton Woods conference. That is, a surplus recycling scheme that would not rely on some bright officials and the unaccountable financial sector of a single country, as the Global Minotaur was, but on a well-run, global organisation that consciously and transparently sets the parameters for the recycling of goods, profits, savings and demand.

Two years later, Strauss-Kahn's daring statement appears more like 'famous last words' than a genuine programme for policy change on a planetary scale. Indeed, the very image of a handcuffed Strauss-Kahn being forced into a NYPD car, a few weeks after he had made that statement to the BBC, is deliciously symbolic of the flicker-like nature of the elites' post-2008 rethink. Since then, dominant politicians, heads of the IMF and the World Bank, private and central bankers alike, generally the stewards of world capitalism, seem to have chosen to un-learn very quickly the lessons of 2008. They resemble drivers who, upon being fined by the police for speeding, drive within the speed limit for a few dozen miles before gradually returning to the original speed, hoping that this time 'it will be different'.

The omens are thus not good. Never before have so many powerful people understood so little about what the world economy needs in order to recover. Never before have history's actors been so painfully absent. Our only hope is that history often forges new possibilities at a time when none seems present. So, let us allow optimism to shine through the darkness and pose the question: if the Global Minotaur is to be replaced by a well-designed, collectively agreed GSRM, who might act as the agent of this birth? Who will emerge as history's actors this time?

Previously, I argued that this time historical agency might spring out of the emerging economies. However, I must make a confession a few sentences before the book's end: I do not believe it will. With Europe out of contention, and the emerging nations buffeted by both the Crisis and a lack of tradition in mould-breaking on a global scale, once more it is the United States that must provide, perhaps for the last time, the missing agency. Put simply, I just cannot see how genuine progress towards building a wholesome GSRM can be made otherwise.

Of course, the prerequisite for this is that America's policy makers grasp the meaning and irreversibility of 'their' Global Minotaur's demise, and are energised by the dystopian prospect of a permanently stagnation-prone world economy. Then and only then is there a chance of a collective future that is rational, stable and pregnant with an iota of hope that our latest Crisis will be allowed to unleash its creative potential.

While emerging countries like China, Brazil, India, South Africa and so on *must* contribute important building blocks in the construction of this brighter future, America must nevertheless lead. If it does, perhaps centuries later its own Minotaur's death will inspire the poets and the myth-makers to mark its demise as the beginning of a new, authentic humanism. If it does not, then our generation's postmodern 1930s will last a lot longer than a decade.

Notes

Chapter 1

1. Monday, 19 October 1987, when the world's stock exchanges suffered the worst one-day loss in their history.
2. Greenspan was addressing the Congressional Committee for Oversight and Government Reform on 23 October 2008, presided over by California Democratic Senator Henry Waxman.
3. These packages went by the mystical name collateralized debt obligations, or CDOs.
4. I concentrate on CDOs because they were the most common form of so-called structured financial vehicles. There were, of course, many other varieties of such toxic paper.
5. US Treasury Bills are IOUs issued by the US Treasury. They are widely considered to be the safest form of debt, as they are backed by the US government. For this reason, they tend to pay some of the lowest interest rates on the market.
6. By law, banks are forced to restrict their loan-making to below a certain percentage of their deposits, so that there is enough capital in their vaults in case some loans go bad and/or more than the usual proportion of depositors want their money back. But if the banks used depositors' money to buy CDOs, that money was treated as though it remained in the bank; as though, in other words, the CDOs had never been bought!
7. This explains why, on that fateful day in September 2008, Lehman Brothers was caught out with mountains of CDOs on its books.
8. In a bid to prevent another 1929, the Act forced a separation between (a) normal bread-and-butter banks, which took deposits

from the common man and woman, and (b) investment banks, which were allowed to gamble on shares, futures, commodities, etc. but were banned from taking deposits. Normal banks were thus prevented from gambling with other people's money, while investment banks could sink or swim in an ocean of high risk.

9. It took a couple of months for the markets to recover fully from a shock so large that many feared a new Great Depression.

10. In 1991, after the housing market downturn; in the late 1990s, following a series of crises (e.g. the LTCM collapse following Russia's default, the East Asian Crisis); in 2001 when the dotcom bubble popped; and, lastly, the run on the stock market following the 9/11 tragedy of that same year.

11. These words were written by Karl Marx in 1844, in the text entitled *Economic and Philosophical Manuscripts*.

Chapter 2

1. See Jared Diamond (2006) *Guns, Germs and Steel*, New York: Norton.

2. Ibn Khaldun (1967) *The Muqaddimah: An introduction to history*, trans. Franz Rosenthal, Bollingen Series XLIII, Princeton, NJ: Princeton University Press.

3. For a good account of such calamities, see Carmen Reinhart and Kenneth Rogoff (2009) *This Time Is Different: Eight centuries of financial folly*, Princeton, NJ: Princeton University Press.

4. Once all your music, films, applications, addresses, etc. are on iTunes and readily accessible by any Apple product (iPod, iPhone, iPad, etc.), the opportunity cost of buying a Nokia or a Sony device is huge (even if these companies bring a better device to market) – you need to spend literally hours setting the new gadget up. Thus, iTunes gave Apple immense monopoly power, of the same type that Edison and Westinghouse were trying to create for themselves.

5. John Steinbeck (1939) *The Grapes of Wrath*, New York: Viking Press, chapter 25. This remarkable novel has a plot that unfolds during the Great Depression.

6. J. M. Keynes (1936) *The General Theory of Employment, Interest and Money*, London: Macmillan, chapter 12.

7. Recall the late-sixteenth-century play by Christopher Marlowe, in which Dr Faustus famously contracted, using his own blood to sign on the dotted line, to sell his body and soul twenty-four years hence to Mephistopheles in exchange for a great deal of current pleasure.

Chapter 3

1. White was an ardent New Dealer and avowed Keynesian. A Harvard PhD economist, he served in the US Treasury as assistant to Secretary Henry Morgenthau. A committed internationalist, he not only helped create the IMF but also became its director. In 1947, he resigned abruptly under a cloud of innuendo that he had acted as a Soviet spy. He died the following year of a heart attack.

2. To be more precise, the IBRD is the original institution of the World Bank, which today also includes the International Development Association, founded in 1960.

3. His very words on the subject were: 'Now is the time to do it and I think we are ready to do it.' Interviewed on 'Inside the IMF', BBC Radio 4, 17 January 2011.

4. White's unequivocal words were: 'We have been perfectly adamant on that point. We have taken the position of absolutely no.'

5. It is important to note that, as the war was coming to its conclusion, all war-torn European nations were highly indebted to the USA and transferred large amounts of gold to it, a fact that contributed to the US determination to turn the dollar into the Bretton Woods system's central axis.

6. It was at this point that successive British governments began clutching at straws – namely, the 'special relationship', which turned the UK into a minor executor of US policy in exchange for privileged access to the US market for British multinationals and the linkage of the City of London to Wall Street.

7. Interestingly, Marjolin had spent his formative pre-war years as a Rockefeller fellow at Harvard. In fact, while there, he participated in a reading group dedicated to understanding Keynes' General Theory. The other two participants were John Kenneth Galbraith (1908–2006) and Paul Samuelson (1915–2009). Galbraith was to spend the war as Roosevelt's 'price czar', determining the prices of all major commodities. Samuelson won the Nobel Prize for Economics and is credited with introducing Keynes (albeit in an oversimplified and, I would argue, toxic form) to Americans.

8. In a radio interview some years ago, linguistics professor and political activist Noam Chomsky pointed out an interesting fact about the Marshall Plan – one that links the United States, France and Holland with European imperialism in Asia. A large part of France's share of Marshall Plan aid went to recolonizing Indochina, a prelude to the Vietnam War that was, eventually, to have such catastrophic effects for everyone involved, and also for the Global Plan itself. Another example is Holland. It used its portion of Marshall Plan aid to reconquer Indonesia, a Dutch colony that

had managed to liberate itself from Japan toward the end of the war. Interestingly, the United States, quite furious with the Dutch, leaned on them heavily in 1950, pressurizing them to send troops to Korea (so as to make amends for the misuse of Marshall Plan money in pursuing their delusions of colonial grandeur).

9. For example, in 1946 America altered course drastically in Greece, forging an alliance with Greek Nazi collaborators against the Left. At around the same time, it made its peace with the Franco and the Salazar regimes on the Iberian Peninsula. Soon after, it turned decidedly against anti-colonial movements in Africa, Indochina and even Cyprus – movements toward which it had been hitherto, if not sympathetic, at least neutral.

Chapter 4

1. Some 2.3 million dead, 3.5 million seriously wounded and 14.5 million refugees.
2. These estimates are by New Deal economist Robert Eisner, professor at Northwestern University and a one-time president of the American Economic Association.
3. V. H. Oppenheim (1976–77) 'Why oil prices go up: The past: we pushed them', *Foreign Policy*, 25: 32–33.
4. See Sheikh Yaki Yamani's interview at the Royal Institute of International Affairs, as published on 14 January 2001 in the *Observer*. Sheikh Yamani was Saudi Arabia's longest-serving minister of oil (1962–86).
5. Paul Volcker, 'An economy on thin ice', *Washington Post*, 10 April 2005.
6. In Romania, for example, house heating ceased for years, even during the coldest of winter months.

Chapter 5

1. This example is based on an idea by John Lanchester. See his 2009 article 'It's finished', *London Review of Books*, 31(10).
2. Though this is higher than the minimum wage in the United States, it also means that Walmart's workers live permanently below the poverty line, qualifying for US government food stamps.
3. The largest private lawsuit in US history involved Walmart's alleged underpayment of, and failure to promote, more than 1.5 million women workers.
4. New Economics Foundation (2006) *Growth Isn't Working: The unbalanced distribution of benefits and costs from economic growth,*

London.

5. High interest rates, corporate America's success in squeezing labour costs, Wall Street's private money-creation skills, rising US household debt, and the dwindling living standards of the average American worker.

6. Even though, as explained in the previous chapter, the truth was rather different: behind the scenes, the US government had acquiesced rather happily to the oil price rises.

7. The previous chapter highlighted how brutal the Global Minotaur proved toward the average American. It might safely be said that, as a result of its success, never before have so few Americans had so much, while so many have had to survive on so little. See James Galbraith (1989) *Created Unequal: The crisis in American pay*, New York: The Free Press.

8. These were called 'stag' issues: selling shares so cheaply that they were heavily oversubscribed and hence rationed. When the TSB was sold, it did not even belong to the British government, but rather to its account holders. The government had to bend the law to privatize it. In some cases, like British Petroleum, the advisers to the government were also the underwriters of the issue, and disaster following a stock market crash prior to the scheduled initial public offering was averted by the government guaranteeing the price of the shares.

9. Recall the three theories that were discussed in chapter 1: Efficient Market Hypothesis, Rational Expectations Hypothesis and Real Business Cycle Theory.

10. This book is not the place to enter into the proof in any detail. If interested, please consult Y. Varoufakis, J. Halevi and N. Theocarakis (2011) *Modern Political Economics: Making sense of the post-2008 world*, London and New York: Routledge.

11. In more technical language, the formulae used to assemble the CDOs assumed that the correlation coefficient between the probability of default across a CDO's different tranches or slices was constant, small and knowable.

12. Doubt about the constancy of the correlation coefficient (see previous footnote) would have cost them their jobs, particularly as their supervisors did not really understand the formula but were receiving huge bonuses while it was being used.

13. See George Soros (2009) *The Crash of 2008 and What It Means: The new paradigm for financial markets*, New York: Public Affairs. Soros correctly states that: 'The belief that markets tend towards equilibrium is directly responsible for the current turmoil – it encouraged the regulators to abandon their responsibility and

rely on the market mechanism to correct its own excesses.'

14. Paul Volcker, 'An economy on thin ice', *Washington Post*, 10 April 2005.

15. Speech given in New York on 12 May 2002, entitled 'Worldthink, Disequilibrium and the Dollar'.

Chapter 6

1. The term *liquidity trap* is due to Keynes, who discovered a fault in the conventional economic theory, according to which recessions cure themselves as the interest rate falls and investment thus picks up automatically. Keynes pointed out (see chapter 2) that when interest rates hit zero, they cannot fall any further. And as prices continue to fall during a recession, the real interest rate (which is the interest rate we pay minus the inflation rate) rises at a time when the theory says it should fall. The result? The recession deepens.

2. Tim Geithner was President Obama's choice for secretary of the treasury. He had previously served as under-secretary to the treasury when Larry Summers was Bill Clinton's secretary. As for Larry Summers, under President Obama he returned to Washington (after spending the Bush years as president of Harvard University) in his new capacity as director of the president's National Economic Council.

3. J. M. Keynes (1932) 'The world economic outlook', *The Atlantic Monthly*, 149: 521–6.

4. Vandana Shiva, an Indian physicist and ecologist who directs the Research Foundation on Science, Technology and Ecology, offers a compelling explanation for the food crisis that had erupted in the developing nations just before the Crash of 2008. See Vandana Shiva (2005) *Earth Democracy: Justice, sustainability, and peace*, Cambridge, MA: South End Press.

5. Quantitative easing is usually referred to as a species of printing money. This is not strictly true. What the Fed is doing is purchasing from banks and other institutions all sorts of paper assets (US government bonds plus private companies' bonds). It does this by creating overdraft facilities for these institutions, on which they can draw for the purposes of lending to others. But if these institutions do not lend to others (because they cannot find clients willing to borrow), the result is zilch. This is why I say that quantitative easing is an *attempt* to create money. The Fed's tragedy is that it is *trying* to print money but finds it hard to succeed!

6. In Europe, politicians are even terrified of the bankers whose bacon they are still saving, daily, and to the tune of billions per month.

7. The Commission was established as part of the Fraud Enforcement and Recovery Act (Public Law 111-21) passed by Congress and signed by President Obama in May 2009.

8. *Ptochos* is Greek for 'pauper, beggar', but also (in modern Greek) for 'bankrupt'. *Trapeza* is Greek for 'bank'. Originally it meant 'table' and is associated with banking because, in ancient Greek city-states, borrowing and lending transactions were carried out in the *agora* ('marketplace'), with the parties to the transaction seated around long tables.

Chapter 7

1. The US Treasury's equity contribution of $5 would actually come from something called the Troubled Asset Relief Program (TARP), whereas the Fed's $50 would come from the Federal Deposit Insurance Corporation (FDIC), set up by the New Dealers (as part of the Glass–Steagall Act of 1933) to guarantee depositors' savings in case of a bank failure. The Geithner–Summers Plan set aside $150 billion for TARP, $820 billion for FDIC and expected the private sector (hedge and pension funds) to chip in $30 billion of their own money.

2. Under the good scenario, H's net return equals $10. Under the bad scenario, H's net returns are –$5. The 'distance' between these two numbers is $15. Should it take part in this simulated market gain? A simple calculation suggests that H stands to gain only if the probability of the good scenario is better than the possible loss ($5) divided by that 'distance' – i.e. 5/15, or a third.

3. Henry Kissinger reportedly once said that Summers 'ought to be given a White House post in which he was charged with shooting down or fixing bad ideas'.

4. Moreover, if by some miracle its subsidiary H can sell c for more than $100, it will stand to gain an extra sum.

5. The plan was that the EU's own budget would chip in another €60 billion and the IMF a further €250 billion, bringing the total package up to €750 billion.

6. For the idea of the neoliberal predator state, see James Galbraith (2008) *The Predator State: How conservatives abandoned the free market and why liberals should too*, New York: The Free Press.

7. Though it would be offensive to the black community and to other minorities to call the 1950s and 1960s a 'Golden Age', it is still true

that the stable growth of that era helped the civil rights movement to rise up when it did, and to make its voice felt.

8. The reader may object that China is in fine working order. In the next chapter I shall argue that it is not. Its growth is predicated upon unsustainable stimuli that do not have the power to create the long-term demand that will keep it going.

Chapter 8

1. The other purpose of Plaza was to accommodate the United States' determination that its multinationals should play a larger role in the global electronics market that Japan and Germany threatened to dominate.

2. I leave Britain outside this taxonomy. Following its deindustrialization under the Thatcher government, the only thing standing between Britain and Europe's stragglers is the City of London, with its pivotal position in the world of finance. Ireland is also excluded because it is currently undergoing a crisis that may well alter its status quite fundamentally.

3. French philosopher Gilles Deleuze defines a simulacrum as a 'system' 'in which different relates to different *by means of* difference itself'. See G. Deleuze (1968) *Difference and Repetition*, New York: Columbia University Press.

4. At a time when Europe's deficit nations and France had to reckon also with growing deficits with Asia.

5. IKB Bank, and its parent bank KfW, were the first to be burnt by Wall Street scams that exploded in 2008. They ran to Berlin for government assistance. The bill came to €1.5 billion. It was the tip of the iceberg. The Global Minotaur, unbeknownst to the German people (and to most of its politicians) had infected German capital with the virus of financialization. When that disease became full-blown, the German taxpayer had to foot an enormous bill.

6. Greece, Ireland, Portugal, Spain, Italy and Belgium.

7. Technically this could be done by swapping the existing bonds of deficit states that Europe's banks hold for new ones with a much lower face value.

8. Suppose, for instance, that California wanted to exit the United States of America. How could they decide which part of the US federal debt corresponds to California, so that the Golden State can pay its dues and leave gracefully? It simply cannot be done. Similarly with Germany after a common eurobond is issued: it would make the business of extracting itself from the eurozone very messy indeed.

9. In an Australian Broadcasting Company radio interview, Mexican economist Rogelio de la O stated in 2009: 'Even strong companies that are subsidiaries of international firms are very, very discouraged at the way their volumes have fallen and their margins have been totally squeezed. The China effect is kind of overwhelming.'

Chapter 9

1. This is a new chapter, written for this updated edition.
2. For the full story the reader is advised to reread Chapter 6.
3. Most of the data used in the first edition ended in 2009. This edition was written with the benefit of data from the financial years 2010, 2011 and the first three quarters of 2012.
4. For a reminder of President Hoover's role in the Great Depression revisit Chapter 2.
5. With no strings attached that would have seen write-offs of Main Street's debts and/or greater lending to consumers and firms.
6. Even though Tea Party candidates had no qualms about the considerable backing they received from Big Business and Wall Street.
7. One of the curiosities of this Crisis is that it gave impetus to the gold and silver standard revivalists. While it is understandable that both the Fed's loose monetary and regulatory policy (under Greenspan and Bernanke), as well as the experience of Wall Street's effective minting of private money, should make many yearn for money that no one can tamper with (and print more of at will), it is quite startling that so many intelligent people should come to the conclusion that the solution is to tie the money supply to the quantity of some metal (gold, silver etc.). It is as if the Great Depression of the 1930s had never sprung out of a world shackled by the chains of the... gold standard (see Chapter 3).
8. Meaning that interest rates were already close to zero and could not be lowered further (see Chapter 2). Moreover, with money interest rates close to zero, falling prices threatened to boost the real interest rate during a recessionary time (the very definition of a liquidity trap).
9. Measured by nominal gross domestic product.
10. My assertion here is that the unqualified demand that countries like Greece and Portugal eliminate their deficits through deep public-sector cuts, at a time of a debt-deflationary depression, is to ask for the macroecomically impossible – especially when these countries lack a currency whose devaluation would yield some respite.
11. While almost 100 billion euros was written off, Greece was forced

to take on new loans to repay its 'official lenders' (the trio made up of European Union countries, the European Central Bank and the International Monetary Fund) plus the remaining private lenders. With a savage recession raging, the Greek government was made to accept public expenditure cuts and appalling new taxes that, between them, caused national income to shrink so much that the nation's debt-to-national-income ratio rose to levels it had never scaled before.

12. Naturally, no central banker worth his salt will speak such blunt words. Mr Mario Draghi's choice of words, by which to signal unambiguously that he was talking about the Eurozone's dismantling, was that there was now a serious 'convertibility risk' – by which he meant that there was a risk that all prices in the eurozone would be 'converted' to other, new, national (one presumes) currencies!

13. This loss becomes clear the moment one realises that the ECB has chosen to conduct monetary operations that will stop not when the ECB judges they must but when Brussels or the IMF say it should cease and desist. This is, if nothing else, ample proof that the fabled central bank independence was never a real principle but, rather, a pretext for never financing anyone other than 'needy' bankers.

Postscript

1. These words were conveyed to us by Ron Suskind in his article in the *New York Times Magazine*, October 2004. Though not attributed, many believe they were spoken in the summer of 2002 by Karl Rove, a senior aide to President George W. Bush.

2. When my colleague Joseph Halevi and I published an article (the first to use the metaphor of the Global Minotaur) back in 2003, focusing on America's growing 'global imbalances' – that is, its twin deficits – our point was ignored. Since the Minotaur was felled by the Crash of 2008, everyone is now acknowledging that the global imbalances are a problem, both at the international level (i.e. China's surplus with the US and Europe) and within Europe (i.e. Germany's surplus with the rest of the eurozone).

3. 'Inside the IMF – Part Two', BBC Radio 4, broadcast 17 January 2011.

Recommended reading

Many of the arguments in this book are explained in much greater and more scholarly detail in the book that I co-authored with Joseph Halevi and Nicholas Theocarakis: *Modern Political Economics: Making Sense of the Post-2008 World* (London and New York: Routledge, 2011). Readers may be interested in the large relevant bibliography it offers. Having said that, let me warn you that it is a dense, academic book; certainly not one to take along to the beach...

Those interested in the Global Minotaur's lineage may wish to consult the paper that Joseph Halevi and I published on the subject in 2003: 'The Global Minotaur', *Monthly Review*, 55 (July–August 2003): 56–74. This article occasioned a series of questions and answers that were later published as 'Questions and Answers on the Global Minotaur', *Monthly Review*, 55 (December 2003): 26–32.

Turning to something completely different, and far more edifying, I thoroughly recommend two books that will make you smile, laugh and generally lift your spirits thanks to their fine prose and imaginative links between matters of finance and matters of life. The fact that they were penned by two accomplished novelists is no coincidence. They are Margaret Attwood's *Payback – Debt and the Shadow Side of Wealth* (Massey Lecture, Canadian Broadcasting Corporation, 2008); and John Lanchester's *Whoops! Why Everyone Owes Everyone and No One Can Pay* (London: Allen Lane, 2010).

And since I have recommended literary books on the Crisis, I cannot resist the temptation to suggest that those readers who have never read *The Grapes of Wrath* should make amends. No other book, especially not one by an economist, can convey better what a crisis does to people – what it really means to become the plaything of a depression's unchecked forces. Thus: John Steinbeck. *The Grapes of Wrath* (New York: Viking Press, 1939).

Before I recommend books on the Crash of 2008 itself, I want to mention three books by James Galbraith which are an excellent introduction to the period preceding it: *Created Unequal: The Crisis in American Pay* (New York: Free Press, 1998); *The Predator State: How Conservatives Abandoned the Free Market and Why Liberals Should Too* (New York: Free Press, 2008); *Inequality and Instability: A Study of the World Economy just before the Great Crisis* (New York: Oxford University Press, 2012).

Finally, I draw your attention to two books on the Crash of 2008. From a plethora of books that I could have recommended, I have chosen one by a well-known Marxist and one by a well-known financier. It is astonishing how mutually consistent their arguments are: a sure sign that, at a time of crisis, logic brings people of different ideological backgrounds closer – at least if they are hungry enough for the truth and thus prepared to be baptised in the shock of unfolding drama. The books are: Rick Wolff, *Capitalism Hits the Fan: The Global Economic Meltdown and What to Do about It* (Northampton MA: Olive Branch Press, 2010); George Soros, *The Crash of 2008 and What It Means: The New Paradigm for Financial Markets* (rev. edn, New York: Public Affairs, 2009).

Select bibliography

Attwood, M. (2008) *Payback: Debt and the shadow side of wealth*, Toronto: House of Anansi Press.

Bernanke, B. (2004) *Essays on the Great Depression*, Princeton, NJ: Princeton University Press.

Condorcet, M. de (1979) *Sketch for a Historical Picture of the Progress of the Human Mind*, trans. June Barraclough, Westport, CT: Hyperion Press.

Deleuze, G. (1968) *Difference and Repetition*, New York: Columbia University Press.

Diamond, Jared (2006) *Guns, Germs and Steel*, New York: Norton.

Eliot, T. S. (1942) *Little Gidding*, London: Faber & Faber.

Evans-Pritchard, E. E. (1937, 1976) *Witchcraft, Oracles and Magic among the Azande*, Oxford: Clarendon.

Evans-Pritchard, E. E. (1940) *The Nuer: A description of the modes of livelihood and political institutions of a Nilotic people*, Oxford: Clarendon.

Forsberg, A. (2000) *America and the Japanese Miracle: The Cold War context of Japan's post-war economic revival, 1950–1960*, Chapel Hill and London: University of North Carolina Press.

Galbraith, J. (1998) *Created Unequal: The crisis in American pay*, New York: The Free Press.

Galbraith, J. (2008) *The Predator State: How conservatives abandoned the free market and why liberals should too*, New York: Free Press.

Greenspan, A. (2009) 'We need a better cushion against risk', *Financial Times*, 26 March.

Halevi, J. and Y. Varoufakis (2003) 'The Global Minotaur', *Monthly Review*, 55 (July–August): 56–74.

Halevi, J. and Y. Varoufakis (2003) 'Questions and answers on the Global Minotaur', *Monthly Review*, 55 (December): 26–32.

Hobsbawm, E. (1999) *Industry and Empire: From 1750 to the present day*, revised and updated with Chris Wrigley, New York: New Press.

Keynes, J. M. (1920) *The Economic Consequences of the Peace*, New York: Harcourt Brace.

Keynes, J. M. (1932) 'The world's economic outlook', *The Atlantic Monthly*, 149 (May): 521–6.

Keynes, J. M. (1936) *The General Theory of Employment, Interest and Money*, London: Macmillan.

Keynes, J. M. (1980) *Activities 1940–1944. Shaping the Post-War World: The clearing union*, Vol. 25 of *The Collected Writings of John Maynard Keynes*, ed. D. E. Moggridge, London: Macmillan.

Khaldun, Ibn (1967) *The Muqaddimah: An introduction to history*, trans. Franz Rosenthal, Bollingen Series XLIII, Princeton, NJ: Princeton University Press.

Kissinger, H. (1982) *Years of Upheaval*, Boston, MA: Little Brown.

Kuntz, D. (1997) *Butter and Guns*, New York: Free Press.

Lanchester, J. (2006) 'The price of pickles', *London Review of Books*, 28(12): 3–6.

Lanchester, J. (2009) 'It's finished', *London Review of Books*, 31(10): 3–13.

Lanchester, J. (2009) 'Bankocracy', *London Review of Books*, 31(21): 35–6.

Lanchester, J. (2010) *Whoops! Why everyone owes everyone and no one can pay*, London: Allen Lane.

Luxemburg, R. (2003) *The Accumulation of Capital*, trans. Agnes Schwarzschild, London: Routledge.

MacCulloch, D. (2009) *Reformation: Europe's House Divided 1490–1700*, London: Allen Lane.

Marx, K. (1972) *Capital*, Vols. I–III, London: Lawrence and Wishart.

Marx, K. (1973) *Grundrisse: Foundations of the Critique of Political Economy (Rough Draft)*, trans. Martin Nicolaus, Harmondsworth: Penguin.

McDonald, L. with P. Robinson (2009) *A Colossal Failure of Common Sense: The inside story of the collapse of Lehman Brothers*, London: Ebury Press.

Minsky, H. (2008) *Stabilizing an Unstable Economy*, New York: McGraw-Hill.

Parker, D. (2009) *The Official History of Privatisation*, Vol. 1, *The Formative Years 1970–1987*, London: Routledge.

Reinhart, C. and K. Rogoff (2009) *This Time Is Different: Eight centuries of financial folly*, Princeton, NJ: Princeton University Press.

Schumpeter, J. (1942) *Capitalism, Socialism and Democracy*, New York and London: Harper & Brothers.

Soros, G. (2009) *The Crash of 2008 and What It Means: The new paradigm for financial markets* (revised edn), New York: Public Affairs.

Steinbeck, J. (1939) *The Grapes of Wrath*, New York: Viking Press.

Varoufakis, Y., J. Halevi and N. Theocarakis (2011) *Modern Political Economics: Making sense of the post-2008 world*, London and New York: Routledge.

Volcker, P. A. (1978–79) 'The political economy of the dollar', *FRBNY Quarterly Review*, Winter: 1–12.

Wachowski, Larry and Andy Wachowski (1998) '*The Matrix*, numbered shooting script', 29 March 1998, available at: www.dailyscript.com/scripts/the_matrix.pdf

Wolff, R. (2010) *Capitalism Hits the Fan: The global economic meltdown and what to do about it*, Northampton, MA: Olive Branch Press.

Zinn, H. (1998) *The Twentieth Century: A people's history*, New York: Harper Perennial.

Žižek, S. (2006) *The Parallax View*, Cambridge, MA: MIT Press.

Index